SENSE AND
NONSENSE ABOUT IQ

SENSE AND NONSENSE ABOUT IQ

THE CASE FOR UNIQUENESS

CHARLES LOCURTO

PRAEGER

New York
Westport, Connecticut
London

Library of Congress Cataloging-in-Publication Data

Locurto, C. M.
    Sense and nonsense about IQ : the case for uniqueness / Charles
Locurto.
        p. cm.
    Includes bibliographical references and index.
    ISBN 0–275–93803–4 (alk. paper).—ISBN 0–275–93911–1 (pbk. :
alk. paper)
        1. Intelligence levels.   2. Individual differences.   3. Nature and
nurture.   4. Intelligence levels—History.   I. Title.
    BF431.L548   1991
    153.9'3—dc20   90–23133

British Library Cataloguing in Publication Data is available.

Library of Congress Catalog Card Number: 90–23133
ISBN: 0–275–93803–4 (cloth)
        0–275–93911–1 (paper)

First published in 1991

Praeger Publishers, One Madison Avenue, New York, NY   10010
An imprint of Greenwood Publishing Group, Inc.

Printed in the United States of America

The paper used in this book complies with the
Permanent Paper Standard issued by the National
Information Standards Organization (Z39.48–1984).

10 9 8 7 6 5 4 3 2 1

    Every reasonable effort has been made to trace the owners of copyright materials in this book
and to obtain responses from those who may hold copyrights for materials reproduced in this book.
The publishers will be glad to receive information leading to more complete acknowledgments in
subsequent printings of the book, and in the meantime extend their apologies for any omissions.

To Kasia

There is no arguing with the pretenders to a divine knowledge and to a divine mission. They are possessed with the sin of pride, they have yielded to the perennial temptation.

Walter Lippmann
The Public Philosophy

There are three kinds of lies: plain lies, damned lies, and statistics.

Mark Twain
Autobiography

Contents

Illustrations

APPENDICES

Acknowledgments

As every life has a theme, the same should be true for every area of behavioral science, even the most seemingly muddled areas, including the study of human intelligence. "Nature doesn't play dice" as it were, the thought a determinist-minded Einstein once applied to the subject matter of physics. Finding those themes in the study of IQ has been the purpose of this work.

A portion of this work draws on the Pygmalion myth, and like Pygmalion's hopes for his statue I wanted this work to be perfection itself, to be, that is, the perfect revelation of those themes as they are played out in the study of human intelligence. Unfortunately, as much if not more than any work, this one suffers from the inevitable translation of hope into the hard truths of a complex subject matter. However difficult that translation, it was made far easier than it might have otherwise been by a number of people.

The idea for this book was first supported by the Committee on Professional Standards at The College of the Holy Cross, who awarded me a faculty fellowship for the 1986–1987 academic year. A summer fellowship from the same committee in 1988 carried the work to near completion. Colleagues at the City University of London, particularly Graham Davey, invited me to work among them for a year, during which time the bulk of the research for this book was completed. During my stay in England I profited from the kindness of Ann and Alan Clarke, who generously shared their work and knowledge with a newcomer to the field.

I thank Julian Bach, among others, who helped to see this work through to completion. I owe an unpayable debt to John Walsh, my graduate mentor, who taught me to think like a psychologist. To other colleagues and friends who shared their thoughts about this work and who listened with at least pretended interest as I tried out my ideas on them, a most sincere "thanks."

Any book about IQ attracts its share of criticism; one that challenges some of the prevailing wisdom of the discipline will probably attract more than its share. I accept full responsibility for the errors, both thoughtful and factual, contained herein that may add fuel to those fires.

Introduction

My own interest in IQ and intelligence testing began with a graduate school course on individual differences. It is a course that seldom is taught today in graduate programs, and the training of psychologists is much the worse for that omission. I say that because, arguably, no other area of psychology illuminates the complexities of human nature and the futility of adopting extreme positions regarding the origins of human nature as does the study of individual differences.

Ironically, the study of individual differences in intelligence has long been the birthplace, as well as the final resting place, for some of the most extreme, single-minded views about human nature that psychologists hold. The question of how various sorts of extreme thinking were able to set down such strong roots in this area has long been of interest to me, and detailing that history forms Part I of this book. The setting down of roots, admittedly fascinating in its own right, is, however, far less important than the ideas spawned by the extreme positions themselves. Part II is devoted to those ideas and to their validity.

There are two forms of extremism to be examined, hereditarianism and environmentalism. Both positions are well known and both are buttressed by long-standing beliefs. Hereditarians, at least the most ardent among them, have historically embraced the idea of the immutability of human nature, cloaked behind the formidable truths of evolution and genetics. Environmentalists, who have more recently dominated the debate, have flirted with a far more provocative idea that has an equally heralded history, one that will be referred to as the Pygmalion myth.

It will here be argued that the extremes, whether the modern embodiment of the Pygmalion myth or one that derives from evolution and genetics, are, in fairly equal measure, incorrect. In the case of the hereditarians this argument is not at all surprising, for documenting their apparent shortcomings has become nothing less than an intellectual cottage industry over the past two decades. It will perhaps be far more surprising to find that the shortcomings of the environmentalists are themselves rather striking. The environmentalists' shortcomings, it also will be argued, derive directly from their reliance on the modern incarnation of Pygmalion, the idea that intelligence can rather easily be improved. To place those shortcomings in their appropriate context requires first a brief exploration of the myth itself and its history.

PYGMALION

According to legend, Pygmalion was a sculptor of uncommon devotion to the perfection of his art who fell hopelessly in love with a statue of his own creation, the figure of a woman so perfect that "her face was life itself," according to Ovid.[1] At an annual festival of the gods, after appropriate supplications and animal sacrifices, Pygmalion was moved to beg for a wife. Too shy or perhaps too embarrassed to reveal his true intentions, he asked only for "one like my virgin." Aphrodite, in her wisdom, sensed his true wish. Upon returning home Pygmalion kissed the mouth of his statue and found her lips warm, her limbs soft to his touch. The virgin blushed as he kissed her a second time and so was brought to life and to marriage with Pygmalion.

History has it that the Pygmalion myth was itself a transformation that began as a primitive, erotic tale of a Cypriot king who attempted sexual union with a statue of Aphrodite.[2] In Ovid's hands the myth became an imaginative, if supernatural, story that nonetheless evoked feelings common to human experience, of romance undeterred and love requited. There are, of course, other transformations. The most well known is George Bernard Shaw's play *Pygmalion*, in which the ivory statue is given life in the form of Eliza Doolittle and Pygmalion becomes Henry Higgins, the incorrigible professor of phonetics.

In Shaw's play the myth is brought yet closer to life and becomes a satire on class distinctions. Eliza is the poor flower girl of Covent Garden whom Higgins regards as a "squashed cabbage leaf," an "incarnate insult to the English language." His plans for her are the stuff of myth: "I could pass you off as the Queen of Sheba. . . . I shall make a duchess of this draggletailed guttersnipe."[3] And so it came to be. Eliza is transformed by Higgins in six months' time into a lady, or more precisely, is given the facade of gentility that allows her to be treated as a lady as her inner dignity and grace blossom.

Eliza's transformation is no less miraculous in its way than that of Pygmalion's statue, particularly so since in Shaw's rendering of the myth there is no emotion, no romance between Eliza and her Pygmalion. Higgins, it seems, considers Eliza as nothing more than an *experiment*. At one point in the play Higgins' friend and accomplice, Colonel Pickering, asks: "Does it occur to you, Higgins, that the girl has some feelings?" Higgins replies: "Oh, no, I don't think so. Not any feelings that we need bother about."[4] The lack of romance was fully rectified in the Broadway musical adaptation of Shaw's play, *My Fair Lady*. For our purposes, however, Shaw's attempt to see the relationship between Eliza and Higgins in terms of an experiment is quite to the point. There is, as it happens, a modern embodiment of the Pygmalion myth that is itself much of an experiment. In place of Higgins imagine social scientists armed not with lessons in phonetics, but with cherished beliefs about the malleability of human nature. In place of Eliza imagine young children.

This most recent transformation of the myth is not playful fiction, as myth may sometimes be, nor is it merely the contrived reality of ancient legend brought to the present. It is, we are counseled, the stuff of science, and as science it enjoys a honored place in American psychology and education. The myth's scientific origins will themselves be of concern, albeit briefly, but our principal interest with respect to the Pygmalion myth is far more provocative. It is, simply stated, whether the Pygmalion myth in this most modern incarnation is fact or fantasy. Can we alter the potential of children? The answer to that question can be phrased in as many ways as we can define potential, but one way has clearly dominated the thinking of social scientists for the better part of this century: Can we alter intelligence?

We might, as is at times done, hide behind the many definitions of intelligence to obscure a clear-cut answer, but it is undoubtedly true that one definition of intelligence has the force of history and common usage behind it. Intelligence is most often measured by standard intelligence tests and is represented—rightly or wrongly—by the summary score derived from those tests, the intelligence quotient, or IQ. Whatever the faults of IQ, and they are many, as we will see, a simple fact cannot be escaped: Social scientists have invariably used IQ as the principal measure of intelligence and as the preferred measure to document the outcomes of attempts to alter the intellectual capacity of children.

THE ACCURACY OF EXTREMISM

The contention that intelligence is highly malleable usually embraces several assumptions. Most important for our purposes, that proposition often carries with it the idea that genetic influences on intelligence are negligible. It is assumed as well that preschools, the focus of institutional attempts to alter intelligence over the past twenty-five years, are effective. That assumption may mean many things, among them the idea that having children master a common curriculum and share a common experience—in short, being in school as compared with, say, being at home—is the best way to enhance intelligence. And perhaps of equal importance, it is assumed that an early start on malleability is essential, that there is some sort of critical period in intellectual development that, if bypassed, cannot easily, if ever, be recaptured.

These assumptions are part and parcel of modern social science, together constituting a portion of the received wisdom of the discipline, as it were. For that reason alone it will undoubtedly be rather disturbing to find that each of them fails, in the main, to capture the nature of IQ and its malleability. The challenges to conventional thinking do not end there, however, for the paradoxes that emerge from the study of intelligence far outweigh the simple and straight conclusions to be drawn.

Naturally, if both the hereditarians and the environmentalists are, in large measure, incorrect, it is reasonable to ask what is left. What remains is in fact neither myth nor mystery, but it will lead to a heretofore unrecognized appreciation of what I have called *uniqueness*, and with it the certainty that the particular array of abilities that constitutes our intelligence is very much the product of our own idiosyncratic pathways and less the result of imposed common experience. This idea of uniqueness and some thoughts about the nature and status of IQ in the context of uniqueness form Part III of this work.

NOTES

1. Anderson, W. S. (Ed.). (1972). *Ovid's Metamorphoses, Books 6 - 10* (pp. 495–501). Norman: University of Oklahoma Press.
2. Ibid.
3. Shaw, G.B. (1916). *Pygmalion*. Edinburgh, Scotland: Penguin Books, pp. 27, 41.
4. Ibid., pp. 43–44.

Chronology

1884	Galton's Anthropometric Laboratory
1911	First version of Binet's intelligence test
1912	Goddard publishes *The Kallikak Family: A Study in the Heredity of Feeblemindedness*
	George Bernard Shaw publishes *Pygmalion*
1916	Terman's first version of the Stanford-Binet
1923	Brigham publishes *A Study of American Intelligence*
1928	Goddard's "recanting"
1937	Terman's revision of the Stanford-Binet
1946	Bernardine Schmidt's study
1949	Hebb publishes *The Organization of Behavior*
	Skodak and Skeels final report
1961	Hunt publishes *Intelligence and Experience*
1964	Bloom publishes *Stability and Change in Human Characteristics*
1965	Head Start initiated
1969	Jensen publishes "How Much Can We Boost IQ and Scholastic Achievement?"
1974	Kamin publishes *The Science and Politics of IQ*
1978	First publication of the French Adoption Study
1982	Comprehensive report from the Consortium for Longitudinal Studies
1988	Final report of the Milwaukee Project
1989	First publication of French Cross-Fostering Study
1990	First Comprehensive publication of the Minnesota Study of Identical Twins Reared Apart

Part I
A History of Extremisms

1

Case Study of a Miracle

If the misery of our poor be caused not by the laws of nature, but by our institutions, great is our sin.

—Charles Darwin[1]

It was a moment in history when anything and everything must have seemed possible. In 1946, the United States entered the postwar era in sole possession of the atomic bomb, its industrial reconversion to a peacetime economy nearly completed, and on the cusp of an unparalleled baby boom. If presidents do well to gauge the spirit of the people and embrace it as their own, then Harry Truman seemed to be right on the mark when he confidently predicted the peaceful use of atomic energy, the spread of democracy throughout Eastern Europe, and called upon the American people to become the "most powerful pressure group in the world." Perhaps simply because unbridled optimism should never go unpunished, the people, in their wisdom, soon responded by presenting Democrat Truman with a Republican Congress in the midterm elections of that year.

It was, it would seem, the best of times for changes in conventional wisdom, a time for the unexpected. The perfect moment for the publication of a study unique in the history of psychology. In the *Psychological Monographs* of that year Bernardine G. Schmidt published an article titled "Changes in Personal, Social, and Intellectual Behavior of Children Originally Classified as Feeble-minded."[2] Contrary to the limited space usually given to scientific publications, Schmidt's article ran 144 pages. The article was accompanied by a quite unusual prefatory statement, one never seen before or since in a scientific publication. It was co-signed by the editor of the journal, Dr. Schmidt, and two psychologists who had served as members of her doctoral examination committee.

In view of intense and critical advance interest in the following study . . . it seems appropriate to call the attention of readers to a somewhat unusual situation in respect to scientific policy in publication. Where a piece of research produces results which appear to be in sharp contrast to conventional professional opinion, and especially if there is an element of controversy, a scientist might be expected to withhold publication pending a repetition of the research, preferably under independent auspices. In the present case, however, although several such repetitions of this investigation are, we understand, at the point of being initiated, the unusual scope of the experiment, involving some eight years for the collection of the data plus several more for preliminary planning and the subsequent analyses, would entail a delay of many years if publication were to be held up. Because of the desirability of making available the full report of the study for those who may wish to repeat various aspects of it for verification or extension, the undersigned believe it desirable to publish at this time.

The space allocated to the article and the unprecedented prefatory statement seemed justified, for the article described in incredible and dramatic detail nothing less than the rescue of children who would otherwise be lost to lifelong institutional care. The subjects were 254 adolescents aged twelve to fourteen who had been classified as feebleminded, a term that in the vernacular of the times designated those whose intellectual functioning left them minimally educable and virtually incurable. As Schmidt pointed out, the problem of treating feebleminded children in postwar America was not a small one: In one census 98,000 children and adolescents classified as feebleminded were enrolled in special schools throughout the country; another 22,000 were in private or public homes and institutions. An untold number of children, probably many times more than those located by the census, had yet to be identified.

At the start of Schmidt's training program the children's IQs averaged 52. The nature of that average can be illustrated by the hypothetical distribution of IQ scores shown in Figure 1. As are many measurements, the distribution of IQs is normal or bell-shaped. The largest frequency of scores as well as their mean or average occurs at 100. That the mean falls at 100 is not a stroke of luck; intelligence tests are constructed deliberately so as to have this property.

To describe a distribution of scores fully the mean must be known as well as something about the spread of scores around the mean. The vertical lines perpendicular to the mean spaced at 15-point intervals are a measure of that spread called standard deviations. As illustrated in the graph, about 68 percent of all scores are encompassed by the standard deviations on either side of the mean, that is, IQs of 115 and 85. Two standard deviations above and below the mean encompass about 95 percent of all scores, and three standard deviations include 99 percent of all scores.

The feebleminded children in Schmidt's study began with IQs that were more than three standard deviations below the mean (52 is less than the value of 55 that marks the third standard deviation below the mean). That average can be expressed in another way by subtracting 52 from the average of 100 and then dividing by the standard deviation: $52 - 100/15 = -3.20$. The result is called a deviation score, and these scores are useful because the probability of any one of them occurring in a normal distribution is known precisely. In the case of -3.20

Figure 1
The Normal Distribution of IQ Scores

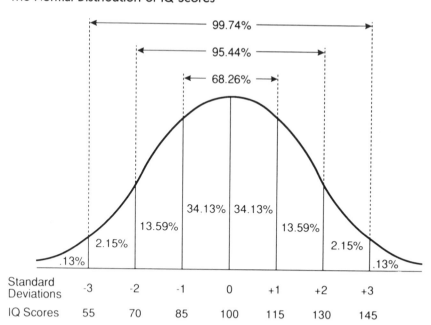

the probability of a score that low is .0007, meaning that the average IQ of Schmidt's adolescents fell well below the lowest 1 percent of all IQs.

As might be expected from the position of the adolescents' IQs, their backgrounds and family lives were extremely disadvantaged. Nearly half of the fathers were unemployed, their families on public assistance; those who were employed worked in semiskilled or unskilled occupations. Many of the parents had long histories of mental or physical illnesses. Fifty-nine percent of the homes fell below the average of adequate housing for the city of Chicago, where the study had been conducted in the late 1930s. The adolescents themselves were plagued by numerous physical abnormalities and behavioral problems in addition to low IQs.

The three-year training program was conducted in three special schools in which Schmidt was head teacher. The program was both intensive and comprehensive. It included the development of "desirable personal behavior," improvement of fundamental academic skills, manipulative arts, work-study habits, and even vocational pre-employment experience. By the end of the program the adolescents' IQs had risen to an average of 72, an increase that placed them within two standard deviations of the mean with a deviation score of −1.90.

More important, these gains were not the end of the program's successes. The adolescents continued to improve after the end of training when they returned to regular schooling or to jobs. Five years after the end of the program Schmidt again tested her subjects and found their average IQ now to be 89, a deviation score of −0.70, or within the general range termed low-normal to normal. None of the adolescents had an IQ below 50; 27 percent of them had IQs that were above 100. The average gain in IQ had exceeded 30 points; more than one-quarter of the adolescents had gained more than 50 points. Presumably the program had allowed the youths to take better advantage of life experiences after training, the direct effects of the program spiraling into even greater posttraining gains.

The cumulative effects of Schmidt's program, by far the most remarkable ever published, were not confined to gains in IQ. Eighty-five percent of the adolescents had continued some form of voluntary schooling or training after the end of the program. More than half had completed some high school education. Ninety-three percent were employed; none were in need of financial assistance from public agencies. Stated another way, by the end of the follow-up study when the subjects were twenty to twenty-two years of age, they had the profile in every respect—intellectually, socially, and personally—of average adults.

These results are even more remarkable if we consider some additional facts. Schmidt reported that the families of these feebleminded adolescents had remained at virtually the same low socioeconomic level during the training and follow-up periods, conditions that would presumably have maintained the adolescents' intellectual and adjustment problems. This prediction was born out by examination of a control group of sixty-eight feebleminded adolescents that Schmidt had constituted at the start of her study. These subjects, none of whom experienced Schmidt's training program, actually performed more poorly on tests at the end of the follow-up period than they had eight years earlier. In addition, their overall adjustment, as judged by contacts with public agencies, mental health clinics, and the criminal court system, was far below that of the adolescents who had received Schmidt's training program. Presumably, for these adolescents the cumulative negative effects of their environments had slowly eroded even their modest levels of intellectual and social functioning.

The details provided by Schmidt might seem to have left little in the way of unresolved questions. She presented an exhaustive number of measurements in seventy-seven tables and twenty-three graphs. In addition, she provided a unique comparison in the form of eleven pairs of identical twins, one member of which had received Schmidt's training program, the other placed in the control group or into regular schooling. As identical twins share identical heredity, any differences between them must be due to environmental factors. Separating the twins into the training and control groups would seem a somewhat ethically curious procedure in that one twin was denied treatment, but it was deemed essential to separate the twins in these eleven pairs because of their growing dependence on each other.

One such separated twin pair was Gloria and Lavern. The twins lived in one of the poorest sections of Chicago, in a home their family had once owned but had lost at the start of the Depression and now rented. Their father was employed by the Works Projects Administration and earned $18 per week. Lavern had been referred for special examination because of her severely poor school achievement. At the age of thirteen she was unable to read and was only in the second grade. Her tested IQ was 69. Gloria was in the fifth grade with a measured IQ of 71. After testing, Lavern was assigned to one of Schmidt's training groups, Gloria to a regular classroom.

The separation reportedly was difficult for the twins. They had fallen into a destructive pattern of using each other as mutual scapegoats to avert the emotional pressures that arose from their academic deficiencies. Once in the training program, Lavern was at first extremely withdrawn but gradually found herself through her artistic ability, a talent that allowed her to gain some recognition from her classmates. She progressed slowly but determinedly; as she did her IQ rose from 69 to 87, then to 92 by the end of the three-year program.

After the program Lavern wanted to continue her studies, but because of her mother's illness, she was forced to take a job as a concession attendant at an amusement park for $25 a week. Commenting on Lavern's progress, even her mother expressed surprise. Only a short time before, Lavern had seemed unable to do anything for herself, much less for others. "Now," her mother said, "I find I actually rely on her to take care of things for us."[3] Lavern moved on to become a clerk in a department store and attended a commercial high school, where she completed a business training course. By the end of the follow-up period she had become head of the credit department of the store, earning $48 per week. Her IQ was now 102.

Gloria, on the other hand, graduated the eighth grade nearly two years after Lavern. She was unable to find work and at the end of the follow-up period had just begun high school—and that only at the urgings of Lavern. Gloria's tested IQ was 68. The results for Gloria and Lavern conformed to that for all eleven twin pairs. In each case the twin who had received Schmidt's training program exceeded his or her co-twin on every measure.

The response to Schmidt's study was predictable. An article in the October 1947 *Reader's Digest* titled "They Are Feebleminded No Longer" described Bernardine Schmidt as a child prodigy who had graduated Chicago's Teacher's college in 1931 at the age of nineteen. With no teaching jobs in sight during the Depression she had started her program for feebleminded adolescents out of desperation, saying, "I need them and they need me."[4] A similar piece appearing in the *Woman's Home Companion* one month earlier led with the banner "Feebleminded Children Can Be Cured."[5]

The scientific community was more skeptical. As is made clear by the prefatory statement, Schmidt's data at the time of their publication were unparalleled. No one before her had shown that children or adolescents labeled as feebleminded could be treated so successfully. The only sure confirmation of a finding of that magnitude comes not from the data contained in the original report, no matter how compelling or extensive, but from replication, preferably by other scientists. Schmidt in fact acknowledged that requirement in the prefatory statement and referred to several ongoing replications that would soon document her findings.

After publication of her article, Samuel Kirk, a psychologist also interested in the education of the feebleminded, asked for a list of Schmidt's subjects so that he might examine their school records and retest them himself. Schmidt denied Kirk access to her records, stating that she wanted to protect the confidentiality of her subjects, who had been much-studied by other psychologists since the publication of her article. This "continued spot-light scrutiny cannot help those young men and women preserve the adjustment they have worked so hard to win. . . . If human lives were not the cost, they could be so disclosed."[6]

Without the names of the subjects Kirk was left to substantiate Schmidt's study based on two strategies: his reanalysis of Schmidt's published data and the results of his own efforts to locate Schmidt's subjects from the records of the Chicago schools that Schmidt had listed. His criticisms were summarized in an article published in 1948.[7] On reading the article one might be struck by the limited, tempered nature of his argument. Kirk found no damaging evidence of fraud, of school records invented or altered. He found nothing in fact to question directly the gains reported by Schmidt for the adolescents. What he did note were a number of relatively minor statistical discrepancies in the original article. Also, from his perusal of the school records, it appeared that the initial IQs of the adolescents in these schools might have been somewhat higher than Schmidt stated. He reported those errors and something a bit more curious: In the schools listed by Schmidt as the training sites he could find no evidence to validate her claims of having been the head teacher.

Schmidt immediately published a reply to Kirk's article.[8] Although not directly addressing his arguments concerning statistical discrepancies, she pointed out that others had critically evaluated her work and had validated its successes. Moreover, as her study took place nearly ten years before Kirk's reanalysis, it would be understandable that the records he located would be incomplete, the memories of people he interviewed to substantiate her claims to have been head teacher would be flawed. She made the aforequoted statement that she was protecting the confidentiality of her subjects, and ended with the strongest scientific rebuttal of all: there were at the time four separate replications of her work under way. Soon there would be little question about the success of her training program to save feebleminded children.

And there, for the moment, the matter will rest. Before discovering what finally became of Bernardine Schmidt's claims it is necessary to place them in context. To do so we need to know something about the history and the meaning of intelligence tests, for to understand each of these issues is to marvel even more at Schmidt's results, coming as they did at a time when prevailing scientific thought could not, in some ways, have been less prepared for them.

NOTES

1. Darwin, C. (1909). *The voyage of the beagle*. New York: P. F. Collier & Son.

2. Schmidt, B. G. (1946). Changes in personal, social, and intellectual behavior of children originally classified as feebleminded. *Psychological Monographs, 60* (5, Serial No. 281).

3. Ibid., p. 110.

4. Clark, B. (1947, October). They are feebleminded no longer. *The Reader's Digest*, p. 43.

5. Stern, E. M. (1947, September). Feebleminded children can be cured. *Woman's Home Companion*, pp. 34–35, 156–158.

6. Schmidt, B. G. (1948). A reply. *Psychological Bulletin, 45*, 343.

7. Kirk, S. A. (1948). An evaluation of the study of Bernardine G. Schmidt entitled: Changes in personal, social, and intellectual behavior of children originally classified as feebleminded. *Psychological Bulletin, 45*, 321–333.

8. Schmidt (1948).

2
Intelligence Testing and the Rise of Hereditarianism

Now if one considers that intelligence is not a single indivisible function with a particular essence of its own, but that it is formed by the combination of all the minor functions of discrimination, observation, retention, etc., all of which have proved to be plastic and subject to increase, it will seem incontestable that the same law govern the ensemble and its elements, and that consequently the intelligence of anyone is susceptible of development. With practice, enthusiasm, and especially with method one can succeed in increasing one's attention, memory, and judgment, and in becoming literally more intelligent than before; and this process will go on until one reaches one's limit.

—Alfred Binet[1]

THE FIRST INTELLIGENCE TEST: GALTON AND BINET

The history of intelligence testing is at times a sordid tale, often spectacular and always provocative. We might begin almost anywhere in history, but there is good reason to start in London in the late nineteenth century, at the International Health Exhibition in South Kensington in 1884, to be exact.

If you were a visitor to South Kensington that year you would probably come across an unusual exhibit called the Anthropometric Laboratory. Just outside the exhibit you would read an announcement that read, in part:

This laboratory is established by Mr. Francis Galton for the following purpose:

1. For the use of those who desire to be accurately measured in many ways, either to obtain timely warning of remediable faults in development, or to learn their powers.

2. For keeping a methodical register of the principal measurements of each person, of which he may at any future time obtain a copy under reasonable restrictions. His initials and date of birth will be entered in the register, but not his name. The names are indexed in a separate book.

3. For supplying information on the methods, practice, and uses of human measurement.

4. For anthropometric experiment and research, and for obtaining data for statistical discussion.[2]

If you then were to wander inside, you would see a long series of benches with various testing stations set along them. At each station a different task would be required: Your reaction time would be measured at one station, your keenness of color vision at the next, hearing acuity at a third station, your height and weight at another, and so on through a number of such stations. If you participated, you would be among the nearly 10,000 persons who did so over a span of six years, and you may have come into contact with one of the most notable and notorious figures in psychology's early history, Sir Francis Galton.

Galton, a half-cousin of Charles Darwin, was a man of many talents. As an explorer, he was the first to publish weather maps. As an inventor, he pioneered the study of fingerprints, developing techniques that were later used in criminal investigations. As a scientist, he was interested in the role of heredity in individual differences. He had by the time of the Anthropometric Laboratory established his reputation in the area of genetics by founding and giving name to the science of eugenics, the improvement of offspring through selective breeding.

More to our purposes, in 1869, only ten years after Darwin's announcement of his theory of evolution by natural selection, Galton published *Hereditary Genius*, a voluminous study of the emergence of eminence.[3] In it he traced success of many sorts, ranging from the talents of statesmen and scientists to those of oarsmen and wrestlers, through the life histories of their families over the span of many generations. Galton noted curious regularities in the appearance of eminence in these families. Of the 977 eminent men he identified, only 48 percent of their sons became eminent. That trend of declining eminence continued through succeeding generations. Only 6 percent of the grandsons of eminent men and 1 percent of their great grandsons achieved comparable eminence. Galton called this trend the "law of filial regression to mediocrity." As he later discovered at South Kensington, this law of regression seemed to hold as well for physical stature. Tall fathers tended to have sons who were not quite as tall as them. In like manner, short fathers had sons who were not quite as short.

Sons, then, tended to be more average than were their fathers, both for height and eminence.[4] For Galton, all of this tied neatly together into a explanation true to his hereditarian convictions. If eminence ran in families and behaved as a trait like physical stature, it must have its foundation in the same sort of genetic substrate that was undoubtedly true for height. The genetic basis for the law of regression might seem difficult to divine, but for Galton it was palpably logical: Regression was produced by the "blending of inheritances"—the unique parental heredity pulling in one direction, the mediocrity of more distant generations pulling in another. The result, Galton reasoned, was that the rare inheritance that produced eminence in the father was unlikely to be expressed quite so fully in the son; less so in succeeding generations.[5]

For one so talented, Galton's conclusions seem inexplicably simplistic when cast in a modern light. He gave scant attention to possible environmental similarities that must also run in families and may reasonably give rise to success. The regression effect, too, might be thought to have environmental origins in the unique confluence of factors for one individual that would not likely occur in quite the same manner in succeeding generations. But regardless of the correctness or limitations of Galton's explanations, there can be little doubt as to what he was up to in South Kensington in 1884. He was collecting the first systematic data on individual differences in basic abilities in the hope that these abilities would predict differences in intelligence. He was, in short, in the business of constructing the first intelligence test, using performance on simple tasks as the contents of the test. Given his interests in eugenics, it should not be surprising that Galton believed that individual differences in intelligence were inherited, and that he entertained fanciful ideas as to the uses for his constructed test, including the improvement of human nature through some unspecified form of selective breeding.

Although the body of data Galton collected on individual differences was of considerable interest in its own right, his hope of using these simple tasks to measure intelligence failed. The failure was due, in part, to the fact that differences in these basic processes bore little relation to real-world measures of intellectual performance like academic grades or teachers' ratings.[6] As will soon be apparent, however, Galton's influence extended well beyond the limited successes of his Anthropometric Laboratory.

A decidedly different approach to the development of an intelligence test was taken in France by Alfred Binet. Earlier in his career Binet had been briefly enamored with assessing intelligence by the measurement of physical characteristics such as head size, an approach not far removed in theory from that of Galton. But Binet found, as had others, that these measurements showed only modest relation to real-world measures of intelligence. By 1904 he had abandoned that line of research in favor of one that used complex tasks of reasoning and thinking to measure intelligence. It was to that strategy that he turned when appointed to a commission in that year by the minister of public instruction to develop techniques to identify children in need of special education.

Binet's response to the minister's charge was entirely practical. Instead of attempting a formal definition of intelligence, Binet assumed only that whatever intelligence was, it must be measured with a variety of tasks that tapped higher mental processes. He assumed, too, that intelligence meant nothing absolute, but referred only to a child's relative standing within his or her age group. This second point meant that intelligence should vary regularly with age; a child of ten should be able to perform more tasks correctly than a child of six. Intelligence was cumulative.

With these assumptions in mind, Binet began to construct what would become the first successful intelligence test. His ideas went through several revisions before the final form of his test in 1911. That version, completed just before Binet's untimely death, included five tasks or items at each age level through age fifteen, and five adult items. The items were chosen to reflect on average what about one-half of the subjects at each age could answer correctly. This may seem at first like an odd criterion, but true to Binet's intentions, it was a most practical one. If too many items were included that most children at a given age could answer correctly, the test would not distinguish bright children from those in need of help. That same consideration argues against the inclusion of too many items that almost no child at a given age would answer correctly. Items that span a range of difficulty but that average in the middle of these extremes provide the best "discriminability," a criterion still used to select items for intelligence tests.

Each subject began the test at an age level below his or her chronological age and continued until he or she was unable to answer correctly several items in a row. The items increased in difficulty at the test progressed. The items at age six, for example, included one that asked the child to count thirteen pennies. Another asked the child to distinguish between morning and afternoon. The age ten items included one that asked the child to arrange five same-shaped blocks in order of weight. Another asked the child to draw two designs from memory.

Each item passed was worth one-fifth of the mental age associated with a given chronological age. With a refinement offered by the German psychologist William Stern in 1912, a child's IQ was computed by dividing the child's mental age as determined from the test by the child's chronological age, a division from which we get the notion of "intelligence quotient." The resulting fraction was multiplied by one hundred to eliminate decimals. Thus, if an eight-year-old child passed all the items for age seven and below, four out of five items at age eight, one item at age nine, but none thereafter, that child's mental age would be 8.0 (7 years + 4/5 at age eight + 1/5 at age nine). The child's IQ would be 8/8 × 100 = 100. Note, too, that if that same child could pass only the same number of items at age ten, his or her IQ would have fallen, since 8/10 × 100 = 80. This comparison gives the relativistic flavor of Binet's age-scaled test: the IQ score denoted nothing more than an individual's *standing* within his or her age group.[7]

The differences between Galton and Binet can easily be seen in their approach to the construction of an intelligence test. Whereas Galton believed that the measurement of simple sensorimotor processes would reveal the intellect, Binet opted for the measurement of complex mental tasks. Galton was principally interested in identifying superior adult intelligence; Binet was interested in children with learning difficulties, and from there was led to the idea of developmental changes in intelligence.

Another difference between them is perhaps not so apparent, but for the purpose of assessing the impact of Bernardine Schmidt's study it is far more important. Galton, with his belief in the genetic basis of intelligence, considered what he was attempting to measure to be a unitary ability, inborn and unalterable. Binet thought differently. For him intelligence was far from a singular, genetic-based entity. The very diversity of the items chosen for his test underscored Binet's conviction that intelligence was multifaceted and needed to be measured in various ways. He attempted no formal definition of intelligence beyond referring at some points in his writing to "judgment" as the principal faculty tapped by his test.

Binet also believed that intelligence was not fixed: "We must," he wrote in a now-classic statement, "protest and react against this brutal pessimism."[8] In rebuttal he wrote passionately about the ability of better schooling to contribute to changes in intelligence, as is evident in the quote that begins this chapter.

INTELLIGENCE TESTING IN THE UNITED STATES

The outcome of the different approaches to intelligence and test construction taken by Binet and Galton constitutes one of the dramatic ironies of psychology's history. Whereas Galton's attempts to construct a test failed, Binet's age-scaled test was immediately successful in identifying children in need of special educational attention. More, it was equally successful for this practical purpose not only in France, but also in Belgium, the United Kingdom, and Italy, thereby adding credibility to the test. However, while Binet's test was widely adopted, the interpretation of the summary score derived from it became increasingly congenial to the hereditarian views of Galton and his followers. To understand how that happened requires an understanding of what became of Binet's test in the United States. And that story will return us to feebleminded children and, eventually, Bernardine Schmidt.

Binet's test would likely have met its eventual fate irrespective of who first promoted the importance of mental testing in the United States. It is a curious historical accident, however, that the idea of mental testing and the term itself came to the United States not from a follower of Binet, but from James McKeen Cattell. Cattell had worked in Galton's Anthropometric Laboratory after securing his Ph.D. in Germany in 1888. He returned to the United States from that experience proposing the widespread use and development of mental tests. His convictions met with considerable interest. In 1895, for example, the American Psychological Association, under Cattell's presidency, set up a special committee to study the coordinated development of tests of physical and mental abilities.[9]

A second curious bit of history, not at all accidental, secured the fate of Binet's test and tied its early use inexorably to the views of those committed to Galtonian hereditarianism. The test was first translated into English by H. H. Goddard, director of the Vineland Training School for Feebleminded Girls and Boys in New Jersey. Goddard had established his reputation, and his politics, in a study published in 1912 titled *The Kallikak Family: A Study in the Heredity of Feeblemindedness*.[10] That was the same year that George Bernard Shaw first published *Pygmalion*, and the coincidence in publication dates should not be lightly dismissed, for Goddard's study at first blush bears more than a passing resemblance to Shaw's play.

In true Galtonian tradition it was a pedigree analysis of the family of one of the residents at Vineland, whom Goddard referred to as Deborah. The study of the Kallikaks is very much the story of Deborah. Goddard found her in an almshouse and later arranged her transfer to Vineland. At the time of the study she was twenty-two, and much as Professor Higgins might have pictured Eliza Doolittle, Goddard presented many photographs of Deborah and her progress at Vineland. In one photograph she is seen at a sewing machine working contentedly. Another shows samples of her "handiwork," chairs, a dresser and nightstand, wood carvings that she has made. The photographs provided by Goddard are of interest in their own right, and later we will return to them to describe something reportedly curious about them. But for the moment it is Deborah's family that must capture our attention.

Her family had descended from a Revolutionary War soldier whom Goddard named Martin Kallikak, Sr., a surname coined by Goddard to combine the Greek words for beauty (*kallos*) and bad (*kakos*). As described by Goddard, Martin Kallikak, Sr., "in an unguarded moment steps aside from the paths of rectitude and with the help of a feeble-minded girl, starts a line of mental defectives that is truly appalling."[11] Kallikak had, it seems, engaged in a brief affair with a feebleminded tavern maid during the war. The result of this fateful union was Martin Kallikak, Jr., the great great grandfather of Deborah and one whose sexual proclivities were pronounced enough to warrant the nickname "Old Horror." Goddard traced 480 descendants of Old Horror and found that 143 were feebleminded, 46 were normal, and the rest were of doubtful status.

After the war Martin Kallikak, Sr., married a proper Quakeress. From this more respectable union Goddard located 496 descendants, among whom he found none to be feebleminded. To be accurate, three of these family members were "somewhat degenerate, but they were not defective": two were alcoholics and one was "sexually loose."[12] But Goddard claimed to have found no illegitimate children from this lineage, and no criminals.

It occurred to Goddard, as it had to Galton before him, that such evidence was compatible only with a genetic explanation of intelligence. Goddard's views were reinforced by the striking similarity he noted between the frequencies of feeblemindedness he found in the *kakos* side of the Kallikak family and the newly rediscovered laws of Mendelian inheritance. Goddard's views on intelligence, and of feebleminded children, flowed straightforwardly from the Kallikak study. Intelligence was best represented as a single, underlying function transmitted in true Mendelian fashion. As for feebleminded children, Goddard held out little hope of the sort entertained by Bernardine Schmidt. At their best the mental ages of his students, as measured by the Binet test, fell into the range of eight to twelve years even in late adolescence and early adulthood. These mental ages correspond to the later-used metric of IQs of about 50 to 75. Goddard coined the term moron (from the Greek word *moros*, meaning dull or foolish) to denote the highest-scoring individuals within this range.

Goddard combined his views on intelligence and feeblemindedness into a social theory that was quite compatible with his interest in eugenics. Morons were, in a sense, his greatest problem because they, as "highest grade defectives," were on the cusp of being capable of escaping detection and living on their own. Lower level feeblemindedness, the cases of idiots and imbeciles, would surely be in need of institutions like Vineland. To standardize the treatment of all the feebleminded, Goddard proposed that morons, too, were to live in institutions. His intentions were to provide them with custodial care, and something more:

If both parents are feeble-minded all the children will be feeble-minded. It is obvious that such matings should not be allowed. It is perfectly clear that no feeble-minded person should ever be allowed to marry or to become a parent. It is obvious that if this rule is to be carried out the intelligent part of society must enforce it.[13]

Institutions, then, would serve as a socially acceptable form of sterilization; "segregation through colonization," Goddard called it.[14]

Some of Goddard's writings also suggest that he was not content with this treatment of native-born feebleminded, but sought as well to prevent the immigration of others. The suggestion comes from some haphazard testing of incoming immigrants that Goddard undertook at Ellis Island in 1912 and again, more extensively, in 1917. Not surprisingly, the results revealed that a large percentage of immigrants tested at the level of the feebleminded.

This testing of immigrants has often been cited as clear evidence of the simpleminded, racist mentality of Goddard and the other early hereditarians. In fairness, Goddard's view of these data reflects, at least to some extent, his recognition of the complexities of interpretation. He wrote at one point that "we may argue that it is far more probable that their condition [the low test performance of Ellis Island immigrants] is due to environment than it is due to heredity. ... We know their environment has been poor. It seems able to account for the result."[15]

But having granted that much, it is also clear that Goddard's prevailing disposition was far less open-minded. At one point he relates: "We picked out one young man whom we suspected was defective, and, through the interpreter, proceeded to give him the test. The boy tested eight by the Binet scales. The interpreter said, 'I could not have done that when I came to this country,' and seemed to think the test unfair. We convinced him that the boy was defective."[16] Interestingly, this "picking out" of the feebleminded was a learnable skill, according to Goddard: "After a person has had considerable experience in this work, he almost gets a sense of what a feebleminded person is so that he can tell one afar off. The people who are best at this work, and who I believe should do this work, are women. Women seem to have closer observation than men."[17] Irrespective of the precise characterization of Goddard's intentions at Ellis Island, it is clear that in his hands Binet's test underwent a rather dramatic transformation in function, from a practical tool to identify schoolchildren in need of help to an index—albeit imprecise and controversial—of genetic worth.

That trend continued when the most popular form of Binet's test was developed by Lewis Terman at Stanford University.

THE STERILIZATION LAWS AND THE "SURVEILLANCE" OF THE FEEBLEMINDED

In Terman's autobiography he relates a story that traces his interest in testing to an itinerant book peddler and amateur phrenologist who visited the family farm in Indiana when Terman was nine or ten.[18] After feeling the contours along Terman's head the peddler predicted a bright future. The impact of this prediction was not lost on Terman, who for several years thereafter maintained a keen interest in phrenology. Beyond that it must be said that Terman lived up to the peddler's prediction. He did more than simply translate Binet's test. Whereas Binet had used only 50 subjects to develop and standardize his scales, Terman in 1916 produced a revision that used 1,400 subjects. The resulting instrument was referred to as the Stanford-Binet, and has come to serve as the benchmark against which other intelligence tests are measured.

In the opening pages of the manual accompanying the 1916 Stanford-Binet, Terman made clear what he had in mind for the test:

It is safe to predict that in the near future intelligence tests will bring tens of thousands of these high-grade defectives under the surveillance and protection of society. This will ultimately result in curtailing the production of feeble-mindedness and in the elimination of an enormous amount of crime, pauperism, and industrial inefficiency. It is hardly necessary to emphasize that the high-grade cases, of the type now so frequently overlooked, are precisely the ones whose guardianship it is most important for the State to assume.[19]

Even granting that the word surveillance might have had different connotations when Terman wrote, the paragraph has a chilling air about it. It is Galton's thinking traced through Goddard and infused with a sanctimonious and perverse faith in the singular power of IQ. And the goal was quite explicit: nothing less than a biologically based ordering, a channeling of people into professions based on the IQ as a measure of "vocational fitness." According to Terman, those with IQs below 75 were destined for unskilled labor; for those who scored between 75 and 85 semiskilled occupations awaited. Only if one's IQ exceeded 113 could substantial success be predicted.

It is a recurrent and not surprising observation in the history of intelligence testing that scientific thinking invariably impacts public policy. That influence undoubtedly arises from the volatile nature of the issues surrounding intelligence and its assessment, a fact well understood by the interested scientists. Perhaps as well those concerned with public policy matters are eager to make use of test results to provide a supposed ideologically free basis for their decisions. Yet, as is likely already apparent, it is folly to suppose that science is ever divorced in these matters from ideology.

And so it was with the position of the early intelligence testers. It cannot be entirely coincidental that the rise in mental testing, and more to the point, the rise in the hereditarian view of intelligence, seems to have coincided with a particularly malicious chapter in American legal history, that of the enactment of sterilization laws.[20] The first such law, passed by Indiana in 1907, well preceded the use of IQ tests in the United States. Within ten years five more states had enacted similar laws, each of them quite loosely based on two assumptions: first, that traits such as feeblemindedness, along with criminality, moral perversion, drunkenness, and a host of putatively related disorders, were inherited and, therefore, unchangeable and second, that feeblemindedness could be accurately detected using, among other tools, intelligence tests.[21]

It is apparent that many such laws, although enacted, were never enforced. Yet some were. In Goddard's study of the Kallikaks he notes that although eight states had passed laws authorizing sterilization, actual practice was "carefully restricted to a few inmates of various specified institutions."[22] In 1927, Judge Oliver Wendell Holmes, Jr., in delivering the Supreme Court's decision in the most famous challenge to the sterilization laws, *Buck v. Bell*, argued in part: "We have seen more than once that the public welfare may call upon the best citizens for their lives. It would be strange if it could not call upon those who already sap the strength of the state for these lesser sacrifices. . . . Three generations of imbeciles are enough."[23]

Carrie Buck was a seventeen-year-old girl who had been chosen in 1924 for the first sterilization performed in Virginia. She had tested at a mental age of nine on the Stanford-Binet. Her mother, Emma, then fifty-two, had tested at a mental age of seven. Carrie's daughter, Vivian, seven months old at the time of the decision to sterilize Carrie, was tested and also judged to be feebleminded.[24] Making so harsh a judgment on so young a child should be kept in mind even apart from its cruelty, for as we will see, mental tests for infants and young children are notoriously unreliable, meaning that scores can change appreciably from one testing to another. The dangers attendant to that unreliability have never been more dramatically illustrated than in the case of Carrie Buck: Labeling Vivian as feebleminded gave Justice Holmes his three-generation requirement. The Supreme Court voted eight to one to allow the sterilization to proceed, and in the process upheld the constitutionality of the sterilization laws.

Two subsequent incidents further elaborate this tragedy. Vivian Buck completed the second grade before dying of an intestinal disorder in 1932. Her teachers reportedly judged her to be very bright. As if that singular fact is not sufficiently distressing, Carrie's sister, Doris, was sterilized under the same law in 1928. Doris Buck, however, was never informed of the nature of the surgery she had undergone. "They told me that the operation was for an appendix and rupture," she later said. She tried over the years to conceive, consulting physicians repeatedly. None apparently recognized that her fallopian tubes had been severed. It was only in 1980 that Doris Buck finally discovered the truth. That was the same year that an article in the *Washington Post* revealed that the Virginia sterilization law had been upheld—and enforced—from 1924 to 1972, resulting in more than 7,500 sterilizations.[25]

Numbers, irrespective of their magnitude, can at times not capture tragedy as can a single voice. In this instance that voice belongs to Doris Buck: "I broke down and cried. My husband and me wanted children desperate—we were crazy about them. I never knew what they'd done to me."[26]

In the midst of this tragedy it may seem a cruel joke to point out that Terman dedicated the manual accompanying his 1916 Stanford-Binet to Alfred Binet. Even apart from the aberration of the sterilization laws, Binet surely would have been horrified to see the uses to which his test was being put. Yet to Terman his proposed use of the test seemed compatible with Binet's original intent of identifying those in need of special education. And even in the midst of pronouncements like his "surveillance" quote, Terman at least entertained—cynically, to be sure—the question of whether environmental circumstances might contribute to individual differences in intelligence:

Without such tests we cannot know to what extent a child's mental performances are determined by environment and to what extent by heredity. Is the place of the so-called lower classes in the social and industrial scale the result of their inferior native environment, or is their apparent inferiority merely a result of their inferior home or school training? Is genius more common among children of the educated classes than among the children of the ignorant and poor? Are the inferior races really inferior, or are they merely unfortunate in their lack of opportunity to learn? Only intelligence tests can answer these questions and grade the raw material with which education works. Without them we can never distinguish the results of our educational efforts with a given child from the influence of the child's original endowment.[27]

IQ AND THE "WAR TO END ALL WARS"

The intended usage of Terman's test aside, its publication resulted in a bit of confusion. There were now two versions of Binet's test in the United States, Goddard's and Terman's, and in practice they yielded different results. Some sort of uniformity seemed in order, and the opportunity for just that came from an unexpected source—World War I. The unification was brought about by the then president of the American Psychological Association, Robert Yerkes. Yerkes' convictions about intelligence and its origins seem apparent from the fact that in 1917, he was appointed chairman of a Committee on Inheritance of Mental Traits for the Eugenics Research Association. As World War I began Yerkes, a colonel and the ranking psychologist in the army, brought together a working group of psychologists, including Terman and Goddard, to develop a test that could be used on all army recruits. Their express goal was to be able to identify recruits with respect to intellectual functioning for placement purposes, and in particular to keep the feebleminded out of the army.

The group gathered at Goddard's Vineland school from May through July in 1917. By virtue of the demands of testing nearly two million soldiers, the resulting instrument was a group test. It was drawn up in two forms, Alpha and Beta, the latter a nonverbal form to be used with illiterates and non–English-speaking men. A third test, Terman's Stanford-Binet, was included for cases in which an individual might be in need of more extensive testing beyond the group forms.

It has been said that the Armistice in 1918 came too soon to make much use of the results of Yerkes' efforts. It may be true with respect to the intention of using the testing for personnel decisions, but in point of fact the testing program had yielded a body of results that would take years to assimilate and would have continuing repercussions.

In one sense the data seemed to provide generous support for the hereditarian position of Goddard, Terman, and Yerkes. White recruits scored highest, immigrants below them, and blacks lower still. But there were problems. Conscientious objectors scored well above average despite their obvious moral depravity, as did disloyalists. Worse, for immigrants there seemed to be a correlation between environmental conditions and test scores such that their scores rose consistently with their years of residence in the United States. Indeed, with twenty years of residence immigrants seemed equivalent to white Americans, whereas with only five years of residence immigrants scored only at the level of the feebleminded.

This latter finding might presumably have led to an environmental interpretation: The longer an immigrant had lived in the United States, the greater the mastery of the skills necessary to perform well on the test. But as one might expect, given prevailing dispositions, that sort of explanation was passed over for another. Carl Brigham, who later assisted in the development of the Scholastic Aptitude Test, provided the needed interpretation. In *A Study of American Intelligence* in 1923 Brigham reanalyzed the army test data and offered the conclusion that the higher test scores of longer-resident immigrants meant only that there had been systematic declines in the genetic fitness of each succeeding group of immigrants. Immigrants who had been in the United States longer than newer immigrants were simply of better stock; it was not the case that their intelligence had improved with their length of residence.[28]

Brigham went on to conjecture that with the increasing postwar flood of lower-intelligent immigrants to the United States, particularly from Italy, Poland, and Russia, there would follow a decline in the general intellectual (genetic) fitness of the U.S. population. Brigham concluded his book with an ominous warning:

Immigration should not only be restrictive but highly selective. And the revision of the immigration and naturalization laws will only afford a slight relief from our present difficulty. The really important steps are those looking toward the prevention of the continued propagation of defective strains in the present population.[29]

Immigration and a Country of Morons

It seems but a small step from there to subsequent political events. If the earlier views of Goddard and Terman had given rise, at least indirectly, to the sterilization laws, the new evidence of the genetic inferiority of immigrants was related in equal measure to the passage of the 1924 Johnson-Lodge Immigration Act. The law limited immigration to 2 percent of the number of immigrants from a given country based on the 1890 census. The choice of 1890 is instructive, for it was after that date that the influx of southeastern Europeans had begun, precisely those immigrants who had seemed to perform so poorly on the army tests.

Admittedly, the immigration law, as any other, had several sources of influence, including the desire of labor leaders to restrict job competition. Indeed, political coalitions in favor of restrictive immigration existed long before the emergence of intelligence tests in the United States. The law would undoubtedly have been ratified without the convenient evidence of immigrant inferiority provided by the army data.[30] But it is also clear that enactment of the law was congenial to the views of Brigham and advocates of his position. Perhaps even more important, the law seems intuitively to be a fitting outcome of the speculative interpretation given to the army data and of Goddard's earlier warnings—uncompromised by his qualifying comments—about the percentage of morons at Ellis Island.

The Immigration Act of 1924 was, however, but one outcome of the army testing. The earlier stated fact that immigrants residing in the United States for twenty years scored at the level of the average white recruit needs further elaboration. We did not consider what that level was, and the answer must have produced an initial reaction that was nothing less than astonishing. Terman had previously set the mental age of the average white adult at sixteen. That figure in fact became the divisor in computing adult IQ (mental age/16 × 100). One can only image the expressions of Terman, Goddard, Yerkes, and Brigham when scores on the army tests were converted to mental ages. The average white recruit tested at a mental age of thirteen—13.08 to be exact—or an IQ of about 81. It didn't escape their notice that one implication of this figure was particularly disastrous: Given the normal distribution of test scores, an average mental age of thirteen must mean that nearly one-half of the recruits were blow that average and must be, in Goddard's terms, morons. Could the country survive an army of morons?

There is no one answer to how this fact was eventually assimilated. There is evidence that the first reaction, at least by hereditarians, was to hold fast to the goodness of the test. It was then simply the case that moronity must be far more prevalent than previously suspected, a fact that fueled the growing fires of restrictive immigration. If, after all, the average mental age is already so endangered, further immigration could do nothing more than lower it still. It is likely as well that social assistance programs suffered in the belief that if the average mental age were thirteen, then those under public assistance must be in the lowest reaches of genetic inferiority, and beyond remediation.

HEREDITARIAN "RECANTINGS"

Another effect of the army data admittedly is more suggestive. Soon after the debates about creeping moronity and restrictive immigration the principal hereditarians in the mental testing movement, Goddard, Terman, and Brigham, underwent apparent changes of heart. Goddard, for example, in 1928, wrote:

Then it was for a time rather carelessly assumed that everybody who tested 12 years or less was feebleminded. . . . We now know of course that only a small percentage of the people who test 12 are actually feebleminded . . . the *problem of the moron is a problem of education and training.* . . . It may still be objected that moron parents are likely to have imbecile or idiot children. There is not much evidence that this is the case. The danger is probably negligible. . . . I have no difficulty in concluding that when we get an education that is entirely right there will be no morons who cannot manage themselves and their affairs and compete in the struggle for existence. . . . If we could only hope to add to this a social order that would literally give every man a chance, I should be perfectly sure of the result.[31]

Goddard's statement surely has an air of unreality about it, particularly the last sentences, which exude an almost environmentalist's bravado. It should be noted, however, that Goddard was not referring here to increasing intelligence, only to the possibility of the "highest grade defectives" living largely independent lives. In this supposed recanting in fact he argued strongly against the idea that the intelligence of morons could be raised. Nonetheless, the palpable contradiction between even this modest sentiment and his earlier writings did not escape Goddard, who admitted: "As for myself, I think I have gone over to the enemy."[32]

Terman's change of heart took the form of the manual accompanying his 1937 revision of the Stanford-Binet. In it Terman seemed quite sensitive to the complexities of what was measured by the test. In one part of the manual he cautioned that mental age is relevant only to a particular intelligence test and does not measure other kinds of intelligence, such as musical or mechanical ability, or social adjustment. With respect to IQ differences in social class he warned that

it is hardly necessary to stress the fact that these figures [referring to a table of IQs for different occupations] refer to mean values only, and that in view of the variability of the IQ within each group the respective distributions greatly overlap one another. Nor should it be necessary to point out that such data do not, in themselves, offer any conclusive evidence of the relative contributions of genetic and environmental factors in determining the mean differences observed. . . . Even if the trend were reliable it would require an extensive research, carefully planned for the purpose, to determine whether the lowered IQ of rural children can be ascribed to the relatively poorer educational facilities in rural communities, and whether the gain for children from the lower economic strata can be attributed to an assumed enrichment of intellectual environment that school attendance bestows.[33]

For Brigham the recanting was, if anything, more pronounced. Perhaps remembering his role in the 1924 Immigration Act, Brigham wrote in 1930:

Most psychologists working in the test field have been guilty of a naming fallacy which easily enables them to slide mysteriously from the score in the test to the hypothetical faculty suggested by the name given to the test. . . . That study [referring to his *A Study of American Intelligence*] with its entire hypothetical superstructure of racial differences collapses completely. . . . Tests in the vernacular must be used only with individuals having equal opportunities to acquire the vernacular of the test. . . . One of the most pretentious of these comparative racial studies—the writer's own—was without foundation.[34]

Where did these changes of heart originate? They have been characterized by some as rather sudden, almost inexplicable recantings. Stephen Jay Gould, for example, puzzling over the apparent change in tone in the manual that accompanied the 1937 Stanford-Binet revision, offered that "common authorship [Terman's] seems at first improbable."[35] Improbable or not, the origin of these apparent recantings is determinable and derives from two sources. First, of course, were the army tests. There were abundant hints and numerous bits of evidence of environmental influences on test scores in the army data, only some of which we've discussed. It could not have entirely escaped attention, for example, that the average mental age of thirteen corresponded roughly to the average age at which most recruits had left school. Then, too, the percentage of feebleminded in the U.S. population, as implied by the army test results, was simply too extraordinary to be believed. That fact alone must have called into question the very definition of feeblemindedness as judged principally by IQ. Each bit of evidence or uncomfortable conclusion might be explained away in isolation from the rest, but to dismiss the entire body of evidence must have produced considerable dissonance.

The second influence stems from the fundamental character of American psychology. From examination of the mental testing movement it may appear that American psychology was, at the time, firmly rooted in hereditarian thinking. Nothing, however, could be further from the truth. The operative forces in American psychology were in fact quite disparate during these years. One of the dominant forces in experimental psychology of that era, behaviorism, was in fact quite clearly opposed to hereditarian thinking. That opposition can easily be seen in a quote from John Watson, the founder of behaviorism. In 1930 Watson did nothing less than bring the Pygmalion myth to life in the form of a thought experiment that soon became one of psychology's most quoted statements:

Our conclusion, then, is that we have no real evidence of the inheritance of traits. I would feel perfectly comfortable in the ultimate favorable outcome of careful upbringing of a *healthy well-formed baby* born of a long line of crooks, murderers and thieves, and prostitutes. Who has any evidence to the contrary? . . .

I should like to go one step further now and say, "Give me a dozen healthy infants, well-formed, and my own specified world to bring them up in and I'll guarantee to take anyone at random and train him to become any type of specialist I might select—doctor, lawyer, artist, merchant-chief and, yes, even beggar-man and thief, regardless of his talents, penchants, tendencies, abilities, vocations, and race of his ancestors.'' I am going beyond my facts and I admit it, but so have the advocates of the contrary and they have been doing it for many thousands of years.[36]

The supposed recantings of the hereditarians may then be better characterized, at least in part, as expressions of the fundamental conflicts in American psychology rather than as sudden changes of mind. Surely, the ambiguities in the army data had their cumulative effect, perhaps largely as a catalyst. But there simply were profoundly different ideas rummaging around the collective consciousness of American psychology during these years, and they likely had the counterbalancing effect of mitigating attempts at extreme thinking, hereditarian oriented or otherwise. And, intuitively, Watson's quote and the behaviorism it illustrates seem to capture American impatience, its leanings toward practicality, the desire to intervene and change, ideas likely not entirely lost even on staunch hereditarians.

More important perhaps, these different ideas, particularly those associated with environmentally oriented psychology, were beginning to unearth findings that were inherently contradictory to a hereditarian viewpoint. Some of those findings would in fact soon provide the intellectual foundations for Bernardine Schmidt's study. Others had a more immediate impact. Terman, for example, was regularly attacked for his hereditarian views, not only by other specialists, but also by columnist Walter Lippmann in a vitriolic series of exchanges in the popular press.[37] The impact of these disparate ideas can also be glimpsed in Terman's 1932 autobiography, in which he listed Galton as the founder of modern psychology whom he most admired, but in the very next sentence cited Binet as his "favorite of all psychologists."[38]

There were, then, the shadowy stirrings of educational possibilities, the necessary precursors to Bernardine Schmidt's later demonstration of the malleability of IQ. And these stirrings were evident even in Terman's earlier writings. Recall his earlier-cited quote concerning the role of tests in separating the effects of schooling from that of genetic endowment. Expanding that premise into a challenge, he had written in 1925:

There are . . . many persons who believe that intelligence quotients can be manufactured to order by application of suitable methods of training. . . . If it is possible it is time we were finding out. Conclusive evidence as to the extent to which IQs can be artificially raised could be supplied in a few years by an experiment which would cost a few hundred thousand or at most a few million dollars. The knowledge would probably be worth to humanity a thousand times that amount.[39]

There is here, as earlier, an unmistakable cynical flavor to Terman's writing. He was not arguing that there is such malleability, only that one ought to find out. We might note in this regard that the recantings of the hereditarians were far from complete changes of mind. In Terman's 1932 autobiography, despite his affection for Binet, he referred to Watsonian behaviorism with its "denial of heredity'' as a ''cult'' that was essentially ''ridiculous,'' and argued ''that the major differences between children of high and low IQ will never be fully accounted for on an environmental hypothesis.''[40]

Even in Goddard's 1928 recanting there is a healthy dose of rather standard hereditarian thinking. His recanting, it should be remembered, referred only to morons, the ''highest grade defectives.'' As for idiots and imbeciles, Goddard suggested that they remain ''outside the pale of citizenship,'' and that they be given the name ''mental cripples,'' and live, as before, in segregated colonies.[41] The equivocal nature of Goddard's recanting can also be seen as late as 1942, when he published a vigorous and indignant defense of his Kallikak study to combat the growing criticisms that his methodology fell considerably short of perfection, and defending as well his use of Mendelian principles to describe the genetic character of the Kallikak lineage.[42]

It was, at best, a tortured and ironic defense. Tortured because by the time Goddard wrote it his Kallikak study had taken on the character of an indefensible joke. The army data decades earlier had called into question the ability of even standard intelligence tests to identify the feebleminded. How could Goddard have been so certain of his assessments when all he had to go on were incomplete records, the faulty memories of family members, and some photographs?

The photographs of Kallikak family members, specifically something later claimed about them, bring us to the irony of Goddard's defense. In studying Goddard's work several years ago Stephen Jay Gould noticed something he thought was rather curious about those photographs.[43] The relevant photographs are reproduced here in Figure 2.

In the top photograph we can see Deborah, the Kallikak saved from the depravities of her family by residency in Vineland. As though to emphasize her well-being, she is pictured seated reading a book, serene and pretty in a white dress, a flowery bow in her hair, a cat nestled in her lap.[44] The lower photograph provides the dramatic contrast of Kallikak family members outside their rural poverty-ridden shack. Look closely and you can see something that Gould noticed and later verified. The photograph of the family members has been retouched, albeit somewhat crudely, with the result that the family members look distinctly different from Deborah. And surely we wonder: What was the reason for the retouching? The obvious implication of the retouching is that Goddard in 1942 may have been defending a fraud as well as an indefensible joke.

Although this argument fits neatly with the charges made against Goddard and the other early hereditarians, it is almost certainly incorrect. Most important, Goddard had little to gain by the retouching, inasmuch as one of his contentions about the feebleminded was that they often were difficult to identify without the aid of an intelligence test. It also has been demonstrated that the retouching of outdoor photographs (as contrasted to the indoor photograph of Deborah) was not at all uncommon in the early part of this century.[45] This particular retouching it should be noted, lacks a certain artistry if merely highlighting facial features were the only goal. Whatever the circumstances surrounding the retouching,

Figure 2
Photographs of the Kallikak Family

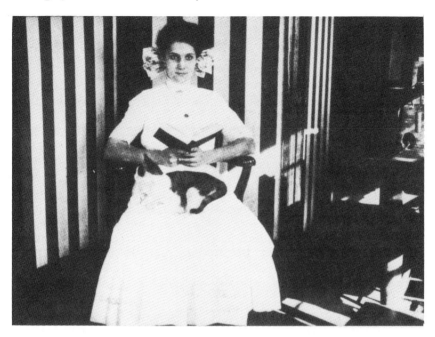

Source: *The Kallikak Family: A Study in the Heredity of Feeble-Mindedness* by H. H. Goddard. New York: Macmillan, 1912.

however, there is no need to suggest skulduggery to grasp the important point about the photographs. The contrast between Deborah and her relatives is sufficiently powerful without additional interpretation.

And so, what to make of that comparison? Was it an attempt to illustrate something about Deborah, to demonstrate her improvements at Vineland? Is the entire setting in which she is presented as compared with her family a statement of her educability, of the success of Vineland, and perhaps a prescient foreshadowing of Goddard's later recanting?

To be sure, no. The presentation of Deborah as seemingly well adjusted, clear-eyed, and normal is illusory. Goddard, at least in his initial description, entertained few hopes for her outside the cloistered confines of Vineland:

Here is a child who has been most carefully guarded. She had been persistently trained since she was eight years old, and yet nothing has been accomplished in the direction of higher intelligence or general education. . . . We may now repeat our ever insistent question, and this time we have good hope of answering it. The question is, "How do we account for this kind of individual?" The answer in a word "Heredity"—bad stock. We must recognize that the human family shows varying stocks or strains that are as marked and that breed as true as anything in plant or animal life.[46]

The Kallikak photographs, whatever the motive behind their retouching, were not intended to suggest anything positive about Deborah—except perhaps the difficulty of identifying her as feebleminded by sight. As though to provide ironic complement to the photographs, Goddard informs us that at the time of the study, Deborah's mental age, like that of Carrie Buck's, was nine years, well within the moron range. Goddard, like George Bernard Shaw, may have been suggesting that appearances are deceiving, but there the similarity most definitely ends. Shaw's point in *Pygmalion* was that the idiosyncrasies of lower class language and manner obscure a deeper, more fundamental equality; Goddard's point was quite different. And although he may later have seemly joined the enemy, Goddard did not offer as his credentials of membership the ability of Vineland to change the *intelligence* of Deborah or other residents of Vineland. In like manner Terman offered no evidence to answer his question about the effects of education to raise IQ.

But evidence was soon to come. It was only four years after Goddard's last defense of the Kallikak study that Bernardine Schmidt published her study of feebleminded children. And it is to the fate of that study that we now turn.

NOTES

1. Quoted in Tuddenham, R. (1962). The nature and measurement of intelligence. In L. Postman (Ed.), *Psychology in the making: Histories of selected research problems* (p. 488). New York: Alfred Knopf.

2. In Dubois, P. H. (1970). *A history of psychological testing* (p. 13). Boston: Allyn & Bacon.

3. Galton, F. (1869). *Hereditary genius: An inquiry into its laws and consequences.* London: Macmillan Co.

4. The law is entirely symmetrical in the sense that we might start with eminent sons and find the same trend: Fathers would not be quite so eminent as were their sons, and so on as we moved farther from the son.

5. Galton's speculations about "blending" came before the rediscovery of Mendel's laws. Regression cannot be used to infer anything about the genetic—or the environmental—influences on a trait. See Mackenzie, B. (1980). Fallacious use of regression effects in the IQ controversy. *Australian Psychologist, 15*, 369–384.

6. Kelves, D. J. (1985). *In the name of eugenics: Genetics and the uses of human heredity.* New York: Alfred Knopf.

7. The fourth revision of the Stanford-Binet in 1986 eliminated age-grouping and instead placed different item types within separate subtests. There are fifteen subtests, and items are arranged in ascending order of difficulty within each subtest.

8. Kamin, L. J. (1974). *The science and politics of IQ* (p. 5). Potomac, MD: Lawrence Erlbaum Associates.

9. Dubois, p. 23.

10. Goddard, H. H. (1912). *The Kallikak family: A study in the heredity of feeble-mindedness.* New York: Macmillan.

11. Ibid., p. 50.

12. Ibid., p. 29.

13. Quoted in Gould, S. J. (1981). *The mismeasure of man* (p. 163). New York: W. W. Norton.

14. Goddard, p. 117.

15. Goddard, H. H. (1917). Mental tests and the immigrant. *The Journal of Delinquency, 2*, 270.

16. Goddard, H. H. (1913). The Binet tests in relation to immigration. *Journal of Psycho-Asthenics, 18*, 105.

17. Ibid., p. 106.

18. Terman, L. M. (1932). Trails to psychology. In C. Murchison (Ed.), *A history of psychology in autobiography, Vol. 2* (pp. 297–331). Worcester, MA: Clark University Press.

19. Terman, L. M. (1916). *The measurement of intelligence* (pp. 6–7). Boston: Houghton Mifflin.

20. The sterilization laws might be thought of as a most extreme form of "negative eugenics." There was as well during these years a "positive" eugenics movement, more in line perhaps with the spirit of Galton's earlier speculations about creating improvements in human nature. And, unlikely as it may seem, positive eugenics attracted a rather broad array of supporters, including George Bernard Shaw. In the preface to *Man and Superman* Shaw foresaw a time when "there should be no possibility of such an obstacle [social class barriers] to natural selection as the objection of a countess to a navvy or of a duke to a charwoman." The result, otherwise, would be to "postpone the Superman for eons, if not forever." Quoted in Kelves, p. 87.

21. Kelves.

22. Goddard (1912), n. 1, p. 109.

23. Quoted in Gould, p. 335.

24. Kelves, pp. 111–112.

25. Gould, p. 335.

26. Quoted in Gould, p. 336.

27. Terman (1916), pp. 19–20.

28. Brigham, C. C. (1923). *A study of American intelligence*. Princeton, NJ: Princeton University Press.

29. Ibid., pp. 209–210.

30. See Chronbach, L. J. (1975). Five decades of controversy over mental testing. *American Psychologist, 30*, 1–13; Scarr-Salapatek, S. (1976). Science and politics: An explosive mix. *Contemporary Psychology, 21*, 98–99; Samelson, F. (1975). On the science and politics of IQ. *Social Research, 42*, 467–488; and Snyderman, M., & Herrnstein, R. J. (1983). Intelligence tests and the Immigration Act of 1924. *American Psychologist, 38*, 986–995.

31. Goddard, H. H. (1928). Feeblemindedness: A question of definition. *Journal of Psycho-Asthenics, 33*, 220–223.

32. Ibid., p. 224.

33. Terman, L. M., & Merrill, M. A. (1937). *Measuring intelligence: A guide to the administration of the new revised Stanford-Binet tests of intelligence* (pp. 48–49). Boston: Houghton Mifflin.

34. Brigham, p. 139.

35. Gould, p. 191.

36. Watson, J. B. (1930). *Behaviorism* (pp. 103–104). Chicago: University of Chicago Press.

37. See Block, N. J., & Dworkin, G. (1976). *The IQ controversy*. New York: Pantheon.

38. Terman (1932), p 331.

39. Quoted in Herrnstein, R. J. (1973). *IQ in the meritocracy* (p. 73). Boston: Atlantic Monthly Press.

40. Terman (1932), p. 330.

41. Goddard (1928), p. 226.

42. Goddard, H. H. (1942). In defense of the Kallikak study. *Science, 95*, 574–576.

43. Gould.

44. For a follow-up study of what became of Deborah, see Doll, E. E. (1983). Deborah Kallikak: 1889–1978, a memorial. *Mental Retardation, 21*, 30–32; see also Smith, J. D. (1985). *Minds made feeble: The myth and legacy of the Kallikaks*. Rockville, MD: Aspen Systems Corporation, for an independent follow-up on the entire Kallikak lineage.

45. Fancher, R. E. (1987). Henry Goddard and the Kallikak family photographs: "Conscious skulduggery" or "Whig history?" *American Psychologist, 42*, 585–590. See also Glenn, S. S., & Ellis, J. (1988). Do the Kallikaks look "menacing" or "retarded?" *American Psychologist, 43*, 742–743, for an empirical demonstration that subjects rating these photographs do not in fact see the Kallikaks as essentially retarded or menacing; and Zenderland, L. (1988). On interpreting photographs, faces, and the past. *American Psychologist, 43*, 743–744.

46. Goddard (1912), p. 12.

3

The Paradigm Shift to Environmentalism

> The social scientist is trained to think that he does not know all the answers. The social scientist is not trained to realize that he does not know all the questions. And that is why his social influence is not unfailingly constructive.
> —L. J. Chronbach[1]

THE FATE OF A MIRACLE

The ambivalent recantings of the hereditarians provide a context within which to understand the impact of Bernardine Schmidt's study. There were hints, some of which will shortly be examined more closely, of the possibilities of education, of special training inducing changes in IQ. These hints, however, shouldn't obscure the still-powerful prevailing idea that IQ measured something fundamentally innate and constant about human nature. The combination of these contradictory ideas might be said to have left a large segment of American psychology skeptical, but receptive, to just the sort of study Bernardine Schmidt provided.

Recall that she was working with feebleminded children whose initial IQs were 52. With that average they would have been labeled Low Morons in a classification system devised by Terman. One of Samuel Kirk's contentions in his reanalysis of Schmidt's data was merely that the adolescents' initial IQs were perhaps 10 points higher, a value still within the moron range. In the context of the times, Schmidt's subjects had started from a level of functioning that would certainly have brought them into institutions similar to Goddard's Vineland school, and possibly—just possibly—into contact with the sterilization laws.

By the end of the follow-up period Schmidt reported the adolescents' average IQs to be 89, a value that placed them within Terman's Low Normal range, and, incidentally, above the level of functioning of the average army recruit in World War I. Twenty-seven percent of the subjects had IQs of 100 or better, in Terman's High Normal range. And so, what was the final disposition of this most spectacular and provocative study?

In one sense, nothing. There were no further criticisms from Kirk, no additional rebuttals from Schmidt. But, as well, and perhaps most damagingly, there were no reports of successful replications of her work, although she had listed several of them as in progress in her reply to Kirk. In one article published in 1949 an investigator cited by Schmidt in her prefatory statement as performing one of the replications wrote simply that "there is no study of this type in progress at this institution."[2]

The failure to find evidence of replications can mean one of two things. One might think that negative and positive findings—that is, for example, knowledge that an educational program works and knowledge that it does not—are of equivalent value to science. But judging at least by publishing practices, something quite different is true. Scientific publications are strongly inclined to publish articles that report positive findings. It is in fact quite difficult to publish an article that merely fails to replicate an announced finding, or, more generally, one that reports nonsignificant results. The failure to find subsequent research articles pertaining to Schmidt's work may then mean only that the replications were unsuccessful.

Or, it may mean something else. In 1951 an article in the *American Journal of Mental Deficiency* referred to Schmidt's work as "highly controversial . . . many persons in the field would prefer to reserve judgement."[3] In that same year Kirk, in a textbook about the education of retarded children (the new terminology for Goddard's high-grade defectives), called Schmidt's results "most sensational. . . . Until Schmidt's study is verified, little stock can be placed in the results."[4]

By 1960, fourteen years after Schmidt's publication, the final disposition of her study had been settled in the subdued manner that often, but not invariably, marks scientific controversies. Typical of the verdicts that had by then been rendered was one in a textbook titled *The Education of Slow Learning Children*. Schmidt's study was pronounced to be "one well-known but doubtful claim" that was "much greater than anything else that has been published." And then, a simple summary that implied far more than it stated: "She claimed that similar investigations were being undertaken but so far these have not been reported upon."[5]

No definitive charges of fraud by Kirk, no confessions by Schmidt, no defense of her from colleagues who had signed the prefatory statement. So promising a study had ended so quietly, in an understated tone that would have seemed unfathomable, given its beginnings.

And one has to wonder: Had Bernardine Schmidt uncovered something that was too unusual to be accepted by less successful scientists? Was she alone in her ability to rescue feebleminded children from the fate predicted for them by their initial IQs? And what of those children, of Gloria and Lavern? Could they not have been located and again studied?

Or, more to the point, did they ever exist?

One might expect that the controversial ending to a study as well publicized as Schmidt's might revive hereditarian views concerning the malleability of IQ. But precisely the opposite occurred. The Watsonian behaviorism exemplified in Schmidt's study was about to have its day on a scale unimagined by Bernardine Schmidt. The transformation of prevailing ideology from the hereditarians to the environmentalists was in fact already under way when Schmidt published.

A SHIFTING OF TIDES

It is most unlikely that patient E. B., a thirty-eight-year-old female, had an interest in contributing to the history of intelligence testing when she first visited a doctor seeking relief from severe headaches in 1935. That visit led to the discovery of extensive calcification in the right frontal region of her brain. Soon thereafter surgeons proceeded with the first of three operations, each of which removed successively larger portions of her cerebrum. By the end of the last operation she had lost almost the entire right hemisphere of her brain. Figure 3 shows both the section of brain removed in the third operation, and patient E. B. recovering from that operation.

It is reported that E. B. experienced a slow return to normal functioning after the third operation with the exception of a "mild loss of inhibitions with a tendency to over-activity of speech."[6] We might be curious about precisely which inhibitions were lost, but E. B.'s talkativeness is of more direct interest with respect to her performance on standard intelligence tests. Before the first operation E. B. had a Stanford-Binet IQ of 115. With nearly one-half of her cerebral hemispheres removed, her IQ after the third operation remained the same.

This outcome, along with numerous others, confirmed the surprising fact that a large portion of cerebral tissue could be lost in adults without a corresponding loss of intelligence, at least as measured by an intelligence test. And the absolute level of intelligence seemed not to matter. In one case an epileptic patient lost 10 percent of his cerebrum in a left frontal lobectomy but nonetheless scored above 150 on the Stanford-Binet after the operation, and later successfully completed medical school.[7] Was intelligence—or at least success in medical school—brainless?

Not quite, thought psychologist Donald Hebb, because the opposite pattern seemed to hold for children. Brain damage to a young child, no matter how minimal, seemed capable of disrupting intellectual functioning rather permanently. Hebb combined this evidence with the results of his own experiments with rats and monkeys that illustrated the damaging effects of early sensory deprivation on later functioning.[8] He proposed that the body of these findings could be understood only by assuming that the organization of the brain was a function of cumulative experience. Once organized, the brain was capable of compensating for damage, but early damage led to a failure in the development

Figure 3
Portion of Brain Removed and Patient "E. B." after Neurosurgery

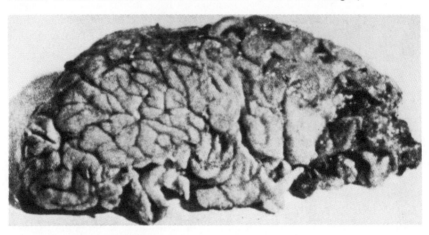

Source: S. N. Rowe (1937). Mental changes following the removal of the right cerebral hemisphere for brain tumor. *American Journal of Psychiatry, 94*, 605–614. Copyright 1937, the American Psychiatric Association. Reprinted by permission.

of necessary brain pathways. Early experiences were, therefore, critical to the later development of normal intellectual functioning.

Hebb summarized his ideas in 1949 in a book titled *The Organization of Behavior*.[9] The pace of science usually is such that most ideas scarcely survive more than a few years; it is rare indeed to find a book or an article published more than forty years ago that might still be thought relevant. Hebb's book, however, survives. Not because he was correct about cerebral organization; many of his ideas about brain functioning and organization are today considered simply incorrect. But Hebb knew how to ask the right questions, and his answers, particularly those concerning the primacy of early experience in providing the foundation for later success, were, at least indirectly, to inspire decades of research.

Ideas, no matter how reasonable or powerful, do not, however, long survive in a vacuum. At the time of Hebb's publication other findings were emerging that seemed to provide essential corroboration for the two implications of his environmental emphasis: The first, deriving from his own work, was that early deprivation might culminate in lasting intellectual deficits; the second, more speculative at the time that he wrote but clearly commensurate with Bernardine Schmidt's work, was that early enrichment might lead to enhanced intellectual performance.

Evidence for the first proposition was already available. In 1945 Raymond Spitz had published a comparison of the destinies of children reared in two sorts of homes, a "foundling home" and a "nursery."[10] The foundling home was little more than an orphanage that provided the minimum of care and stimulation for babies after their mothers separated from them at three months. The nursery, in contrast, was attached to a penal institution for delinquent girls that allowed the incarcerated mothers to care for their babies each day. Presumably, the physical needs of the children were equally met in both residences. If anything, the babies in the foundling home might be thought to have an advantage, as their mothers were judged normal, whereas the mothers of the nursery children were serving sentences for criminal offenses of one sort or another.

Yet, the results revealed precisely the opposite pattern. During the first year of life the Developmental Quotients of the foundling home children, measures of their social and emotional progress, declined from 131 to 72. For the nursery children the scores remained at about the same level, 97 to 100, over the same period. More startling were the mortality rates: In the foundling home thirty-seven of the babies died during the first two years of life; none of the nursery babies died. In interpreting these findings Spitz pointed to the lack of stimulation and mothering provided in the foundling home, using the term hospitalism to describe the environment of these children. In a later study he noted the withdrawal and susceptibility to infection of children so raised, calling it "anaclitic depression." The term anaclitic denotes an abnormal attachment to early childhood parental figures.

Spitz's study was criticized on several grounds, particularly on the merits of assuming that the two residences were equal in providing for the physical needs of the children. Further, it was not at all clear that the Developmental Quotients reported by Spitz were in fact reliable.[11] Yet the criticisms went little noticed amid the immediate reaction to Spitz's descriptions. Spitz had reinforced Hebb's emphasis on the potentially detrimental effects of the early environment, and it wasn't long before the terms hospitalism and anaclitic depression were part of psychology's working vocabulary.

The supporting evidence for Hebb's second proposition, the effects of an enhanced early environment, came not, to be sure, from Bernardine Schmidt's study. There were, however, other studies that seemed much like Schmidt's in principle, if not in the magnitude of their results. The most important of these came from investigators at the University of Iowa led by Harold Skeels, Marie Skodak, and Beth Wellman. The Iowa group produced a number of studies that seemed to indicate that dramatic environmental changes might result in large increments in intelligence test scores. Much of their work concerned placing babies who were being raised in orphanages into special nursery schools.

One study published by the Iowa group came in for quite special attention and scrutiny. It, like Hebb's book, was published in 1949, and perhaps more than Hebb's book it is still regarded as a valuable source of information. Referred to simply as Skodak and Skeels, it is nothing less than the most famous and most controversial adoption study in psychology's history. Its influence has been such that it is worth a healthy pause to consider its complexities in detail.

SKODAK AND SKEELS

Social scientists are incalculably attracted to adoption studies. That affection derives from the very special nature of adoptions. Adopted children are placed into families where they share a common environment but not a common heredity with the adoptive family. In turn, adopted children share a common heredity but not a common environment with their biological parents. There is a complication here because even if children are adopted away from their biological mothers soon after birth, they share a prenatal and postnatal environment arguably an environmental effect, at least in part. Leaving aside that complication for the moment, we can ask a question of adopted children that would seem to provide information about the nature and nurture of intelligence: Who does the adopted child come to resemble more closely in intelligence, the biological or the adoptive parents?

Skodak and Skeels began in 1934 as a service project to collect information about adopted children and the families into which they had been placed.[12] One hundred eighty children were part of the original study; 97 percent of them had been placed in foster homes before six months of age and had been separated from their biological parents earlier. They were followed over the ensuing fifteen years and were retested with the Stanford-Binet at four intervals, when they averaged two, four, seven, and fourteen years of age. Data also were obtained

Figure 4
Types of Correlations

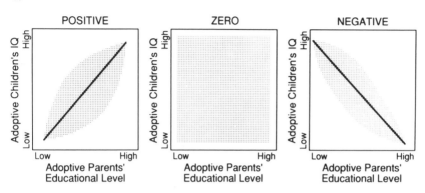

about the educational levels of the biological parents, and IQ measures were obtained for sixty-three of the biological mothers. The educational levels, but not the IQs, of the adoptive parents were also collected.

As is typical of adoptions, the biological and adoptive parents differed considerably. The average educational level of the biological mothers and fathers was ten years, about average for Iowan adults of comparable age according to the 1940 census. The biological mothers' average IQ was 86. In contrast, the adoptive mothers and fathers averaged slightly better than 12 years of education. The biological parents also were described as below average in occupation; nearly one-half of the biological fathers were classified as slightly skilled or day laborers. The adoptive fathers, on the other hand, were principally drawn from the professional and managerial levels and skilled trades; none of them fell into the category of slightly skilled or day laborers.

To answer the question of resemblance posed above, we may, as did Skodak and Skeels, compute the degree of correspondence between the adopted children's IQs and the educational levels of their biological and adoptive parents, respectively. Degree of correspondence is computed by a statistic known as a correlation coefficient, or r. Correlations have the property of assuming values between -1.00 and $+1.00$. The higher the absolute value of the correlation, the closer the correspondence between the two variables being measured. Three idealized correlations between the children's IQs and the educational levels of their adoptive parents are shown in Figure 4. In each graph the plotted points represent two measures of each adopted child: his or her IQ and the educational level of that child's adoptive parents.

The graph on the left illustrates a positive correlation: In general, the higher the child's IQ, the higher the educational level of the adoptive parents. The points cluster close to the line bisecting them, known as the line of best fit, or the regression line. The closer the points cluster around the line, the higher the absolute value of r. In the ideal case of $r = 1.00$, all the points would fall on the line. The middle graph shows a zero correlation, meaning that there is no relation between the children's IQs and their adoptive parents' educational levels. There also is no line of best fit in the sense of a line around which the points tend to cluster. The bottom graph shows a negative correlation: The higher the children's IQs, the lower their adoptive parents' educational levels. If the correlation were perfectly negative ($r = -1.00$), all the points would again fall on the regression line.

In practice, the correlation between two variables almost never reaches perfection. But it can approach zero, which is just what Skodak and Skeels found as the correlation between the adopted children's IQs at age fourteen and the educational levels of their adoptive mothers and fathers. Those correlations were .04 and .06, respectively. These low values mean that the adopted children's IQs were essentially unrelated to the educational levels of the adoptive families into which the children had been placed. In sharp contrast, the correlation between the children's age fourteen IQs and the educational levels of their biological mothers from whom the children had been separated soon after birth was .31.

This pattern of correlations has been taken as evidence of some genetic influence on individual differences in IQ. The evidence for that influence is even more impressive if we correlate the children's IQs with the IQs of their biological mothers. That correlation was larger than it was for educational level, .38 (.44 on a second test given to the children at age fourteen). This higher correlation stands to reason in that educational level and IQ are imperfectly correlated even within the same individual (the average is about .40 to .60). The biological mothers' IQs should then correlate better with their children's IQs than would the mothers' educational levels.

In concentrating on correlations, however, something quite important about the adopted children's IQs has been overlooked. Correlation expresses the degree of relation between two measures, but it does not reveal how close are their averages. The average IQ of the adopted children at age fourteen was 107. Recall that their biological mothers' IQs averaged 86. Although we do not know the IQs of the adoptive parents, it is clear that the above-average IQs of the adopted children are far more compatible with the status of their adoptive families than with the IQs of their biological mothers.

It would seem, then, that there are two ways to answer the question of "resemblance" that was posed for adopted children. The correlation answer tells us that the adopted children's IQs seemed to be *rank-ordered*—for this is what correlations express—generally according to the rank-ordering of their biological mothers' educational levels and IQs. But their *average* IQs suggest that the adopted children seem to resemble more their adoptive families.

How did the adopted children's IQs come to average 107 if their IQs don't correlate with the educational levels of their adoptive parents? The answer to that question will turn out to be elusive and complex. One complication—there are many—stems from what our guess would be about the children's IQs had they not been adopted. Based solely on the biological mothers' IQs, we might guess 86, but this value would be an underestimate. The reason it is an underestimate takes us back to Francis Galton and the law of regression.

Recall that Galton noticed that the sons of eminent men tended to be somewhat less eminent than their fathers. The same general trend occurred for height: tall fathers had sons who were not quite so tall; short fathers had somewhat taller sons. The same trend is true of IQ. The IQs of children whose mothers average 86 will tend, on average, not to be quite as low as that value. Just how much higher they will be can be estimated by using the mothers' average IQ along with the correlation coefficient to predict the expected average of the children. The mothers' IQ average was 14 points below their assumed population average of 100. Multiplying -14 by the correlation between children and mothers' IQs ($.38 \times -14 = -5.32$ and subtracting from the assumed average IQ in the population ($100 - 5.32$) gives us the expected average for the children, or about 95. An average of 95 is then an estimate of the children's IQs had they been raised by their biological mothers.

The inevitability of this regression effect is simply a statistical truism. It tells us nothing about the genetic or environmental influences on test scores, but it does tell us something about the limitations of the correlation coefficient. If two variables correlate imperfectly, that is, if r is less than 1.00, or -1.00, it means that *unique factors* must be influencing one set of scores and not the other. In the case of the IQs of biological mothers and their adopted-away children, the moderate correlation of .38 means that, to a large extent, unique factors must be affecting their IQs. What those factors are we cannot be sure. Children receive, on average, only one-half of their genes from their mothers, so there is room for other genetic influences that would be unique to mother and child. There may also be unique environmental factors that influence each score. The mothers, for example, were tested while they were still pregnant, soon after they agreed to release their children for adoption, a situation that may have affected their test scores.

Unique factors like this are present in all sets of scores that are not perfectly correlated. If the correlation were perfect, then there would be no regression effect, that is, there would be no factors influencing one set of scores and not the other. We can estimate the importance of these other influences by squaring the correlation to yield a statistic known as the coefficient of determination. In the present case that coefficient is $.38 \times .38 = .14$. The interpretation of this squared number is that only 14 percent of the variation in the adopted children's test scores is associated with variation in their biological mothers' IQs.[13] It does not mean that 14 percent of an individual child's IQ is due to the influence of his or her mother. Fourteen percent leaves 86 percent unaccounted for by the biological mother–adopted child correlation. Stated another way, *the adopted children's scores vary importantly for reasons not explicable by knowledge of the IQs of their biological mothers.*

Oddly, this remaining variation is not explained by variations in the adoptive families either, at least as captured by the adoptive parents' educational levels.

Those correlations, recall, were .04 and .06. If squared, they together account for less than 1 percent of the variation in the adopted children's IQs.

So, we have two puzzles. What is producing variation, that is, individual differences, in the adopted children's IQs in addition to their relation to their biological mothers and to their adoptive parents? And, how did their average IQs come to be 107? Our guess is that without adoption, the children's average IQs would have been about 95, so there are at least 12 points still to be accounted for by factors other than the children's similarities to their biological mothers. But if the adoptive families are responsible for the increase, shouldn't the children's IQs correlate with the adoptive parents' educational levels?

It will take some time before those questions can be answered, but the historical importance of Skodak and Skeels should not be lost amid its statistical complexities. It is a study that seemed to offer something for everyone, demonstrating at once both genetic influences on individual differences in IQ and the malleability of IQ. As we will see, both of those conclusions can be seriously questioned and seemingly incompatible facts can co-exist. But then that is part of the enduring intrigue of Skodak and Skeels.

ENVIRONMENTALISM AS PARADIGM

If Skodak and Skeels provided evidence that was susceptible to various interpretations, other results were beginning to accumulate that decidedly favored environmentalists. Much of the evidence derived from or was inspired by Hebb's research with animals, which had suggested that enriched environments might accelerate intellectual functioning. His ideas in these respects were harmonized in the early 1960s with the publication of two influential books, each of which was, in its own way, a fitting continuation of Hebb's legacy.

In *Intelligence and Experience* James McViker Hunt argued forcefully that the malleability of human intelligence was within a range of 20 to 50 points. His conclusions were based, to a considerable degree, on the types of findings relied on by Hebb and the Iowa group. To those he added theoretical ideas about the newly emerging discipline of information processing and coupled them with accepted ideas about child development. The combination gave rise to a quite straightforward optimism about large-scale changes in IQ that were to be had with appropriate psychological intervention:

The problem for the management of child development is to find out how to govern the encounters that children have with their environments to foster both an optimally rapid rate of intellectual development and a satisfying life. . . . It is no longer unreasonable to consider that it might be feasible to discover ways to govern the encounters that children have with their environments, especially during the early years of development, to achieve a substantially faster rate of intellectual development and a substantially higher adult level of intellectual capacity.[14]

In *Stability and Change in Human Characteristics* Benjamin Bloom went beyond even Hunt's optimism and attempted to gauge just how much of adult intelligence was determined by early life experiences. His strategy involved a comparison between the development of intelligence and that of a more easily assessed trait, height. It is a historical irony that Bloom, as had Galton before him, used comparisons between intelligence and height to determine the nature of human intelligence. Bloom, however, arrived at a vastly different view of intelligence than had Galton. In the case of height Bloom noted that as children grow older, there is an increasingly higher correlation between their height at a given age and their eventual adult height. By the age of two and one-half, for example, the correlation surpasses .70. The coefficient of determination of that correlation (r^2) is .50, a value Bloom referred to as the "half-life" of height.

Bloom used the same logic to assert that the half-life of intelligence occurred by age four or five. From this fact he then reasoned that attempts to alter intelligence would be most effective before that age. The assumption was that while intelligence was still weakly correlated with eventual adult intelligence, it would be most susceptible to change. It was an idea that could not have been more consonant with Hebb's suggestions about early experience. Bloom seemed to capture the growing spirit of the times, if not to be limited by scientific caution, when he concluded: "The nature of the individual's pursuit of life, liberty, and happiness may be largely determined by the nature of the environmental conditions under which he has lived in his formative years."[15]

Given the explicit urgency that conclusion accords early educational intervention, it is little wonder that Bloom's ideas were widely cited in events that were quickly to follow. There would soon be a government-sponsored effort to ensure increased opportunities for children not born with middle-class advantages. In that effort few bothered to correct the widely accepted interpretation of half-life that referred to it as the age when one-half of adult intelligence was achieved. The mistake was that half-life is based on correlation. As was noted with Skodak and Skeels, correlation reveals the rank-ordering between two sets of scores but nothing about their respective magnitudes. *The proper interpretation of half-life, then, is the same as that for the coefficient of determination: It indicates only the proportion of common variation between two sets of scores.* Bloom's half-life for intelligence means only that four-year-old children can be ranked with respect to IQ. Their ranking as adults is predictable, to a large extent, from this age four ranking. That fact alone is striking, but it tells us nothing about the eventual *level* of adult intelligence, or about the proportion of adult intelligence evident in age four IQs.

It is true, however, that the IQs of very young children do correlate very poorly with eventual adult IQ. Scores obtained during the first year of life, for example, correlate only about .05 with performance at age seven. It is not until the age of two years that the correlation with age seven IQ reaches .40. As might be expected from this pattern, measures of infant intelligence show little or no correlation with adult intelligence. The correlations, however, do grow higher with age. By age three the correlation with adult intelligence is almost .60, and by age four or five (or six, or seven, or eight, depending on the study cited) the correlation does reach .70, Bloom's half-life.[16]

This pattern seems to be due, to some extent, to differences in the characteristics of infant and adult intelligence. The content of intelligence tests for young children is quite different than the content of adult tests. Whereas adult tests are essentially verbal and conceptual, tests for young children must per force involve sensorimotor skills. As the child grows older, the tests become more similar to adult tests. This increasing similarity in the skills measured by the test is undoubtedly one reason for the higher correlations with adult intelligence observed later in childhood. As a consequence, the low correlations between infant and adult IQs tell us nothing about the most appropriate age, if any, to expect the largest intellectual gains from educational intervention. We might just as easily argue that intervention should not begin until childhood intelligence, at least as captured by IQ, becomes similar to adult intelligence. Although there is no consensus as to when that similarity emerges, it may not occur until late childhood or early adolescence.[17]

Irrespective of the proper interpretation of Bloom's ideas, there is no uncertainty as to their impact. The idea of half-life along with Hunt's enthusiasm for the malleability of IQ represent a historical watershed, a coming together of trends that were destined to become the dominant scientific view of the nature of intelligence and its malleability. With hindsight one can sense a certain modesty in the foundation of these new ideas. In truth, the evidence for the malleability of IQ and particularly for the primacy of early experience was far from compelling. In fairness, however, that evidence was far more rooted in research than had been the earlier hereditarian views of immutable IQ. That sort of progress is as it should be in any science. In fairness as well it should be added that the evidence for Bloom's and Hunt's contentions seem as much rooted in an ideological faith in the power of the environment as were the earlier hereditarian views based on the appeal of genes.

The views of the hereditarians had found expression in public policy, at least indirectly, in the form of the sterilization laws and the Immigration Act. So, too, environmentalists' ideas about the malleability of IQ were entirely congenial to the fabric of John Kennedy's New Frontier and Lyndon Johnson's Great Society in the early and mid-1960s. The domestic political climate of that era was dominated by the civil rights movement and the related programs of what was termed the War on Poverty. Government was much in search of ways of implementing effective social action and found it in the 1964 Economic Opportunities Act. That legislation provided for three types of interventions into the lives of disadvantaged Americans: the Job Corps, Vista, and Community Action Programs. From this last initiative came the compensatory educational programs called Head Start.[18]

HEAD START

In February 1965 a planning committee reporting to President Johnson on the feasibility of implementing early educational interventions stated:

There is considerable evidence that the early years of childhood are the most critical point in the poverty cycle. During these years the creation of learning patterns, emotional development and the formation of individual expectations and aspirations take place at a very rapid pace. For the child of poverty there are clearly observable deficiencies in the processes which lay the foundation for a pattern of failure—and thus a pattern of poverty—throughout the child's entire life.[19]

Soon thereafter Johnson ushered in the era of compensatory educational programs with the announcement of Project Head Start. He had received cautious recommendations that the initial effort should be a small pilot program for no more than 100,000 children. But the president also heard the voice of the first lady, who had been party to the development of Head Start from its beginnings: "Head Start," Mrs. Johnson affirmed, "will reach out to one million young children in a gray world of poverty and neglect and lead them into the human family." The program President Johnson announced served 560,000 children and cost $86 million in its first year.[20]

As though to provide a needed complement for Head Start's rationale, soon after the program began Harold Skeels published another study, this one a long-term follow-up of infants raised in an institution for the feebleminded.[21] It had begun years earlier with a "clinical surprise" that Skeels noted concerning two infants aged thirteen and sixteen months who had been transferred from an orphanage into an institution for the feebleminded because of their low intelligence test scores. The children's IQs were 35 and 46, respectively, before transfer to the institution. They were placed in a ward with women aged eighteen to fifty whose mental ages ranged from five to nine years. Six months after their placement a psychologist visiting the ward noticed what appeared to be remarkable improvements in the two infants. They were accordingly retested and found to have IQs of 77 and 87, respectively. Within two years their IQs had risen to 95 and 93, and both were adopted into middle-class families.

What had happened to these infants in the institution to promote these changes? Skeels hypothesized that they had been, in a sense, "adopted" by the ward attendants and by the older and more capable feebleminded residents, who were reported to have lavished attention on the children. To confirm this impression Skeels transferred eleven more children to similar wards. These children, aged seven to thirty months, had IQs that averaged 64 at the time of their placement. They remained in the institution for an average of nineteen months at which time they were retested. Their retested IQs had risen to 92. Of the total of thirteen children so placed, eleven were eventually adopted and all had shown significant increases in IQ.

To determine whether placement in the institution had indeed produced the changes, Skeels composed a "contrast" group taken from an earlier study. The group consisted of twelve infants who had remained in an orphanage until the age of four years. These infants had IQs that averaged 87 initially. Despite that surprisingly high value, however, when retested at age four, their IQs had fallen to 61.

The adopted children eventually completed nearly twelve years of education; all had married and had produced twenty-eight children whose average IQ was 104. If the pattern of results sounds familiar, it should. It is nearly identical to the pattern reported twenty years earlier by Bernardine Schmidt, although it is undoubtedly a touch of uncommon historical irony that the gains made by Skeels' orphans were attributed to the caring and attention given them by *feebleminded* adults.

Irony aside, there were numerous problems with this study, although certainly none that questioned its veracity, as had been done with Schmidt's work. From much of the descriptive data it appears that the transferred children were superior to the contrast children at the start of the study, at least as judged from their mothers' and fathers' educational levels, fathers' occupation, and, perhaps most important, mothers' IQs. Yet, as noted earlier, contrast children's initial IQs were far above those of the adopted children (87 vs. 64). The reason for this discrepancy might be that, as we've seen, IQ estimates from children so young tend to be unreliable and not predictive of later IQ. If the groups were different at the start of the study, or if we cannot be certain as to the starting points themselves, then nothing can be inferred from subsequent changes in IQ. These and related problems led one critic to conclude of Skeels' study that "commendable as it was from a humanitarian viewpoint, it is worthless from a scientific viewpoint. It offers no convincing support for the malleability of early IQ."[22]

But that criticism did not come until 1981. At the time that Skeels published, his study was praised as unassailable evidence of the malleability of IQ and of the eventual value of Head Start. It was little noted, even granting Skeels' conclusions, that the children in his study had been living in far more disadvantaged circumstances than was the average child earmarked for Head Start. Also relatively unnoted were the results of an intervention program for children who were more like the children entering Head Start programs. That study was conducted by Schmidt's critic Samuel Kirk. In 1958 Kirk reported that children who were placed in special educational programs had shown some gains in IQ after one year, as compared with a control group. Unfortunately the differences between the two groups disappeared soon after the children entered regular schooling.[23]

It was to be a prophetic finding.

NOTES

1. Chronbach, L. J. (1975). Five decades of controversy over mental testing. *American Psychologist, 30,* 13.

2. Nolan, W. J. (1949). A critique of the evaluations of the study by Bernardine G. Schmidt entitled "Changes in personal, social, and intellectual behavior of children originally classified as feebleminded." *Journal of Exceptional Children, 15,* 226.

3. McCandless, B. (1951). Environment and intelligence. *American Journal of Mental Deficiency, 56,* 686.

4. Kirk, S., & Johnson, G. O. (1951). *Educating the retarded child* (p. 32). London: George Harrup & Co. Ltd.

5. Tansley, A. E., & Guilford, P. (1960). *The education of slow learning children* (pp. 29–30). London: Routledge & Kegan Paul.

6. Rowe, S. N. (1937). Mental changes following the removal of the right cerebral hemisphere for brain tumor. *American Journal of Psychiatry, 94,* 609.

7. Hebb, D. O. (1939). Intelligence in man after large removals of cerebral tissue: defects following right temporal lobectomy. *Journal of General Psychology, 21,* 73–87.

8. Hebb, D. O. (1942). The effect of early and late brain injury upon test scores, and the nature of normal adult intelligence. *Proceedings of the American Philosophical Society, 85,* 275–292.

9. Hebb, D. O. (1949). *The organization of behavior.* New York: John Wiley & Sons.

10. Spitz, R. A. (1945). Hospitalism: An inquiry into the genesis of psychiatric conditions of early childhood. I. *Psychoanalytic Study of the Child, 1,* 53–74.

11. Pinneau, S. R. (1955). The infantile disorders of hospitalism and anaclitic depression. *Psychological Bulletin, 52,* 429–459.

12. Skodak, M., & Skeels, H. (1949). A final follow-up study of children in adoptive homes. *Journal of Genetic Psychology, 75,* 85–125.

13. There are cases in which r, not its square, serves as the best measure of "variance accounted for," or common variance. Here, following standard practice, r^2 is used. But see Ozer, D. J. (1985). Correlation and the coefficient of determination. *Psychological Bulletin, 97,* 307–315; also, Jensen, A. R. (1971). Note on why genetic correlations are not squared. *Psychological Bulletin, 75,* 223–224.

14. Hunt, J. McV. (1961). *Intelligence and experience* (pp. 362–363). New York: Ronald Press.

15. Bloom, B. (1964). *Stability and change in human characteristics* (p. 193). New York: John Wiley & Sons.

16. There is recent controversy on this point. See Kolata, G. (1989, April 4). Infant IQ test found to predict scores in school. The *New York Times,* pp. C1 and C8.

17. This argument is consistent with stage theorists like Piaget who contend that the actual character of intelligence changes with age. Alternatively, perhaps early intelligence measurement is simply inherently unstable because of idiosyncrasies in the child's test-taking performance itself. Either condition, or both together, would produce the age-patterning of test-retest correlations.

18. For a concise history of the development of Head Start, see Condry, S. (1979). History and background of preschool intervention programs and the Consortium for Longitudinal Studies. In Consortium for Longitudinal Studies, *As the twig is bent: Lasting effects of preschool programs* (pp. 1–31). Hillsdale, NJ: Lawrence Erlbaum Associates; also Zigler, E., & Valentine, J. (Eds.). (1979). *Project Head Start:A legacy of the war on poverty.* New York: The Free Press.

19. Quoted in Richmond, J. (1979). Entering the arena of Head Start. In E. Zigler

and J. Valentine (Eds.), *Project Head Start: A legacy of the war on poverty* (p. 122). New York: The Free Press.

20. See section in Zigler & Valentine titled "A retrospective view: The founders," section I (pp. 43–71); see also Caruso, D. R., Taylor, J. J., & Detterman, D. K. (1982). Intelligence research and intelligent policy. In D. K. Detterman & R. J. Sternberg (Eds.), *How and how much can intelligence be increased* (p. 51). Norwood, NJ: Ablex.

21. Skeels, H. M. (1966). Adult status of children with contrasting life experiences. *Monographs of the Society for Research on Child Development, 31* (3, Serial No. 105).

22. Longstreth, L. E. (1981). Revisiting Skeels' final study: A critique. *Developmental Psychology, 17,* 620–625.

23. Kirk, S. (1958). *Early education of the mentally retarded: An experimental study.* Urbana: University of Illinois Press.

Part II
Environment, Genetics, and the Malleability of IQ

4

Preschool Programs and IQ

The country may be full of potential geniuses for all we know, and it should be a pressing concern for psychology to discover the conditions that will develop whatever potential abilities a child may have.

—D. O. Hebb[1]

THE EVALUATION OF HEAD START

The outcomes of early Head Start programs were similar to the results Samuel Kirk had reported—early gains in IQ that soon disappeared. These failures led to a most influential and now-infamous analysis of Head Start in 1969 by Arthur Jensen in an article titled "How much can we boost IQ and scholastic achievement?" The first sentence of the 121-page article well captured its tone: "Compensatory education has been tried, and it apparently has failed." Jensen followed with something equally blunt:

Why has there been such uniform failure of compensatory programs wherever they have been tried? What has gone wrong? In other fields, when bridges do not stand, when aircraft do not fly, when machines do not work, when treatments do not cure, despite all conscientious efforts on the part of many persons to make them do so, one begins to question the basic assumptions, principles, theories, and hypotheses that guide one's efforts. Is it time to follow suit in education?[2]

The notoriety of Jensen's article came not from his conclusion about the ineffectiveness of Head Start, but from his analysis of the causes for its failure. Based on an extensive review of the genetic bases of human intelligence, Jensen concluded that IQ was a highly heritable trait, one that, although not entirely fixed, was not easily altered by the types of training offered by Head Start programs. That conclusion alone would likely have evoked little controversy, for even in this era of environmentalism Jensen was doing little more than summarizing a position held by other psychologists.

But Jensen went further. A portion of his article dealt with racial differences in IQ and suggested that these differences might be gentically based. Jensen offered this portion of his analysis as an untested hypothesis; the bulk of his article was devoted to genetics and intelligence, not to racial differences in intelligence or to their origins. But there can be little doubt about the conclusion that might reasonably be drawn from juxtaposing arguments about the genetic basis of IQ with those concerning racial differences. As the vast majority of Head Start children were black, the inference was unavoidable: The specific genetic limitations of these children might be part of the reason for Head Start's failures. It was, as one critic put it, a case of "blaming the victim."[3]

Our concern for the moment is not with Jensen's arguments on the genetic bases of IQ, or with his highly speculative and untested analysis of racial differences, but with malleability. In the furor that followed his article it went relatively unnoticed that at least insofar as the failures of compensatory education were concerned, Jensen had concluded nothing more than had other investigators, including the U.S. Commission on Civil Rights in 1967. But those early evaluations, including Jensen's, were based on the first few years of Head Start's implementation. In 1969 more than one-half of Head Start programs were only two-month summer interventions. It was not until 1972 that full-year programs became the standard. It would seem, then, altogether necessary to evaluate Head Start and other interventions against a more substantial record.

In 1985 a summary of seventy-two separate evaluations of Head Start was published by the Head Start Bureau.[4] The data were reported as a meta-analysis, so named because it combines all research reports into a single, summary analysis. The result of this meta-analysis can be expressed in the form of a deviation score called an "effect size," in which the preschool group average minus the control group average is divided by the standard deviation. As an example, assume that children enrolled in a Head Start program have an average IQ of 110 at the end of the program; a comparable group of children not receiving Head Start averages 100. The effect size for this study would be 110–100/15, or .67. If the effect size equalled .50, it would mean that the Head Start children averaged about one-half a standard deviation above the control group, or 7.5 IQ points. Negative effect sizes would indicate an advantage to the control group; zero would mean no difference. As a rough rule of thumb, educators typically consider effect sizes of .25 or better to be "educationally meaningful."

Figure 5 summarizes the effect sizes for all Head Start programs evaluated in the meta-analysis.[5] Results are shown for the end of the programs and for follow-up periods of one, two, and three or more years. The children were, on average, five to five-and-one-half years old at the end of the programs and into the first two or three years of regular schooling when the follow-up results were obtained. Along with IQ, two other measures are plotted: readiness, a preschool measure of language usage and understanding, and school achievement.

The results seem to speak for themselves. At the end of the typical Head Start program the preschool children averaged nearly .60 above control children, or about a 9- to 10-point advantage in IQ. Similar gains are evident in the other

Figure 5
Results of the Head Start Meta-Analysis

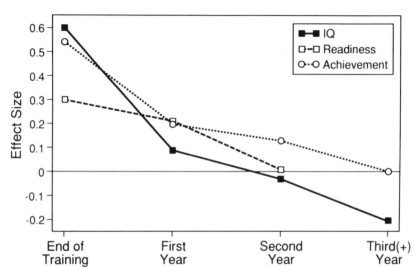

measures. But as the posttraining evaluations reveal, the gains do not last. Two years after the end of the program the effect size for readiness is not different from zero; IQ has fallen slightly below zero, indicating, if anything, a marginal superiority of control group children over Head Start children.

By the third year and beyond, achievement has reached zero. Readiness is not measured at the third year simply because most children have by then entered regular schooling. The effect size for IQ has fallen further below zero. This finding seems provocative, suggesting long-term negative effects for Head Start, but a strong caution is in order. Relatively few studies reported follow-up evaluations for the third year and beyond, and these studies differed greatly in their format and results. Thus, although it seems clear that Head Start has no long-term positive effects on IQ, it is impossible to conclude from these results—indeed it is highly unlikely—that it has any reliable negative effects.[6]

Interpretation

Before drawing other conclusions from these results, it should be noted that in this type of analysis, two problems invariably arise. One is whether the preschool and control groups were equivalent at the start of the study. The best way to ensure equality is to assign subjects randomly to each group, but this was seldom possible. Head Start children often were those whose parents enrolled them first; control subjects often came from waiting lists or from a list of children living in the same community. There may be differences between children who belong to these different natural groupings. Another problem, particularly related to long-term evaluation, concerns attrition, the dropout of subjects over time. In evaluating a program over several years' attrition can become a significant problem if the subjects dropping out of one group differ from those dropping out of another group, thereby making the remaining groups different even if they were comparable at the start.

Although it is impossible to rule out problems caused by equivalence or attrition, it seems, from attempts to evaluate these problems in this meta-analysis, that they were at least not severe. There are, however, other potential problems that relate specifically to performing a meta-analysis. The advantage of performing this sort of evaluation is that it gives a global picture of the outcome of a large number of studies. By combining all studies, however, a meta-analysis may obscure significant differences between studies. This point might be particularly important here because Head Start programs vary widely in their quality as research evaluation projects. Head Start, although it may properly be described as one of the most important social experiments in history, was begun as a service project, not as a research program. Many of the individual projects were simply not designed to be properly evaluated. It is also true that there is no standard Head Start program or curriculum. Each individual project is given wide leeway to design a program most appropriate to the needs of its particular community. These different programs are then combined, their differences possibly obscured by the data reported in Figure 5. For example, certain types of curricula may have worked better than others, or perhaps certain types of children benefited more than others from Head Start.

These possibilities were considered in detail as a part of the meta-analysis, but none was found to be appreciable. Different types of programs seemed to work equally well, and no significant trends emerged from the examination of many other possible factors. It didn't seem to matter how many hours per day a program ran, or the number of children in a class, the minority composition of the class, the socioeconomic status of the families, the age of enrollment of the children, or the pretest IQs of the children. In short, the 9- to 10-point or so gain in IQ and its eventual dissipation seems an inherent outcome for a wide variety of programs.

Other Measures

It might yet be argued that by focusing on IQ, other outcomes of Head Start have been overlooked. Indeed, IQ is undoubtedly a relatively narrow measure of whatever may be meant by general intelligence; other facets of these children's development are probably missed by focusing solely on the single reified number derived from intelligence tests. Examination of achievement and readiness effect sizes revealed the same trend as IQ, but these measures seem intuitively to be similar to the abilities tapped by an intelligence test. As might be expected, achievement tests in fact show a substantial correlation with IQ, averaging about .50 to .60, and can be even higher for more verbally oriented tests.

The meta-analysis evaluated this proposition by reporting on a number of other possible differences between preschool and control group children, including self-esteem, achievement motivation, and social skills. Measuring these sorts of traits, it should be noted, poses problems not encountered in measuring IQ. Despite all the criticisms that might reasonably be leveled against intelligence tests, these tests have two advantages over most other psychological tests: they are, by midchildhood, highly reliable, meaning that the correlation between two successive tests for the same group of individuals is quite high, averaging about .85 to .90 for adults. Reliability is the principal requirement for any psychological test; without it there can be no certainty about the stability of the obtained score. Intelligence tests also offer the advantage of having been standardized on large samples of individuals, and norms are available through which to interpret an individual's score. The same is not always true for measures like self-esteem, achievement motivation, and social behavior, particularly as used with children. Nevertheless, the results from the meta-analysis seem clear. Each of these other measures showed a pattern similar to the results for IQ: The effect size for each measure was less than .40 at the end of training, and none was above 0 after three years.

And so, we are left to make something from this pattern of results. For the purpose of assessing malleability, the most important outcome is the immediate gains in IQ followed by subsequent losses. In one sense the gains alone seem to document amply the malleability of IQ. There are at least two interpretations of these gains, however, that do not involve assumptions about changes in intellectual ability. It may be argued, for example, that what is really changed by Head Start, albeit briefly, is children's motivation to perform well on tests. As children leave the program and enter regular schooling that motivation is lost or discouraged, as reflected in lowered scores. This interpretation does not make trivial the children's gains, but points instead to the harmful effects that lack of motivation may have in attenuating the expression of these children's potential.[7] This idea also assumes, however, that the transient gains evidenced from Head Start programs may not reflect actual changes in intelligence. If true, this interpretation carries with it an interesting thought: If Head Start principally affects motivational deficits, perhaps a one-year or two-year program of educational intervention is not required to produce this change. As a corollary, we might ask whether such a temporary motivational change—if otherwise unsupported—is worth the cost of intervention.

From a different perspective, it might be argued that an educational program for four- and five-year-old children probably involves some training in just those skills tapped by intelligence tests. If so, the program might be expected to have a sort of coaching effect, increasing scores temporarily but in the long run having no permanent change in intelligence. This argument need not be true; one might, in theory, imaging testing young children with tasks that are unlikely to be included in an educational program. But out of necessity it probably has some reasonable basis, given that intelligence tests have their origins in attempts to predict school success. The tests, therefore, assess abilities that are part and parcel, to some extent, of educational programs. For example, the items contained in the 1972 revision of the Stanford-Binet at the four-year level included the following:

1. Naming common objects in pictures
2. Naming objects from memory
3. Opposite analogies (e.g., "A brother is a boy; a sister is a . . .")
4. Pictorial identification (e.g., "Show me the one that catches mice.")
5. Comprehension (e.g., "Why do we have houses?")

It is not unlikely that these sorts of tasks and the abilities tapped by them might be included in an educational program for four-year olds. If so, what does this explanation, or the motivational account, tell us about the effects of Head Start? One thing to recognize is that these two explanations are not incompatible. Motivational changes may attend Head Start participation; coaching on test-related items may be an inevitable part of the process as well. Each explanation does have the curious property of suggesting that what is measured by an intelligence test may not entirely be a pure estimate of reasoning or thinking or intellectual ability, but may include other, more transient influences. If so, it seems all the more important to assess the long-term results from these programs.[8]

We might, on the other hand, hold to the idea that changes in IQ principally indicate changes in intellectual ability. We might, then, speculate that what is captured by IQ seems, in some sense, to be different from, say, learning to ride a bicycle, an ability that carries with it the adage "once you learn, you never forget." If not practiced, any ability would be expected to deteriorate. But, oddly, the differences between Head Start and control group children begin to disappear just as both groups enter regular schooling, presumably just when intellectual skills would be more demanded and the positive effects of Head Start might lead to greater gains. To be sure, part of this shrinking difference between the groups is due to increases in the IQ of control group children as they enter school. But gains by control group children are not the entire story, as we will see, for preschool children return to their initial IQ levels over the course of the early school years. All of this may tell us more about the efficacy of schooling than anything else, or about the combined effects of these children's disadvantaged family circumstances and their schools, but to be sure it allows no convincing interpretation about the rise and fall of IQs associated with Head Start programs.

It also reveals nothing about the influences of nature and nurture on IQ. From a hereditarian perspective, the lack of long-term changes in IQ might be taken as evidence that the fundamental ability tapped by an intelligence test is relatively difficult to change. This position is compatible with the idea that there is a general ability, or g, that informs performance on most portions of these tests.

Other portions of any test, however, consist of items unrelated to g and are perhaps more susceptible to coaching. One might expect, then, a short-term rise in IQ owing to better performance on these coachable items, but in the long run IQ will return to its starting point owing to the pervasive, stable influence of g.

Environmentalists argue that IQ is in fact quite malleable. Given the advantageous environment offered by Head Start, scores rise. Given the less supportive environment of these children's regular schools, scores fall. We have to asume that the children's family environments remain relatively constant during these years and that schools are in fact deleterious in these respects, points we will later consider in more detail.

Unfortunately, the data on Head Start simply don't permit a decision among these various alternatives, in part because few Head Start programs are ideally designed to address issues of this nature. In addition, as most Head Start programs provide only one year of intervention, it is simply unreasonable to expect so limited an influence to shelter a child against pervasive, environmental disadvantage.

THE CONSORTIUM FOR LONGITUDINAL STUDIES

In part to overcome these limitations, the Consortium for Longitudinal Studies was formed in 1976. The consortium consisted of eleven interventions that were initiated in the 1960s, nine of which were not Head Start programs. The consortium members pooled their results and conducted a long-term evaluation of their programs in the late 1970s, when their subjects were ten to seventeen years old. Of the 3,656 original children, most of whom were similar to the children in Head Start programs, more than 2,000 were located for the follow-up. Most of these programs were better funded and more professionally staffed than the average Head Start program, represented more intensive educational interventions, and were better designed for evaluation purposes. This is not to say that these programs were coordinated in terms of their curricula or structure. They seem to differ as widely from one another as do Head Start programs, but the pooling of results and the conduct of a long-term evaluation makes them unique and useful. Indeed, the evaluation reported by the consortium is, to date, the most systematic long-term assessment of the effects of early interventions.

Seven of these projects reported IQ data. Despite the care with which the programs had been designed, only four of the seven were considered to be "more nearly randomized," meaning that they met the criterion of equivalence.[9] For these four, the results seem quite similar to those reported for Head Start. At the start of the programs preschool children tested at an average IQ of 88, control children at 83. Although this 5-point difference was not significant, it does demonstrate the difficulties encountered even in well-designed programs in achieving equivalence between groups. At the end of the various training programs the average IQs were 95 and 88 for the preschool and control groups, respectively. Three to four years later the group averages had fallen to 90 and

87, and by the time of the long-term evaluation preschool subjects averaged 83, control subjects averaged 82.

The consortium also reported the results of achievement tests for mathematics and reading ability. These results were also similar to those reported by Head Start. By grade 6 there were no significant differences between the preschool and control groups on either test. Earlier there had been some differences in mathematics in favor of preschool children, although these differences were not consistent across the different programs; no one program reported significant results in favor of preschool children for more than one year between grades three and six. Interpretation is also confounded both by attrition problems and by the fact that not all programs reported results for each year. Beyond grade 3 there were no differences in reading ability.

The Consortium's Social Competence Results

The consortium's results have been given much attention and have been characterized as demonstrating more pervasive gains from early interventions as compared with Head Start programs. Yet, based on the results of IQ and achievement tests alone, it seems unnecessary to conclude anything about these programs that differs from the conclusions drawn from Head Start. The consortium did, however, report other results. As a way of assessing what might be called the "social competence" of children in addition to the results of formal tests, the consortium examined the extent to which children had been retained in grade or had been in need of some form of special education. Social competence judged in this manner also was reported in the Head Start meta-analysis, but the results came from only three studies.[10]

For the consortium, across all projects, 25 percent of preschool children and 30 percent of control group children were retained in grade. For the four more nearly randomized designs the results were better, 26 percent and 37 percent, for preschool and control group children, respectively. For special education the results for all programs combined also suggested an advantage for preschool children: Only 14 percent of these children, as compared with 29 percent of control group children, received some form of special educational placement.[11]

These results have been characterized as demonstrating a sort of real-world effect of early interventions that seems to be quite independent of the assessments made by standard intelligence and achievement tests. This pattern suggests again that standard tests may indeed miss something important about a child's abilities, even in school settings. It is reasonable to question just how large scale these effects are, for in the case of grade retention the differences seem quite small when all programs are averaged together. It also has been argued that the differences in social competence seem greater during the elementary school years than later on.[12] Then, too, averaging all projects together can, as noted earlier for the Head Start meta-analysis, obscure the results for individual programs. With respect to grade retention, only one of the eight programs reporting on this factor showed a statistically significant difference in favor of preschool children. Some of the remaining projects showed "trends" in favor of preschool children, however, so when they were all averaged together the result was judged to be significant.[13] Something similar was true for special education placement: Only three of six programs reported significant differences in favor of preschool children; two of the six programs showed trends in favor of the control group, but the combined results for all programs were significant.[14]

Considerations like these might limit enthusiasm for these results, but beyond these caveats there is clearly a modest but real effect of these programs with respect to social competence as judged by grade retention and special education. The question, then, becomes one of interpretation, and there are at least three possibilities. Perhaps the most straightforward explanation focuses on the fact that intervention programs do result, at least temporarily, in increases in intelligence and achievement test scores. These enhanced scores in turn influence teachers and administrators, who make the decisions about placement and grade retention. In other words, at the time these decisions are made the children who have experienced early intervention are in fact performing better in school, and thereby avoid placement and retention.

The problem with this interpretation is that the majority of decisions regarding grade retention and placement usually are not made until the middle elementary school years.[15] By that time test differences between preschool and control group children have disappeared. Remember as well that achievement test differences were rather small, uneven across programs and school years, and limited to mathematics.

It might be argued that the earlier differences favoring preschool children, no matter how small, still influenced those making education assignments to have more confidence in these children. An alternative explanation, however, is also suggested by these data: Perhaps participation in an early intervention program in itself, apart from any intellectual benefits, influences subsequent decisions regarding placement and retention. Children who have participated in these programs may be identified by that fact on their school records or in other less formal ways and, as a result, are simply judged differently from other children. They are expected perhaps to be better able to take advantage of school opportunities, to recover better from problems, to be less in need of remedial or special attention. Their grades aren't higher, neither are their intelligence and achievement test scores, but they are reacted to differently because of their preschool experience.

There is no direct support for this possibility in the consortium's results, just as there is none for the idea that the temporary differences in measured ability between preschool and control children led to later differences in retention and placement. This second interpretation assumes that placement and retention decisions are made on broader grounds than merely scholastic performance as judged by tests or grades. This undoubtedly is true to some extent. If so, we might take things a step further and ask why was it not so evident for Head Start programs? The answer might be that Head Start programs are more widespread, and therefore no longer regarded as so prestigious as were the consortium's programs. Over the past twenty years it has probably become quite commonplace to find children from disadvantaged environments coming into elementary schools from Head Start programs. Perhaps, then, it is the distinctiveness of some of the consortium programs that contributed to their placement and retention results.

These thoughts lead to a curious possibility: Extrapolating from the consortium's social competence findings we might say that participation in an early intervention has school-related benefits above and beyond the failures to alter IQ and achievement test performance. This argument has in fact become a primary justification for the existence of these programs. But if the distinctiveness of these programs per se contributes to their influence on placement and retention, then *the more widespread these programs become, the less effective they will be in these very respects.*

We might add here some skepticism about whether the lower placement and retention rates for preschool children should be considered an entirely positive outcome. These are, after all, children whose IQs fall more than a standard deviation below average. Are they in fact better off by avoiding special education? The answer undoubtedly depends on one's views about the effectiveness of special education and grade retention compared with the negative effects of being singled out in these respects. Although there is surely no one answer to this question, it is difficult to disagree with Alfred Binet, who once noted that "it will never be to one's credit to have attended a special school."[16] Nonetheless, the lower rates of placement and retention are not an unequivocal benefit of these programs.

As if there weren't already sufficient ambiguities in these results, the fact that IQ and achievement do not wholly predict placement and retention decisions is open to yet another interpretation. Perhaps these programs result in changes that are simply not captured by IQ and achievement test scores, and it is these other changes that mediate the fact that preschool children are somewhat better at avoiding placement and retention. Recall that the meta-analysis of Head Start looked at this possibility with respect to achievement motivation, social behavior, and self-esteem. The consortium reported nothing of similar magnitude for all projects combined, although it was argued that throughout the school years, former preschoolers maintained a slightly higher achievement orientation than did former control group members. Unfortunately this result was not significant across programs.[17] One consortium member, however, separately reported an extensive array of data that went well beyond standard measures of intelligence, achievement, or even social competence. That project is also the most publicized and most highly regarded preschool program.

THE PERRY PRESCHOOL PROJECT

The 123 three-year-old children in this project were recruited by project director David Weikart and his co-workers from the inner city of Ypsilanti, Michigan, in the early 1960s. The children had scored in the range of 70 to 85 on the Stanford-Binet and evidenced no organic impairment. For the next two years half of the children were randomly assigned to receive training in cognitive development activities five days each week. The remaining children served as a control group. The training was supplemented with home visits by the teachers for ninety minutes each week.

Both groups began with IQs slightly below 80. By the end of the program, at age five, the children enrolled in the program had IQs of 95, the control children had IQs of 84. That 11-point difference was reduced to 5 points by the first grade (age seven) and disappeared entirely by the second grade. At age fourteen both groups had IQs of 81, almost identical to their age three averages.

These results seem to match those reported for Head Start and for the other consortium programs, and one might wonder why this program was characterized as so highly regarded, or for that matter why a monograph summarizing the program's results was titled "Changed Lives."[18] The reason comes not from any effects on IQ to be sure, but from the analysis of other results, some concerning achievement tests and social competence, others from more exotic variables like rates of delinquency and pregnancy in adolescence.

Achievement Tests and Social Competence

It has been argued, for example, that although IQ differences disappeared by the second grade, differences in achievement test performance emerged at that age and continued through the school years. Other differences followed a similar pattern, so that by the time these children had graduated high school an entire constellation of academic outcomes in favor of the preschool children had emerged, making them far more successful than their control group counterparts.

For our purposes, the program's results are unusual for a number of reasons, not the least of which is that they, more than perhaps any other results, suggest that IQ may be a relatively uninformative measure of the effectiveness of pre-school programs, even with respect to school achievement tests. The results reported by this project are unexpected because intelligence measures and achievement tests are reasonably well correlated. The correlation is only mod-erately high, however, so there certainly is room for one measure to behave differently from the other. But for achievement test differences to emerge just when IQ differences disappear is indeed unusual, as was the pattern of achieve-ment test results: There were no achievement test differences in first grade when there were still IQ differences between the groups. Differences appeared first at age seven, although they were described as accounting for "marginally signif-icant amounts of variance" over the first four years of school.[19] Curiously, these differences disappeared at age eleven, only to reappear in stronger form at age fourteen.[20]

In itself that pattern is odd, and its interpretation is complicated by two considerations. First, comparisons between groups are usually expressed in terms of the probability that the result occurred by chance. It is standard practice to adopt probability levels termed ".05" or ".01," meaning that a result is considered to be significant if the probability of it occurring by chance is less than five in one hundred or, more stringently, one in one hundred. The Perry program adopted a more lenient criterion, that of ten in one hundred, or .10. Using this criterion, the achievement test differences from age seven onward, with the exception of age eleven, were all significant. Using the standard practice of the .05 level, only the age fourteen result was significant.[21]

Moreover, those achievement test differences themselves were of comparatively small magnitude. For example, at age fourteen where the largest differences occurred, the group averages, expressed as the percentage of items answered correctly on the California Achievement Test, were 36 percent for preschool children and 28 percent for control group children.

The Perry program also reported differences in favor of preschool children in social competence. Nine measures of placement and retention were reported (see Appendix 1).[22] Only three of these measures reached the .05 level of significance, and one of them favored the control group (only four met the more relaxed criterion of .10). Six other measures were not significantly different between the groups. If we define social competence in terms of avoiding remedial education, then in fact the control group was superior. If we define it in terms of avoiding classification as mentally retarded, the preschool group was superior. If we define it in terms of rate of grade retention, there was no difference between the groups. Nor was there a difference in perhaps the most straightforward measure of social competence: the percentage of children placed in any sort of special education. In short, it is unclear which measure or measures constitute the most important evidence of the program's effectiveness. Some measures, like "percent of all years of education in which group members were in special education," seem contrived, and one wonders how many other measures could be similarly constructed so as to yield at least a trend in favor of the preschool group.

The same pattern of emphasizing portions of a large body of items may be a factor in other reported advantages of the preschool group with respect to social competence. Many of these outcomes were reported as summaries taken from self-report forms, rating scales, and interviews (see Appendix 2).[23] Of the eighty-five questions reported in this manner, fifteen favored the preschool group at the .05 level of significance. Of these, some were highlighted as indicative of the superiority of the preschool children. For example, on a scale labeled "Aspects of School Commitment" at age fifteen, only three items in eight were significantly different between the groups. One item that did reach significance entailed responding to the statement "Does your school work require preparation by you at home?" From that item it was concluded that preschool children displayed a greater commitment to schooling than did control group children. Items that did not differentiate the groups, such as "What is the average grade you got in your classes last year?" or "Compared to others in your grade, how do you rate yourself in how smart you are?'' were not taken as evidence of equal commitment to education.

Other Measures and the Search for a Mediator

Similarly, it was claimed that ''youths who attended preschool came to the attention of juvenile court authorities less frequently than their no-preschool counterparts.''[24] As evidence, eight measures from ''Official juvenile delinquency records'' were summarized, only one of which was significantly different between the groups. That item was the ''Number of petition requests submitted to juvenile court.'' Petitions to a juvenile court judge must be submitted and accepted before a court hearing on a charge will be arranged. It is certainly a reasonable measure of delinquency, but so is the percentage of people arrested or the total number of arrests, neither of which revealed any differences between the groups.

Even if one were to overlook these interpretative problems and argue instead for the superiority of the preschool children, there would still be the question of what produced the differences between the groups over so long a time span, particularly in the absence of IQ differences. Surely preschool education at age three cannot be thought to influence adolescent delinquency directly, nor can it be pointed to as the reason why control group females were reported to have become pregnant at a higher rate during adolescence than did preschool females. The pregnancies for the two groups were seventeen (out of twenty-five) and twenty-eight (out of twenty-four—some females had more than one pregnancy) for preschool and control group females, respectively. That statistic was reported as ''teen pregnancies per 100.'' By this measure 68 preschool females (prorated for a group of 100) and 117 control females became pregnant, a difference that failed to reach significance at the .05 level. The comparable statistic for males (''fathering'') failed to reach significance at the .10 level.[25]

In short, a mediating variable is needed, some enduring difference between the groups that might help to explain some of the supposed long-term effects of the program. We are back, then, to the reason for examining the Perry program. Recall that one explanation of the effects of preschool on later social competence was the existence of some difficult-to-detect variable that mediated the success of preschool children in later avoiding placement and retention. The easiest mediator would perhaps be IQ, but in its absence the authors of the Perry program have an alternative:

Preschool may positively affect adaptive functioning in the actual school environment. This improved adaptive functioning creates a more positive social dynamic and thereby supports and maintains itself. Children who attended preschool actually do function better in school, are perceived and treated as functioning better, therefore continue to function better, and so on.[26]

The superior "adaptive functioning" and its companion "social dynamic" seemed difficult to discover in the measures of school achievement and social competence as well as in other measures of commitment to schooling that have been thus far analyzed. They might better be located in less standard measures of school performance, some heretofore overlooked factors that might support the argument of the project staff that "on *achievement* measures the magnitude of the difference [between preschool and control children] tended to increase as children experienced elementary education."[27] The Perry program measured many of these for the first four years of schooling, where one might expect to find evidence of the differences that would later sustain the supposed superiority of the preschool children (see Appendix 3).[28]

Before seeking untapped variables to explain the program's effects, the possibility should be considered that focusing on only one measure of IQ failed to capture differences between the groups in intelligence. To examine this possibility, the Perry project used four intelligence measures (see Appendix 3, top row); none of them showed a trend different from that revealed by the Stanford-Binet, the source of the IQ data reported here for the project. The project also reported three measures of school performance—academic motivation, academic potential (as rated by teachers), and verbal skills—along with six measures of social-emotional maturity (see Appendix 3, middle and bottom rows). Without belaboring a point made obvious by the results themselves, there was no pattern to them: Of thirty-six such measures taken over the first four years of schooling, only five reached statistical significance. There was little to suggest the superior adaptive social functioning alluded to by the Perry project authors.[29]

And so, what can be made of all of this? Simply stated, the pattern of results of the Perry program seem very much like those of Head Start and the other consortium projects. Unkindly, using only the project's reported results, we might marry the large number of nonsignificant and unfavorable findings into a far different picture of the project's outcomes. We might argue that preschool training resulted in no differences in school motivation or school potential at the time of school entry, no changes in IQ, no subsequent reliable achievement test differences. By age fifteen the preschool children placed no increased value on schooling as compared with control group children; both groups were equally certain that they would graduate high school. There were no differences in their average grades, in their personel satisfaction with their school performance, or in their self-esteem. The parents of the preschool children were no more likely to talk with teachers about school work or to attend school activities and functions than were control group parents. And preschool children were more likely to have been placed in remedial education. Their adolescent IQs were 81; 65 percent of them had received special educational services of some kind.

That description depends on a selective reading of the project's results and is, in that way, clearly unfair. It is offered only to illustrate what can be done when only selected results are used to draw conclusions. To be fair, though, the pattern of results from the Perry program in conjunction with other results are clear enough to allow for some general conclusions: Preschools result in no long-term differences in IQ, school achievement, or a host of other frequently measured factors. The most identifiable outcome of these programs is the somewhat better placement and retention record of the preschool children. The interpretation of this outcome, however, need not involve substantive changes in intelligence or achievement, but rather might point to the social status characteristics attendant to preschool participation.

From all of this it would seem that preschool programs are, at best, modestly effective, at least with respect to the types of measurements that usually have been regarded as important. The most important measure, judged at least by the attention accorded it historically, is IQ. The preschool literature seems strongly to suggest that IQ carries with it a certain *stasis*, an inability to be much changed in the long run, despite the earnest intentions of psychologists and educators over the past fifty years to demonstrate otherwise through educational interventions. This generalization seems to have no exceptions.

None but one, that is. Although the Perry Preschool Project might be the most highly regarded intervention, the next program to be described is by far the most notorious. It is known variously as the Miracle—or the Mystery—in Milwaukee.

MISCHIEF IN MILWAUKEE

In comparison with the programs previously described, the Milwaukee project was both longer in duration and more intensive. The children participating in the program were inner-city black children whose mothers had scored below 75 on a standard intelligence test. The intervention, conducted by Richard Heber and his colleagues, consisted of a seven-hour program five days each week that lasted from the time the children were three months old until the time they entered regular schooling at five or six years of age. For the first few months each child was assigned his or her own teacher, nothing less than a sort of co-parent, who dressed, fed, played with the child, and began educational intervention. As they grew older the children were placed into preschool groupings of four of five students per teacher. Health and nutritional care were provided for the children throughout the program. Their mothers received their own educational program that included vocational training and information regarding homemaking and parenting.

The effects of the Milwaukee project were both of far greater magnitude than any other program and more durable. Although the preschool and control group children were similar in IQ at one year of age, by the age of three they differed by almost 30 points (120 vs. 95 for preschool and control group children, respectively). The IQs of both groups decreased as they entered regular schooling at age five, but a nearly 20-point difference remained between them throughout the early school years. At ages twelve to fourteen the preschool children's IQs were, on average, 10 points above the control group average (101 vs. 91).[30]

Nothing in the previous examination of the intervention literature has quite anticipated this sort of result. No other program has ever demonstrated a long-lasting effect on IQ, and certainly no program has shown the magnitude of IQ gain as has the Milwaukee project. As might be expected from this sort of result, the program has been much discussed and evaluated over the years, and it has not escaped without problems of interpretation arising.

One problem derives from the fact that as the program began so early and lasted so long, several different tests of intelligence had to be used—one appropriate for infants, another for preschoolers, another still for the elementary school years. These tests are not equivalent in their reliability or in their standards of measurement. One readjustment of the different test scores against a common standard yielded in fact a different picture of the preschool children's performance.[31] The adjusted results indicated that the IQs of the preschool children never exceeded 108 during any portion of training. That average fell to 95 soon after school entry and declined somewhat further, to about 91 or 92, in adolescence. This readjustment makes more reasonable the preschool children's performance but does not diminish their superiority as compared with control group children. The scores of the control group children would be similarly readjusted downward.

The effectiveness of the intervention with respect to IQ still needs to be explained. Perhaps the first question is what precisely about the Milwaukee project made it work so well as compared with others? Its duration is notable: a five-year intervention as compared with the shorter programs of Head Start and the consortium. It seems reasonable that the longer the intervention, the greater the expected gains from the program. Even for programs of shorter duration there is a correlation ($r = .44$) between the length of the program and the largest differences in IQ obtained between preschool and control group children at any point in the program. By contrast, age of starting per se has no similar effect ($r = .02$).[32]

But duration itself is uninformative. What must count is the nature of the intervention, and here other sorts of problems begin to emerge with the Milwaukee project, for quite surprisingly the precise characteristics of the project were not specified for the better part of twenty years after first news of the project emerged. A brief history may clarify this startling fact.

The Milwaukee project was begun at about the same time as Head Start. By the early 1970s reports began to emerge of large-scale gains in IQ from this project, all the more eagerly received given the insubstantial results coming from the first Head Start evaluations. These reports came not from scientific publications, but from the popular press. *Time* magazine, for example, reported that the project "offers persuasive evidence that mental retardation in the offspring of mentally retarded mothers can be prevented." The *Washington Post* added that "Prof. Rick Heber's group at the University of Wisconsin may have settled once and for all the question of whether the disproportionate mental retardation of slum children is the result of heredity or environment."[33]

Beyond these descriptions the Milwaukee project was seldom reported on, at least in the usual outlet of refereed scientific journals. Matters did not improve in the years to follow. Summaries of the project were published in chapters in edited volumes, but the evidence presented was little more than the average IQ differences that were by then well known. The most substantial presentation of the project came in 1972 with a progress report that promised a final, comprehensive reporting within a year.[34] Heber never published that final report, and in the years after the first reports of the project he showed a marked disinclination to share the specifics of his project with others. Many investigators apparently tried in vain to obtain information from Heber concerning both the project's educational programs and the specifics of the results.

Beyond a general project description it would have been impossible for anyone to detail precisely the sorts of training the children received and, therefore, to replicate the project. As late as 1978 Heber's description of, for example, the training provided for the mothers of the preschool children was little more than that "we provided vocational guidance, jobs outside the home and pocket money. These dimensions seem important because the mothers responded so well to them."[35] Pocket money may indeed be effective, but as was illustrated by the case of Bernardine Schmidt, the failure to provide sufficient data for reanalysis and replication is not a minor quibble, but an essential facet of the verification process in science. This is not to say that all scientists comply with this provision. Probably a good portion do not offer their raw data to others, but at the very least standard practice is to provide sufficient procedural detail to permit replication. To fail to do this in the case of the Milwaukee project seems extraordinary. In the face of the failures of other interventions to alter IQ the Milwaukee project apparently had come upon techniques that worked, yet they were not disclosed. And one is forced to wonder why. Humanitarian considerations aside, the results of the Milwaukee project were by far the most startling ever to be announced. To engender the sort of skepticism that naturally arose over the project seems entirely self-defeating.

One possible reason for the project's communication problems became apparent in 1981 when Heber and an associate were convicted in federal and state courts in Wisconsin for the misuse of institutional funds intended for the Center on Mental Retardation and Human Development at the University of Wisconsin, where Heber was then the director. Heber subsequently served a three-year term in federal prison, concurrent with a four-year conviction on state theft and tax charges. As disclosed in a series of articles in the *Madison Capitol Times* during 1981 and 1982, Heber and his associate had engaged in a "pattern of increasing greed," with the result that at least $165,000 of the center's money had been diverted into personal bank accounts. Heber was described as having a legal residence in Colorado, where he was engaged in breeding champion Arabian horses, despite his full-time position at the Wisconsin center. He was said to own 26 acres of land in Colorado, another 200 in Iowa, and 100 more in Florida and Wisconsin.[36]

Personal problems of this sort should not bear directly on the veracity of the Milwaukee project. But in the context of the pattern of sketchy reporting of the project's results and procedures coupled with the apparent disinterest in responding to colleagues' requests for information, there was, over the years, little to encourage faith in the results. Fortunately this situation was rectified in 1988 when Howard Garber, one of the project's original directors, published a comprehensive accounting of the program's results.[37] After so long a delay this final accounting may reasonably be viewed with caution, but examination of its intricacies reveals a rather detailed picture of the project's outcomes and some most unexpected findings.[38]

The Final Results and Some Surprises

Perhaps the most important surprise is the fact that the effects of the Milwaukee project seem to have been limited to IQ. Within four years after the end of the program it was reported that the preschool children's achievement test performance, including math and reading, had declined to the level of control group children, that is, to the average level of inner-city children.[39] It is a rather unexpected failure, given the IQ differences between the groups and the expected correlation between IQ and school achievement, particularly with reading, an ability that substantially correlates with IQ.[40]

As another oddity, although the groups were comparable academically by the fourth grade, nearly three times as many control group children received special educational services during that year. It might be argued that preschool children still maintained a slight, though statistically nonsignificant academic superiority. Test results aside, however, both groups had C averages across the first four grades in reading, math, and language.

It also might be argued that preschool children maintained more competent social skills—the better "adaptive functioning" alluded to by the authors of the Perry project—and it was these skills that enabled them to avoid placement and retention. Perhaps so, but school grades surely include an adaptive functioning component. More to the point, preschool children actually were rated by their teachers as *less* compliant than were control group children; their deportment was judged to be more in need of control. Apparently, as the preschool children progressed in school, they experienced increased conduct problems, absenteeism, and negative attitudes toward school. It may well be argued that the source of these conduct problems was that the preschool children found their elementary schools unstimulating compared with their preschool experience. Yet, to the extent that these behavioral problems reflect problems in self-discipline, they do not easily lend themselves to an interpretation that emphasizes superior adaptive functioning.

An alternative interpretation of the differences in social competence might be that the social status characteristics attendant to the Milwaukee Project, a highly visible intervention, themselves influenced placement and retention decisions.

On this point there is some evidence. The project staff regularly informed schools of the status of the preschool children with letters that routinely became part of the children's academic folders. As an additional point the schools to which the preschool children were sent were not in all cases their neighborhood schools, but were those that had been selected by the project staff to be most nurturing of the children's nascent academic abilities. These schools in turn may have had different policies and expectations with respect to placement and retention than the neighborhood inner-city schools that control group children attended.

The Isolation of IQ

These results are, oddly, the mirror image of the claims made by the Perry project. Recall that in the Perry project, IQ showed no lasting improvement, whereas a host of other changes reportedly took place. In the Milwaukee Project, IQ was permanently raised, but that improvement did not mean what IQ normally means with respect to school achievement.

The first point to make in this regard is that this lack of predictiveness was not confined to IQ. Virtually every measurement taken of the preschool children revealed above average performance and their superiority to control group children. With respect to cognitive functioning, for example, the preschool children were characterized as "demonstrating more sophisticated early problem solving behavior" and an "earlier tendency to hypothesize test" than control group children. By the time of school entry preschool children were two years ahead of their control group counterparts in language performance and reading readiness. In many respects they were described as performing at the same level as white children from middle- and upper-middle-class backgrounds.[41]

The question raised by these results is both curious and thorny: Why were these measures so unpredictive of the preschool children's academic performance? One possibility is to view these data as powerful evidence of the deleterious effects that substandard schools can have on children's potential, even academically prepared children—and perhaps *especially* on these children. If so, we have to assume that these effects acted rapidly, within the first year of schooling. We also have to assume that the schools selected by the project staff especially for the preschool children were as deleterious in these respects as were the inner-city schools attended by control group children.

As an alternative to focusing exclusively on the failure of schools, perhaps the Milwaukee project somehow enhanced test performance on IQ and other measures without providing for them to function as they usually do to predict real-world performance. This possibility seems particularly applicable to the preschool children's IQs that survived, though by no means intact, the precarious journey through the Milwaukee public schools. Is it possible, in other words, that the Milwaukee project produced an impressive variety of high test scores, particularly IQs, but little else?

MILWAUKEE AS METAPHOR

The possibilities above undoubtedly admit to no sure answer. We might well tend to be cautious of the Milwaukee project for any number of reasons—its inconsistent history, the unparalleled raising of IQ, the seeming isolation of IQ from other academic measures. And yet, despite those thoughts, there is undoubtedly something fascinating about it, the hint perhaps of some heretofore undiscovered potential that goes wasted in the face of our usual efforts. What if it *was* in some undetected but critical ways different from any other attempt to improve the success of disadvantaged children? What to do about that possibility?

Freud once was asked how he could be sure that his patients were being truthful about their recollections of infantile sexual experiences. Might they not be making them up to suit Freud, to meet the unstated obligations of analysis? It didn't matter, was Freud's reply: The experiences patients made up were as revealing as the real thing.[42] An ingenious answer, to be sure. And so it is perhaps with the Milwaukee project. Whether or not its results are to be wholeheartedly embraced, they speak of possibilities, create their own mythical imperative that leaves us wondering where to look for answers.

There is, as it would happen, an important place to look. We might take the Milwaukee project as a hint—and only that, given the preschool children's lack of academic success—about what might happen under the most ideal of circumstances if severely disadvantaged children were truly transported into new and better environments. In a sense, the Milwaukee project, more than any other preschool program, was nothing less than a sort of shared parenting; an adoption of sorts.

And so we return to Skodak and Skeels.

NOTES

1. Hebb, D. O. (1949). *The organization of behavior*. New York: John Wiley & Sons.

2. Jensen, A. R. (1969). How much can we boost IQ and scholastic achievement? *Harvard Educational Review, 39*, 3.

3. Ryan, W. (1971). *Blaming the victim*. New York: Pantheon.

4. Head Start Bureau. (1985). *Final report. The impact of Head Start on children, families, and communities: Head Start Synthesis Project*. DHHS Publication No. (OHDS) 85–31193. Washington, D.C.: U.S. Government Printing Office. Many of the analyses regarding preschool programs presented in this chapter are considered in greater detail in Locurto (*in press*). Beyond IQ in preschool programs? *Intelligence*.

5. Redrawn from Figures 3–3, 3–4, and 3–5, in Head Start Bureau.

6. These follow-up data are not synonymous with longitudinal data. Some Head Start studies reported only a one-year follow-up, others only a two-year follow-up, and so on. Therefore, the data presented in Figure 5 do not represent the same children studied over

several posttraining years—another reason to be cautious about interpreting these follow-up results.

7. For example, Zigler, E., Abelson, W. D., Trickett, P. K., & Seitz, V. (1982). Is an intervention program necessary in order to improve economically disadvantaged children's IQ scores? *Child Development, 53*, 340–348.

8. For a similar analysis see Zigler, E., & Freedman, J. (1987). Early experiences, malleability and Head Start. In J. J. Gallagher & C. T. Ramey (Eds.), *The malleability of children* (pp. 85–95). Baltimore: Paul H. Brooks.

9. Much of the following analysis is taken from Lazar, I., & Darlington, R. (1982). Lasting effects of early education: A report from the Consortium for Longitudinal Studies. *Monographs of the Society for Research in Child Development, 47* (2–3, Serial No. 195). The four "more nearly randomized" programs were those of Gordon, Gray, Palmer, and Weikart.

10. Head Start Bureau, Tables 3–1 and 3–2.

11. The consortium also reported a composite measure termed "failure to meet school requirements" that combined grade retention and special education placement. On that measure the averages for preschool and control group children were 25 percent and 44 percent, respectively. Only two of seven projects, however, reported significant differences in favor of preschool childen on this measure, whereas two other projects reported trends in favor of control group children.

12. Horn, J. M. (1981). Duration of preschool effects on later school competence. *Science, 213*, 1145. But also see a reply by Darlington, R. B. (1981). *Science, 213*, 1145–1146. The original article that spawned this exchange of letters was Darlington, R. B., Royce, J. M., Snipper, A. S., Murray, H. W., & Lazar, I. (1980). Preschool programs and later school competence of children from low-income families. *Science, 208*, 202–204.

13. Lazar & Darlington, Table 6, p. 34.

14. Lazar & Darlington, Table 5, p. 32.

15. This pattern is not true in all cases. Some states require grade retention if basic skills are not mastered even as early as kindergarten.

16. Quoted in Woodhead, M. (1988). When psychology informs public policy: The case of early childhood intervention. *American Psychologist, 43*, 443–454.

17. Lazar & Darlington, p. 50.

18. Berrueta-Clement, J. R., Schweinhart, L. J., Barnett, W. S., Epstein, A. S., & Weikart, D. P. (1984). Changed lives: The effects of the Perry Preschool program on youths through age 19. *Monograph of the High/Scope Educational Research Foundation, No. 8*. The following analyses of the Perry Preschool Program can also be found in Locurto (in press).

19. From Weikart, D. P., Bond, J. T., & McNeil, J. T. (1978). The Ypsilanti-Perry Preschool Project: Preschool years and longitudinal results through fourth grade. *Monograph of the High/Scope Educational Research Foundation, No. 3*, p. 63.

20. Achievement test results are given in Schweinhart, L. J., & Weikart, D. P. (1980). Young children grow up: The effects of the Perry Preschool Program on youths through age 15. *Monograph of the High/Scope Educational Research Foundation, No. 7*, Figures 3, 3A, 3B, 3C, and 5; and in Weikart et al., Figures 6, 7, 8, and 9.

Achievement test results were sometimes reported using different metrics. For example, some reports of these results used the percentage of items passed "to [maintain] some degree of comparability over time," Schweinhart & Weikart, p. 37; see also

Schweinhart, L. J., & Weikart, D. P. (1983). The effects of the Perry Preschool Program on youths through age 15—a summary. In The Consortium for Longitudinal Studies, *As the twig is bent* (pp. 71–101). Hillsdale, NJ: Lawrence Erlbaum Associates. The present analysis is based on this metric. Other reports of these data, however, transformed scores to grade equivalents, which yielded a different picture. See Schweinhart, L. J., & Weikart, D. P. (1981). Perry preschool effects nine years later: What do they mean? In Begab, M. J., Haywood, C. H., & Garber, H. L. (Eds.) *Psychosocial influences in retarded performance, Vol. 2*, Tables 2 and 3. Baltimore: University Park Press. Also, other analyses of these same data yielded somewhat higher *p* levels (compare, for example, Weikart et al., Tables 15 and 17).

21. See Schweinhart & Weikart (1980), Figure 3, p. 38.

22. Berrueta-Clement et al., Table 6, p. 26.

23. Ibid., Tables 7, 19, 20, and 22; Schweinhart & Weikart (1980), Tables 7, 8, and 11.

24. Berrueta-Clement et al., p. 63; see also Tables 19 and 20.

25. Ibid., p. 69.

26. Schweinhart & Weikart (1981), p. 123.

27. Weikart et al., p. 48.

28. From Schweinhart & Weikart (1980), Table 7; Weikart et al., Tables 15 and 18, and Figures 13 through 18.

29. The significance of some measures seems to have changed over time. For example, in Weikart et al. (Table 15) and Schweinhart & Weikart (1980, Table 7) school motivation failed to reach significance at the .05 level, and school potential failed at $p = .10$. In Schweinhart & Weikart (1981, Table 3), however, (''academic'') motivation was reported at $p = .04$ and potential at $p = .06$. In Schweinhart & Weikart (1983, Table 3.4 and p. 83) both measures were again reported to be nonsignificant.

30. See Garber, H. L. (1988). *The Milwaukee Project*: Preventing mental retardation in children at risk (p. 307). Washington, D.C.: American Association on Mental Retardation.

31. Flynn, J. R. (1984). The mean IQ of Americans: Massive gains from 1932 to 1978. *Psychological Bulletin, 95*, 29–51.

32. Data calculated from Ramey, C. T., Bryant, D. M., & Suarez, T. M. (1985). Preschool compensatory education and the modifiability of intelligence: A critical review. In D. Detterman (Ed.), *Current Topics in Intelligence, Vol. 1: Research Methodology*, Table 10.5 (pp. 247–296). Norwood, NJ: Ablex Publishing Corp.

33. Quoted in Herrnstein, R. J. (1982, August). IQ testing and the media. *Atlantic Monthly*, 68–74.

34. Heber, R., Garber, H., Harrington, S., Hoffman, C., & Falender, C. (1972). *Rehabilitation of families at risk for mental retardation: Progress Report, December, 1972.* Madison: Rehabilitation Research and Training Center in Mental Retardation, University of Wisconsin.

35. Heber, R. F. (1978). Sociocultural mental retardation: A longitudinal study. In D. G. Forgays (Ed.), *Environmental influences and strategies in primary prevention* (p. 80). Hanover, NH: University Press of New England.

36. For a complete description see Page, E. B. (1986). The disturbing case of the Milwaukee Project. In H. H. Spitz, *The raising of intelligence: A selected history of attempts to raise retarded intelligence* (pp. 115–140). Hillsdale, NJ: Lawrence Erlbaum Associates. Quote comes from the *Madison Capitol Times*, April 8, 1981, p. 16.

37. Garber.

38. There has been one attempt at direct replication. See Ramey, C. T., & Campbell, F. A. (1984). Preventative education for high-risk children: Cognitive consequences of the Carolina Abecedarian Project. *American Journal of Mental Deficiency, 88*, 515–523; Ramey, C. T., & Haskins, R. (1981). The modification of intelligence through early experience. *Intelligence, 5*, 5–19.

39. See Clarke, A. M. (1984). Early experience and cognitive development. In E. W. Gordon (Ed.), *Review of research in education, 11*, 125–157, especially 135–136.

40. Heber, especially pp. 53–56.

41. Garber, H., p. 120; see also Jensen, A. R. (1981). Raising the IQ: The Ramey and Haskins study. *Intelligence, 5*, 29–40; and Jensen, A. R. (1989). Raising IQ without increasing *g*: A review of The Milwaukee Project: Preventing mental retardation in children at risk. *Developmental Reviews, 9*, 234–258. See also reply by Garber H. L. & Hodge, J. D. (1989). Reply: Risk for Deceleration in the Rate of Mental development *Developmental Review, 9*, 295–300.

42. To be sure, this rendering of Freud's response—indeed the possibility that he was ever asked a question of this sort—is apocryphal, at best a construction intended to make a point. The point conveyed, however, is not incorrect. In his *Introductory Lectures on Psychoanalysis* ([1963]. In James Strachey [Ed. and Trans.] [pp. 367–368] London: Hogarth.) Freud writes:

I have warned you that we still have something new to learn; it is indeed something surprising and perplexing. By means of analysis, as you know, starting from the symptoms, we arrive at a knowledge of the infantile experiences to which the libido is fixated and out of which the symptoms are made. Well, the surprise lies in the fact that these scenes from infancy are not always true. Indeed, they are not true in the majority of cases, and in a few of them they are the direct opposite of the historical truth. . . . It will be a long time before we can take in our proposal that we should equate phantasy and reality and not bother to begin with whether the childhood experiences under examination are the one or the other. Yet this is clearly the only correct attitude to adopt towards these mental productions. They too possess a reality of a sort. It remains a fact that the patient has created these phantasies for himself, and this fact is of scarcely less importance for his neurosis than if he had really experienced what the phantasies contain. The phantasies possess *psychical* as contrasted with *material* reality, and we gradually learn to understand that *in the world of the neuroses it is psychical reality which is the decisive kind.*

5

Adoptions and the Malleability of IQ

> I do not profess to have worked out the kinships of the Italians with any special care, but I have seen amply enough of them, to justify me in saying that . . . the very common combination of an able son and an eminent parent, is not matched, in the case of high Romish ecclesiastics, by an eminent nephew and an eminent uncle. The social helps are the same, but hereditary gifts are wanting in the latter case.
>
> —Francis Galton[1]

Given his other accomplishments, it should perhaps not be surprising that Francis Galton was the first to use adoptions to study the heredity and environment of intelligence. As can be seen from the quote above, taken from *Hereditary Genius*, Galton sought to dismiss the influence of the environment on intelligence by referring to a most unique sort of adoption—that involving Roman Catholic popes, for whom it was once commonplace to "adopt" young boys and raise them as "nephews." Galton studied the eminence of these adoptees under the assumption that they surely received an advantaged upbringing, but did not share heredity—or so he assumed—with their adoptive parent.

Irrespective of Galton's conclusions regarding the social heredity of Catholic popes and their nephews, adoption studies do indeed offer unique opportunities for assessing genetic and environmental influences on IQ. For assessing the malleability of IQ they are equally important. Recall that early intervention programs were essentially conceived as attempts to capture something about advantaged environments and bring it to disadvantaged children. The nature of that "something" may be open to conjecture, and given the results of early intervention programs, it would appear that if there is something to be captured, interventions have as yet, by and large, not identified it. But given that adoptive families usually are well above average in status, adoptions might be thought of as the best possible place to look for positive changes in IQ. In a real sense they fulfill the promise of intervention programs by providing a child with long-term exposure to the type of environment that presumably underlies the optimal development of intelligence.

THE IDEAL ADOPTION STUDY

It is a cruel justice that by offering so rich a source of information, adoptions seem as well to exact an unusual price. In point of fact, as is apparent from Skodak and Skeels, there is arguably no other area of research more complicated and puzzling. Adoption studies differ widely in their design, the quality and quantity of the information they provide, and the types of children and families studied. Instead of detailing the problems wrought by these complications, it might be better to begin by outlining the ideal adoption study and then see how close reality comes to that ideal.

Perhaps the first requirement would be that the adopted child is separated from the biological mother soon after birth. This requirement has in fact been met in several adoption studies to be discussed. Next, we would like to know what the child's expected IQ would be without adoption, if, that is, the child had been raised by his or her biological parents. Unfortunately, this requirement constitutes the most serious interpretative complication. As has been noted before, there are simply no measurements that can be taken of an infant that will predict adult intelligence, or for that matter even that infant's later intelligence at age three or four. In the absence of that information indirect estimates must be relied on. The biological parents' IQs would be the best substitute, but unfortunately only two studies provide useful information about the biological parents' IQs. Skodak and Skeels is one of them.

Lacking that information, and given that any information about the biological fathers often is impossible to obtain, the child's IQ is estimated from the mothers' education, occupation, or income. These measures in turn present problems in that they are only moderately well correlated with IQ. Then, too, many of the biological mothers are young; nineteen to twenty-three seems to be about their average age. Estimating the biological mothers' intelligence from their income or educational level at that age may well be an underestimate. They may reasonably still be in school or just beginning careers, to say nothing of the disruptions in their lives owing to pregnancy and the adoption process.

We would like to have the IQs of the adoptive parents, to estimate the intellectual level of the adoptive families. It also would be useful to have the IQs of any biological children of the adoptive parents for comparison with the adoptive children or, lacking that, perhaps the IQs of children in families that have been matched to the adoptive families. Each of these measures is at times available, but not always. There are in fact several important adoption studies for which no IQ data are given for the adoptive families; Skodak and Skeels is one of them.

If these requirements are matched against every adoption study ever published, only one study substantially meets all of them. That study is the Texas Adoption

Project conducted by Horn, Loehlin, and Willerman.[2] The adopted children were separated from their biological mothers within one week of birth and were eight years old at the time of the study. IQ data were available for the biological mothers as well as for the adoptive parents and their children. And, as compared with many other adoption studies, the Texas study included large numbers of children and parents. There were 343 biological mothers tested, 469 adopted children, nearly 300 adoptive families, and 164 biological children of adoptive parents.

The adoptive children's average IQ was 111. The average IQ of the adoptive parents was 114 on the Revised Beta Examination, a test of performance (nonverbal) IQ and the most frequently used test in this study to assess adult intelligence. It is clear from evidence provided by the Texas Project that the adoptive parents were typical of adoptive parents in general, well above average in education, income, and overall standard of living. The average IQ of the adoptive parents' own children was 112, not different from the average IQ of the adopted children. This pattern of results has been described as follows: "These figures indicate that adopting parents successfully transmitted high IQs to all the children they reared, whether or not they shared genes with them. The relatively low IQs of adopted children's biological mothers simply did not matter."[3]

As judged by the quote, the question of whom the adopted child comes to resemble is answered in the averages reported above. Adopted children resembled their adoptive parents and, we are told, the "relativity low IQs" of the biological mothers were not influential. In this interpretation the pattern of these averages clearly illustrates the malleability of IQ. To complete the picture with respect to the question of resemblance, we might think to look at the pattern of correlations in this study. Recall, however, that correlations are most useful in understanding the respective contributions of genetics and environment to individual differences in IQ. We will in fact turn to the correlations reported for this and other adoption studies at a later time, but for the moment, to assess malleability, the average IQs are most useful.

One critical piece of information has not yet been revealed: the average IQ of the biological mothers. It was 109 on the Revised Beta. That average may be quite surprising, especially given the earlier discussion of Skodak and Skeels in which the IQs of the biological mothers were nearly a standard deviation below average. It must be noted that a private adoption agency was used in the Texas study, and the biological mothers were asked to contribute funds to help defer the costs of adoption. These mothers were, then, likely from above average backgrounds, not unlike those of the adoptive parents. But the fact remains that their IQs were only 2 points less than the average of their adopted-away children fully eight years after adoption had taken place.

One needs, it would seem, a rather insular faith in the power of the environment to draw firm conclusions about the malleability of IQ from this study, particularly as there are factors other than the adoptive environment that might have altered the scores of adopted children as compared with their mothers. One problem, as it was in intervention programs, is attrition. Most adoption studies, including the Texas project, are retrospective, in the sense that the adoptions have already taken place. The investigators solicit the cooperation of the adoptive parents, and only those who volunteer become part of the study. The investigators then try to locate information for the biological mothers of the volunteered adoptive children, a process that can be quite difficult and is one of the reasons sufficient information on biological mothers often is not available.

The Texas investigators were fortunate in that the adoption agency they used regularly gave intelligence tests to the biological mothers as part of their screening process. But, as with many studies, a good portion of the adoptive parents, nearly 25 percent, decided not to volunteer for the study. We have no information as to whether the nonparticipating families were different from those who chose to participate, whether, for example, their children may have been experiencing difficulties and the parents decided against participation. If so, the adopted children studied might be a select sample of all adopted children.

The Texas Adoption Project, then, is special in a number of ways. It provides more information than has any other project, but given the similarities between the biological and adoptive parents, it is inconclusive with respect to the malleability of IQ. We need, it would seem, to look elsewhere. Given the wide divergence in adoption studies, and the fact that no single study contains all the needed information, it might be best to begin by summarizing the data on IQ for the most often cited adoption studies (see Appendix 4).[4]

Two Conclusions

It is indeed hazardous to draw conclusions from any diverse group of studies, but two generalizations are possible. The first is that adopted children have above average IQs: 106 was the average across all studies.[5] The second conclusion derives from studying the averages of the adoptive parents, their own children, and the children in control groups. The adoptive parents averaged 116; their children and control group children averaged 114 and 113, respectively. These three averages might be taken as a sort of global measure of the ambient intellectual level in adoptive families and in similar families in the community. These averages are about one-half to two-thirds of a standard deviation above the average IQs of the adopted children. In a sense, then, the IQs of adopted children usually fall short of the intellectual levels that are characteristic of their adoptive environments.

It might be speculated that ideally, if IQs were highly malleable, adopted children's IQs might reach the average intellectual level provided by their adoptive families. There are, naturally, complications attendant to this interpretation, not the least of which is the danger inherent in summing together so diverse an array of studies. The idea of an ambient intellectual level itself might be questioned, at least as it can be captured by the IQs of adoptive parents, their children, and control families. Should we accept that idea, there nevertheless remain many reasons why adopted children's average IQ might fall below this level. These children may experience a number of adjustment problems in their adoptive families, despite the best intentions of those families. Then, too, not all studies limited themselves to adoptions within the first week of life, as did the Texas project.[6]

And this possibility leads to the critical issue in assessing malleability from any adoption study. The adopted children's average IQ of 106 tells us nothing about the degree of malleability evident in that average unless we can compare it with what would be expected *if the children had not been adopted*. To give even a suggestive answer to that question requires the answer to three other questions. The first is *Who is put up for adoption?* Based on the Texas project, we might say that the average IQ of adopted children is already above average. But that study was special, and we have no reason to think that the biological mothers in that study were more representative of biological mothers in general than were the mothers in Skodak and Skeels. Their average, remember, was 86. There is precious little information about the average IQs of mothers who relinquish their children for adoption, but there is one survey of nearly 3,000 such mothers in Minnesota conducted during the 1950s. In that study the mothers' IQs averaged 100.[7] If we take this as a sort of rule of thumb in the absence of other information, then we expect that adopted children, on average, would have IQs of 100 if not adopted.[8]

That alone suggests a 6-point gain for adopted children averaged across all studies. But there is a second question that makes interpretation of that apparent gain difficult: *Who is adopted?* This question might seem identical to the first, but it may not be in every adoption study. Not all children offered for adoption may be adopted, or at least may not be adopted early in life, as are most of the children studied in adoption research. As a corollary, certain types of infants, those with health problems or those suspected of retardation, for example, might be unlikely to be adopted, a fact noted in several adoption studies. Parents may have a say in all of this, especially with respect to adopting high-risk infants. There also may be a probationary period during which both the parents and the agency assess the correctness of the adoption. This was, for example, true in Skodak and Skeels, although it is not present in every adoption study.

There is a second aspect to the question of who is adopted that involves the subtle, but nonetheless measurable filtering process that agencies and parents engage in during adoptions. Most agencies, for their part, attempt to "fit the child to the family," a process called *selective placement*. The magnitude of this effect can be estimated by correlating characteristics of the biological and adoptive parents—their educational levels, for example. If children are placed randomly in adoptive families, then that correlation should be 0. If agencies attempt to place infants coming from the best backgrounds with the best adoptive families and so on along some sort of continuum loosely judged by the agency, then the correlation should be positive. Most of the major adoption studies have in fact reported positive correlations of this type. Given the above average status of adoptive families, the effect of these selective factors is to make the sample of adopted children special, not unlikely above average in IQ as a group. Ideally, we would like to know what the IQs of the children were at the time of adoption to document this possibility, but given the early age of adoptions, that information is lacking.[9]

The special nature of the children in adoption studies may be further enhanced by the answer to a third question: *Who is studied?* This question concerns attrition. If the adoptive families of lower scoring children tend not to participate, then the group average of the adopted children studied is increased. We have no definitive information on this point, and the authors of the Texas project point out that perhaps adoptive parents with problem children would be more likely to participate to receive an assessment of their child. Just the opposite pattern is apparent in Skodak and Skeels. The subjects lost between the third and fourth testings alone scored 5 points below those remaining in the study on the third testing.

So, what began as the best glimpse into the potential malleability of IQ seems now to be more than a bit messy. Returning to the fact that adopted children are generally above average in IQ, it would seem that we can say little concerning what that value indicates about malleability. It is impossible to estimate precisely the effects that answers to each of our questions have on the group average, but in concert they probably make the gain in IQ for adopted children something less than 6 points.

STUDIES OF CONTRASTED ENVIRONMENTS

One more requirement, it would seem, needs to be added to the list of features that compose the ideal adoption study to assess malleability: Studies are needed in which the adopted children come from disadvantaged backgrounds, more like the backgrounds characteristic of the children treated in intervention programs. What is needed, in other words, are studies of *contrasted environments:* the upper middle-class environment of the adoptive families compared with a below average environment provided by the biological parents. As it happens, there are four studies that conform to this requirement. Skodak and Skeels is one of them.

Skodak and Skeels

The intricacies of this most famous study that make interpretation difficult have already been discussed. It has been argued that the biological mothers' average IQ is an underestimate; if more reliably measured, their average might be closer to 100. As it is, the children's nonadopted IQs were estimated by assuming some regression toward the mean in their scores, given the mothers' low average of 86. There was selective placement; for educational level the correlation between biological mothers and adoptive parents was .27. The authors report that care was taken not to place children suspected of retardation, and as mentioned earlier, there was a long probationary period before an adoption was made final. There also was significant attrition during the study. It began in 1936 with 180 children and ended in 1946 with 100.

These factors combine to make the final sample of 100 children quite special; their average IQ of 107 may not be solely attributable to their adoptive environments. Then, too, nothing is known directly about the IQ levels of those families, only their educational levels. There is the remaining curiosity of why the children's IQs did not correlate with those educational levels. That puzzle will be left for a later discussion concerning the genetics and environment of intelligence. For the moment there is an additional curiosity that might be mentioned before passing on to other studies.

One of the authors, Marie Skodak, did most of the testing of the adopted children. The most frequently used intelligence tests are individually administered, scoring often requires judgment on the part of the examiner, and there is considerable interaction between examiner and subject during the test. That combination surely allows for the examiner's expectations, as well as those of the subject, to become a factor. This potential bias unfortunately is true of many intervention programs and adoption studies. It is cited here because of the duration of Skodak and Skeels. By the time of the final testing the first results of the study had already been published, the expectation of large-scale changes in IQ well known. So well known in fact that by the time of the final testing, at least two of the subjects had read about themselves in earlier publications of the project. They reportedly "cooperated delightfully" in the final testing.[10]

The Transracial Adoption Study

The second study of contrasted environments, the Transracial Adoption Study by Scarr and Weinberg, is unique in that it is the most extensive study of black children adopted into upper middle-class white families. As might be expected, the adoptive families were highly educated, averaging sixteen years of schooling, and were above average in occupational status and income. Their average IQ was 120; the IQs of their own children averaged 117. The biological parents were less well educated, averaging twelve years of schooling, and had lower income levels. The IQs of the biological parents were not available. The biological parents were, on average, twenty-four years old; the adoptive parents, thirty-six years old. The adopted children were placed at an average age of 1.8 years, although that average is misleading; many of the children were adopted before six months of age. The adopted children were tested at an average age of seven years and obtained an average IQ of 106.

On the face of it, these data provide strong evidence of malleability. We might assume that without adoption, black children should have IQs of about 90, at least as judged against the average of the black population in the North Central and Northeast regions of the United States, the place of origin of most of the adoptees.[11] If so, this study seems to show a gain of about 16 points for the black children, placing them above the average of white children in the Minnesota area, although well below the average of the biological children of the adoptive parents. As might be expected, however, some features of this study render that conclusion more tenuous.

Most important, the sample of children studied by Scarr and Weinberg was in fact partly composed of two distinct subsamples: children of two black parents and interracial children. These two samples differed significantly with respect to their IQs: Black children averaged 97, whereas interracial children averaged 109. These two groups also differed with respect to the intellectual levels of the adoptive families into which they were placed, as judged by the IQs of the adoptive parents and their own children. The pattern of the data clearly indicated that the interracial children were adopted into more favorable families. They also were adopted earlier, at an average of nine months compared with thirty-three months for the black children. That in turn indicates that the interracial children spent more time with their adoptive families before testing and were subjected to fewer preadoptive placements (see Appendix 5).

Given the differences in background and IQ between these groups, they require separate analysis with respect to malleability. For the twenty-nine children of two black parents the average educational levels of their biological fathers was about average or slightly above average for black males in Minnesota; the mothers were about one year below average. The children's average IQ of 97 was then 7 points or so above the expected average for blacks in Minnesota.

For the sixty-nine interracial children, their average IQ of 109 is more difficult to place against an expected average if adoption had not taken place. For all but two of these children, their biological mothers were white. The mothers' average educational level of 12.4 years was about average for their appropriate comparison group. The black fathers' average of 12.5 years was one-half year above their comparison group average. The average IQ of whites in the North Central region at that time was about 102. If we assume the mothers to be average and the fathers above average, perhaps as high as 95, then a rough estimate of their children's average IQ without adoption would be about 99, 10 points or so above their expected average in the absence of adoption. Higher estimates for the biological parents would lower the estimate of malleability.

This analysis admittedly owes as much to guesswork as to empiricism, and it illustrates the difficulties encountered when sufficient data are not available. Unfortunately, there are several additional considerations that make interpretation even more approximate. The adopted children in this study, perhaps more than in any other adoption study, may well have experienced difficulties adjusting to their adoptive environments, perhaps more so for the black children than for the interracial children. Also, as in other studies, there was attrition: About 25 percent of contacted families declined to participate. There also may have been appreciable selective placement of one sort or another in this study, given that the interracial children were placed so much earlier and into more highly rated families. The authors state that the adoptive parents were not given a choice of which infants to adopt beyond the freedom to decide whether to adopt an older or a handicapped child. The fitting process, however, came from some source; if not the parents, then the agencies themselves must have had some leeway in deciding at least which infants to place first. The result, as the authors state, was that "this study has an unusual sample of children."[12]

There are additional problems related to our estimates of what the children's IQs would have been without adoption. Those estimates were based on the educational levels, not the IQs, of the biological parents. Recall, however, that the biological parents were, on average, twenty-four years old. One of the typical occupations of the biological mothers was that of a student. As a result, it is possible that their educational levels would increase in subsequent years, thereby raising our estimate of their children's nonadopted IQs.

These caveats aside, it is reasonable to conclude something rather positive from this study. Overall, the adopted children's IQs, both black and interracial, cannot simply be the result of attrition of less able children or the selective placement of only the most desirable infants by adoption agencies. We should note, too, that school achievement measures were available for a small number of the black and interracial children. On these measures the children's performance was slightly above national norms, although appreciably below the achievement of the biological children in the adoptive families. Clearly, the pattern of achievement test results parallels the IQ results for these adopted children.

One final point adds to some of these conclusions, at least as they pertain to long-term changes. A recent ten-year follow-up of this study has been completed for the black and interracial adopted children.[13] At the time of the follow-up the adopted children were fourteen to twenty-four years old. Their IQs and educational achievements were described as having been maintained, although at more modest levels. At the time of this writing more information is not yet available and more complete information is needed before evaluating this follow-up but that summary in itself suggests that it is no easy matter to draw firm conclusions about the long-term effects of this sort of adoption on these children. It may be, for example, that as these children grew older, they experienced severe difficulties in forming an appropriate cultural identity, given the predominant upper middle-class white culture in which they lived. If so, developing and maintaining these children's potential may not simply be a matter of providing a high-status environment, but may involve as well the provision of an appropriate cultural milieu.[14]

The French Adoption Study

The third adoption study of contrasted environments is the French Adoption Study by Michel Schiff and his colleagues.[15] As estimated by the authors, the biological parents in this study fell into the lowest 16 percent in terms of socio-economic status. Their children were adopted into families described as highly advantaged, in the upper 5 percent in terms of social status. The biological mothers were described principally as workers and domestic personnel; the biological fathers were described, for the most part, as unskilled workers. The adoptive fathers, on the other hand, were senior executives, their wives classified as junior executives or as having no occupation outside the home.

We have, unfortunately, no further information regarding the biological and adoptive parents other than these estimates, which are based solely on occupations. Given only these descriptions, then, the French Adoption Study is less informative than either Skodak and Skeels or the transracial study, or for that matter all other adoption studies, and it would be virtually impossible to estimate what the IQs of the children would have been without adoption. This study, however, contained one rather unique bit of information. For twenty of the thirty-two adopted children nonadopted siblings were located and tested. These siblings provide a heretofore untapped way of estimating what the IQs of the adopted children would have been without adoption. The average IQs of these nonadopted sibs was 95, as compared with 107 for the adopted children, on a group intelligence test.

There also were two control groups. One was composed of the upper middle-class schoolmates of the adopted children. Their average IQ was 115. The second control group was composed of the schoolmates of the nonadopted siblings, matched to the nonadopted sibs in terms of social class. Their average IQ was 100.[16] In each case these averages come from a group intelligence test, the only test common to all four groups.

The average IQ of the adopted children in this study was then 12 points higher than their estimated IQs without adoption. It should be noted that with only twenty nonadopted sibs for comparison, this study has by far the smallest sample size of any study. This fact alone might suggest caution in interpretation. Then, too, the adopted sibs average IQ is also 8 points below that of their upper middle-class schoolmates. Despite these caveats, the interpretation afforded this study often has been quite favorable, as witnessed in the following summary:

The investigators managed to locate . . . 20 *biological* siblings of the adopted children; these biological siblings had been reared by their own mothers. Thus, the two groups of siblings are genetically equivalent. . . . The adopted children had an average IQ of 111— a full 16 points higher than that of their stay-at-home siblings. . . . The title of the Jensen article which spurred the renewed interest in IQ heritability was "How much can we boost IQ and scholastic achievement?" The Schiff study gives an unequivocal answer.[17]

This quote is preceded by the following subheading: "A Big Boost for IQ." As if that weren't sufficient, Schiff paraphrased the title of Jensen's infamous article ("How much can we boost IQ and scholastic achievement?") in one report of this study and followed it with the phrasing, "A direct answer from a French adoption study." A later book devoted to the study was titled: *Education and Class: The Irrelevance of IQ Genetic Studies*. The Foreword to the book happily declares that the authors "steadfastly and indeed belligerently declare their ideological bias to environmentalism." It goes on to assert that this study has restored "our confidence that passion can ascend through meticulous science to genuine theoretical advance."[18]

There is, clearly, something special about this study in the eyes of certain beholders, and sufficient time should be taken to explore its intricacies. We might begin with the average IQ of 111 and the 16-point advantage referred to in the quote, which is different from the average of 107 and the 12-point difference described here. The varying descriptions come from focusing on different tests. As noted above, the 12-point difference and the average IQ of 107 for the adopted children come from a group-administered test, the only test common to all four groups in this study. The quote refers to the results of an individual IQ test given to the adopted children and their sibs but not to the control groups.

There are in fact several test results that one might use. Both the group test and the individual test provided total IQ scores and separate verbal and performance IQs. Performance tests include such tasks as constructing puzzles, arranging pictures to form a coherent story, and traversing picture mazes, that is, tasks that do not depend principally on verbal instructions or the interpretation of verbal material. The scores reported here and elsewhere in this book have always been total IQs. The adopted children were significantly above their nonadopted siblings in terms of total IQ and verbal IQ (107 vs. 95 in total IQ; 104 vs. 91 in verbal IQ) but, as noted previously, significantly below their upper middle-class schoolmates on each measure. Interestingly, there was no significant difference between the adopted and nonadopted sibs in terms of performance IQ (see Appendix 6).[19] Performance IQ might provide the most reasonable comparison between these two sib groups, in that on performance tests verbal differences are reduced.[20] That point may be particularly relevant here, in that one-fourth of the nonadopted siblings were described as living in rural districts that have a bilingual tradition (Alsatian and French), whereas the adopted children were raised in families that spoke French exclusively. Moreover, 30 percent of the nonadopted sibs had mothers who were Alsatian.[21]

Then there is the matter of the italicized word "biological" in the quote describing this study. Presumably, the emphasis is added to ensure that the unique properties of the sib comparison, this "genetic equivalence," are not missed. There is, however, a piece of information missing. The "stay-at-home" sibs, as they are called, were not full siblings—as might reasonably be inferred from the term "biological"—but half-siblings. They and the adopted children had a common mother but not a common father. Full siblings share, on average, a random 50 percent of their genes; half-sibs, only 25 percent.

Lastly, there is the matter of the description that the stay-at-home half-sibs "had been reared by their own mothers." This statement is, at the least, misleading and in some cases simply false. Many of the nonadopted half-sibs experienced several forms of parenting. Some were not raised primarily by their biological mothers; others were never raised by their mothers (see Appendix

7).[22] In point of fact, the nonadopted half-sibs experienced what might reasonably be called disruptive childhoods. In one report of this project they were described as having "little family stability." In comparison, the adopted half-sibs were characterized as benefitting from a "more stable emotional climate."[23] More than half of the nonadopted sibs were described as illegitimate children. Only four were raised by "2 parents," meaning the biological mother and a stepfather. Four were never raised by their mother. Curiously, five children were raised wholly or in part by nurses. We are told that in French, the term *nourrice*, or nurse, "refers to a woman who has the general care of a child" and "is a veritable institution in France, especially among the working class."[24] Perhaps so, but it does not translate into being "reared by their own mothers." In fact, the nonadopted half-sibs experienced a total of twenty-nine parenting combinations.[25]

The point here is that the half-sibs are to be used to estimate the IQs of the adopted-away children if adoption had not taken place. The 12- or 16-point difference between the two half-sib groups is attributed by admirers of this study to the "boost" of the adoptive environment. One might be led to wonder, however, whether the disruptiveness of the family lives of the nonadopted half-sibs resulted in the lowering of their IQs, thereby contributing to the IQ difference between the two sib groups. The potential disruptions attendant to births out of wedlock and successive parentings by different adults are just the sort of factors that an environmentalist would point to in interpreting the nonadopted half-sibs' average IQ of 95. That average fell 5 points below the average of their social class–matched schoolmates. In fact, the nonadopted half-sibs fell below their class-matched schoolmates on each IQ measure, a pattern unlikely to occur by chance.

We might add to this the fact that the mothers of the nonadopted half-sibs had placed for adoption at least one other sibling. Were the nonadopted half-sibs perhaps not sufficiently fit to be adopted? Three of those children had tested IQs below 80.[26] We cannot answer these questions without more information than is provided by this study, but it leaves us unable to interpret clearly the differences between the two sib groups. Perhaps the adopted children were simply the more advantaged offspring among children growing up in lower and working-class environments. As the authors of the study point out, within each social class there is considerable variability in IQ such that about 10 to 15 percent of lower class children score above the average of upper middle-class children. Given that the adoptive families were far above average, we might rephrase the second question related to adoption studies to read: Who is adopted by upper middle-class families? The answer, at least in many instances, is that the fittest infants are probably selectively adopted by these advantaged families.

A related concern is the fact that the French study began with 1,136 adoption files from six adoption agencies. That number was reduced to thirty-two to get cases in which both biological parents were unskilled, the adoptive families were high in status, and the children were adopted before six months of age. That combination alone may have produced a highly select group of children. Given this difficulty, possible genetic differences between the half-sibs, and concerns about the family lives of the nonadopted half-sibs, it becomes a formidable task indeed to discern the singular ''boosting'' effects of the adoptive environments.

The effects of the adoptive environment on other aspects of the adopted children's lives seems easier to detect, if not interpret. The authors also reported ''school failure'' rates for the two half-sib groups, defined as grade retention and special education placement. On these measures only 3 percent of adopted children experienced ''serious failure'' compared with 33 percent of the non-adopted half-sibs. Both of these rates correspond to the average rates for children in their respective social classes. Unfortunately, interpretation of these differences carries with it the same problems as those encountered in the intervention literature. Decisions regarding school failure are surely informed by factors that go beyond objective measures of aptitude and achievement, and may well be influenced by differing expectations for children living in different social classes.

The French Cross-Fostering Study

The most recent adoption study involving contrasted environments, the French Cross-Fostering Study, used a unique four-group design in which the biological families of the adopted children were either low or high in socioeconomic status and the adoptive families also were either of low or high status.[27] As was the case in the French Adoption Study, the separation between the two social classes was quite pronounced for both biological and adoptive families: Low-status families ranked at the very lowest levels in education (average years of schooling for all low-status families = 6.6) and on an occupational status measure, with occupational descriptions of ''worker'' or ''diverse unskilled.''[28] Upper class families, on the other hand, ranked high in education (average years of schooling = 16.1 for all high-status families) and in occupational status, with occupational descriptions such as ''physician'' and ''senior executive.''

The results with respect to IQ are given in Table 1. The top row provides the results for children whose biological families were rated low in social status and who were adopted into families either low or high in status. These data represent, in a sense, a replication of the French Adoption Study, if it is assumed that the average IQ of children born and reared in the same low socioeconomic class (average = 92) is a reasonable estimate of what these children's IQs would have been without adoption. If so, this comparison reveals a 12-point enhancement owing to the adoptive environment (92 to 104), setting aside for the moment possible interpretative difficulties. The bottom row provides the results for adopted children born into biological families rated high in status. If we assume that the average for children born in and adopted into that same high social class is an estimate of their nonadopted IQs (average = 120), then this comparison reveals a symmetrical 12-point decrement in IQ (120 to 108).[29] This latter comparison, it should be noted, is unprecedented, given the inclusion of children

Table 1
IQs in the French Cross-Fostering Study

| | | Status of Adoptive Parents | |
		Low	High
Status of Biological Parents	Low	92 (15) n=10	104 (13) n=10
	High	108 (12) n=8	120 (12) n=10

Source: C. Locurto (1990). The malleability of IQ as judged from adoption studies. *Intelligence, 14*, 275–292. Reprinted with the permission of the Ablex Publishing Corporation.

from high-status families who were reared in low-status families (only 1 in 600 adoption files fit this category).

Some caution is in order in interpreting these data insofar as the small sample sizes account for relatively little of the variability in adopted children's IQ scores.[30] However, some of the interpretative problems inherent in other studies of contrasted environments that may serve to mitigate clear-cut conclusions do not appear to be present to a significant degree in this study. For example, vital factors that might affect interpretation, such as birth weight, age of adoption, number of years in the adoptive families (average = 14 years), and the prevalence of perinatal or neonatal disorders, were equated across all four groups. Also, as all subjects who were identified from adoption agency files were subsequently tested, there was no direct effect of attrition.

Moreover, the data regarding the status of the biological and adoptive parents suggest that the 12-point estimate of malleability was not significantly compromised by selective placement. In this instance selective placement might mean that among children born to low-status families, the fitter of those children composed the group that was adopted by high-status families. But that was not the case, at least to the extent that fitness is assessed by measures of parental educational level and occupational status. Children from low-status biological families (top row in Table 1) did not differ in status regardless of whether they were placed in low- or high-status adoptive families. Similarly, children from high-status biological families did not differ in status regardless of whether they were placed in low- or high-status adoptive families.

Given the remarkable absence of selective placement, and considering the other well-designed aspects of this study, these data demonstrate more clearly than have other studies the malleability of IQ, in terms of both enhancement and decrement. Interestingly, by assessing these data in a different way they also demonstrate the limits of IQ's malleability. The limits are revealed by holding constant the status of the adoptive families and considering only the effects of the biological families' status (that is, reading down the columns of Table 1). For example, consider the data for low-status adoptive families. Children both born into and adopted by families rated low in status averaged 92. However, children reared in equally low status families who were born into high-status families averaged not 92, but 108. That 16-point difference suggests a certain stasis to IQ, a resistance to decrement despite long-term exposure to a low-status environment. A similar conclusion comes from considering the group of children born into and adopted by families rated high in status. Their average of 120 was 16 points higher than that of children reared in the same high-status environment but born to low-status families.

Viewed from this perspective, it might be argued that although malleability is quite evident in these data, they also reveal instances in which low and high status profoundly failed to affect IQ. Admittedly, interpretation of the 16-point difference that leads to this conclusion is open-ended. Environmentalists would certainly argue against the invocation of genetic influences, but the environmental alternatives also carry with them interpretative difficulties. For example, reliance on pre-adoptive environmental influences would seem to be hindered by the close matching of all four groups on many of the factors that might be expected to distinguish the two types of biological families. Naturally, it might further be argued that other status-related differences in the preadoptive environments produced effects that could not later be entirely overridden by the adoptive environments. Aside from the ad hoc nature of that argument, it also requires that these influences rather profoundly affect IQ. Whether in fact they do is the subject of Chapter 6, and the answer, at least from an environmentalist's perspective, may indeed be somewhat surprising.

ADOPTIONS AND THE MALLEABILITY OF IQ AS JUDGED FROM ADOPTION STUDIES

It is worth a pause here to look back on the promise of adoption studies and assess how that promise has been fulfilled. That promise began with the observation that although adopted children have above average IQs, by itself that fact is of little meaning unless we can fairly judge what the IQs of these children would have been without adoption. That judgment turned out to be very much a matter of guesswork in most studies and left few clear conclusions with respect to malleability. If the children's IQs without adoption are unknown, another vantage point on malleability might be gained by looking at the overall intellectual levels provided by their adoptive environments. The assumption might be that those levels constitute some sort of ceiling for the growth of the adoptive children's IQs. If IQ is highly malleable, the adopted children's IQs might be expected to reach that ceiling, that is, to match the IQs of adoptive parents, their own children, or those of equivalent control families. On average they do not.

It seems that the average adoption study provides little certain evidence about the malleability of IQ. There is, however, something far more certain to be concluded from the four studies of contrasted environments. Despite their many differences, and setting aside interpretative problems for the moment, there is a commonality about them regarding children from low-status backgrounds who are reared in high-status families: The estimated IQs of the children without adoption in each study was about 10 to 12 points below their measured IQs in their adoptive environments. The French Cross-Fostering Study replicated and enlarged that conclusion by providing evidence that for children born into families of high status and reared in families of low status, decrements in IQ occurred in the same magnitude. Although that gain or loss is subject to various interpretative difficulties—some unique to each study, others common across studies—overall these studies strongly demonstrate that IQ is malleable. The extent of that malleability is, however, far less than the optimistic predictions made during the early 1960s by Hunt and Bloom or other eager environmentalists who spoke of changes on the order of 50 or more points. The range of 10 to 12 points appears to be about the upper limit of IQ's malleability *in these circumstances.* If the interpretative caveats noted here are indeed important, malleability often may be appreciably less than 10 to 12 points, even given the rather pervasive environmental changes of the type inherent in most adoption studies, including those of the transracial study and Skodak and Skeels.[31]

The single most pervasive evidence of extreme malleability comes undoubtedly from the French Cross-Fostering Study. Recall, however, that for children who experienced a change in status between their biological and adoptive environments, their average IQs were 16 points different from the intellectual levels characteristic of their adoptive environments. The same pattern also is evident in the French and transracial adoption studies, and it is that pattern that leads to what is arguably a rather certain conclusion to be drawn from these studies. Simply put, *there appear to be limits in the extent to which even the most substantial environmental changes can affect IQ.* The clarity of this conclusion depends precisely on the failure to find evidence of higher malleability where it might most easily be seen—in studies of contrasted environments. This is not to imply that malleability is insignificant in these studies, only that it seems modest where it might in theory be impressive, given the potential for change provided by the adoptive environments.

Having said that much, there are two unresolved issues raised by the French adoption studies, and each of them deserves further elaboration. The first issue concerns the effects of status, commonly referred to as social class, on IQ. True to their convictions, environmentalists dismiss possible genetic differences between classes and contend that it is solely the environmental differences between social classes that determine IQ differences between classes. They assume, then, that in the studies of contrasted environments, it was the host of sociocultural advantages offered by upper class adoptive families that produced whatever gains in IQ adopted children experienced. We will ask what, for the moment, must seem like an odd question about that assumption: *Do the environmental differences between social classes so neatly produce social class differences in IQ?* The answer may seem obvious, given our expectations about environmental differences between social classes, but it will turn out to be a far more intriguing question than one might suspect.

To provide an answer, we have to look at the average IQs of children in several social classes. Adoption studies are well suited for answering this question, for although the average adoptive family is high in status, there is some range in the social classes found in most adoption studies. As might be expected, severely disadvantaged families are typically not included, but in many studies there is a range that runs roughly from working class to highly privileged. Given that adopted children bear no genetic relation to their adoptive parents, any differences in their average IQs in different social classes would presumably be environmental. There is a caveat here, for agencies match children to families, thereby causing some spread of IQs across social classes irrespective of the influence of the adoptive environment. Chapter 6 examines what is known from adoption studies about the environmental effects of social class on IQ, and attempts to tease these apart from those owing to selective placement.

Having examined the effect of social class on IQ we find ourselves with the second implication of the French adoption studies: Genetic differences matter little in producing individual or group differences in IQ. We have, in a sense, been avoiding genetics while searching for changes in IQ brought about by environmental change. Yet it is probably not surprising to note that some of the results thus far surveyed might well be congenial to a genetic interpretation, at least in part. Paradoxically, the data on social class, presumably the most powerful of environmental factors, make a discussion of genetics unavoidable. And so, finally, we will have backed our way, for better or worse, into the mare's nest of heritability.

NOTES

1. From Fancher, R. E. (1985). *Makers of the IQ controversy* (p. 32). New York: W. W. Norton.

2. Horn, J. M., Loehlin, J. C., & Willerman, L. (1979). Intellectual resemblance among adoptive and biological relatives: The Texas Adoption Project. *Behavior Genetics, 9,* 177–207.

3. Kamin, L. J. (1981). In H. J. Eysenck & L. J. Kamin, *The Intelligence controversy* (p. 121). New York: John Wiley & Sons.

4. These seven adoption studies are Burks, B. S. (1928). The relative influence of nature and nurture upon mental development: A comparative study of foster parent–foster child resemblance and true parent–true child resemblance. *Twenty-Seventh Yearbook of the National Society for the Study of Education, 27,* 219–316; Freeman, F. N., Holzinger,

K. H., & Mitchell, B. C. (1928). The influence of environment on the intelligence, school achievement, and conduct of foster children. *Twenty-Seventh Yearbook of the National Society for the Study of Education, 27*, 103–217; Horn et al.; Leahy, A. M. (1935). Nature-nurture and intelligence. *Genetic Psychology Monographs, 17*, 236–308; Scarr, S., & Weinberg, R. A. (1976). IQ test performance of black children adopted by white families. *American Psychologist, 31*, 726–739; Scarr, S., & Weinberg, R. A. (1978). The influence of "family background" on intellectual attainment. *American Sociological Review, 43*, 674–692; Schiff, M., Duyme, M., Dumaret, A., & Tomkiewicz, S. (1986). In Schiff, M., & Lewontin, R. *Education and class: The irrelevance of IQ genetic studies* (pp. 37–124). Oxford, England: Claredon Press. Oddly, Skodak and Skeels is omitted from this list because it provided no information about the IQ levels in adoptive families, information needed for the conclusions drawn from these studies. A more detailed analysis of the issues raised in this chapter can be found in Locurto, C. (1990). The malleability of IQ as judged from adoption studies. *Intelligence, 14*, 275–292.

5. This average is reliable across studies (including Skodak and Skeels, in which the average was 107) with one exception, that of Freeman et al., in which the average IQ was 95 (see Appendix 4). That average was for 134 adopted children placed into families in which the IQs of the biological children of the adoptive parents (average = 112) were known. The average IQ for all adopted children in that study was 97. That study might be considered unusual in that a subgroup of the adopted children were selected for study because they were suspected of retardation (see Table 11, p. 136).

6. In Freeman et al., the one study in which the average IQs were below 100, the average age of placement was greater than four years of age. Prenatal and postnatal factors before adoption might well retard the children's development, particularly if the environment provided by the biological mother was disruptive or disadvantaged.

7. Pearson, J. S., & Amacher, P. L. (1956). Intelligence test results and observations of personality among 3,594 unwed mothers in Minnesota. *Journal of Clinical Psychology, 12*, 16–21.

8. There is some evidence, admittedly scanty, that children put up for adoption by unmarried mothers are slightly higher in IQ than children not put up for adoption. Leahy (1932, cited in Munsinger, H. [1975]. The adopted child's IQ: A critical review. *Psychological Bulletin, 82*, 623–659), for example, noted that mothers who put up "illegitimate" children for adoption were higher in occupational status and educational level than were mothers who retained their children. Freeman et al. (Table 23, p. 154) noted something similar: The IQs of "illegitimate" children averaged 104, whereas "legitimate" children averaged 94.

9. This information is, however, available in Freeman et al. (Table 3, p. 119). The children in this study were not adopted until an average age of nearly five years. For a subgroup of them, their preadoptive IQs were measured. Children placed into "better" families (n = 33) had IQs at the time of adoption of 95. Children placed into "poorer" families (n = 41) had IQs that averaged 88 at the time of adoption.

10. Skodak, M., & Skeels, H. (1949). A final follow-up study of children in adoptive homes. *Journal of Genetic Psychology, 75*, 95.

11. Norms come from the 1976 revision of the Weschler Intelligence Scale for Children (WISC-R). See Kaufman, A. S., & Doppelt, J. E. (1976). Analysis of WISC-R standardization data in terms of stratification variables. *Child Development, 47*, 165–171. See also Scarr, S. (1984). A reply to some of Professor Jensen's commentary. In S. Scarr

(Ed.), *Race, social class and individual differences in IQ* (pp. 515–522, especially p. 517). London: Lawrence Erlbaum.

12. Scarr & Weinberg, p. 736. For another type of transracial adoption study see Moore, E.G.J. (1986). Family socialization and the IQ test performance of traditionally and transracially adopted black children. *Developmental Psychology, 22*, 317–326.

13. Scarr, S., Weinberg, R. A., & Gargiulo, J. (1987, June). *Transracial adoption: A ten-year follow-up*. Paper presented at the meeting of the Behavior Genetics Association, Minneapolis, MN (abstract).

14. This argument, unfortunately, carries with it a potential paradox: Cultural differences between blacks and whites are often cited as the principal reason blacks score lower on IQ tests. That is, reasonably, aspects of black culture are simply not conducive to performing well on the tasks demanded by white-normed IQ tests (see, for example, Elliott, R. [1987]. *Litigating intelligence: IQ tests, special education and social science in the courtroom*. Westport, CT: Auburn House, for arguments about the cultural bias of IQ). If the *presence* of that culture, however, is in fact involved in this way, it is not an easy matter to argue as well that its *absence*, for the black and interracial adolescents and adults, produced the lowering of their IQs.

15. There have been four reports of this project: Dumaret, A. (1985). IQ, scholastic performance and behavior of sibs raised in contrasting environments. *Journal of Child Psychology and Psychiatry, 26*, 553–580, which includes a larger sample of nonadopted sibs than do the other reports of this project; Schiff, M., Duyme, M., Dumaret, A., Stewart, J., Tomkiewicz, S., & Feingold, J. (1978). Intellectual status of working-class children adopted early in upper-middle class families. *Science, 200*, 1503–1504; Schiff, M., Duyme, M., Dumaret, A., & Tomkiewicz, S. (1982). How much could we boost scholastic achievement and IQ scores? A direct answer from a French adoption study. *Cognition, 12*, 165–196; and an expanded version of Schiff et al. (1978 and 1982) in Schiff & Lewontin. Unless otherwise indicated, descriptions and results come from the version in Schiff and Lewontin.

16. This average is taken from Dumaret, Table 2, p. 562. In other reports of this study a control group for the nonadopted sibs was composed of schoolmates of the nonadopted sibs who were class-matched to the *adopted* sibs. (in Schiff & Lewontin, Table 3–13, p. 72).

17. Kamin, in Eysenck & Kamin, p. 124.

18. Quotes come from Schiff and Lewontin, pp. v, vi.

19. From Dumaret, Table 2, p. 562. This study included a larger number of children in control groups than was the case in other reports of this project. Hence the averages reported here may differ from those given in other reports of this project.

20. See Brand, C. (1987). A touch of (social) class. *Nature, 325*, 767–768.

21. Dumaret, p. 568.

22. Schiff & Lewontin, Table 3.7, pp. 58–59.

23. Dumaret, p. 559.

24. Schiff & Lewontin, footnote *a*, p. 87.

25. This figure refers to all nonadopted half-sibs, not just those closest in age to the adopted sibs who constituted the comparison group of twenty in the first reports of this project (i.e., Schiff et al., 1978; Schiff et al., 1982).

26. Subjects labeled 6B, 10B1, and 12B in Appendix 7.

27. Capron, C., & Duyme, M. (1989). Assessment of effects of socio-economic status on IQ in full cross-fostering study. *Nature, 340*, 552–554.

28. One of the data points for educational levels contains an error. The average years of schooling for low-status biological parents whose offspring were adopted into low-status adoptive families was reported as 6.7 years with a standard deviation of .10, but a range of only 5 to 5.9 (ibid., Table 1).

29. Decrements in IQ have been studied under the rubric of "cumulative deficit." See Jensen, A. R. (1974). Cumulative deficit: A testable hypothesis? *Developmental Psychology, 6,* 996–1019, and Jensen, A. R. (1977). Cumulative deficit in IQ of blacks in the rural South. *Developmental Psychology, 13,* 184–191. See Kamin, L. J. (1978). A positive interpretation of apparent "cumulative deficit." *Developmental Psychology, 14,* 195–196, for an alternative interpretation of some of Jensen's findings.

30. For example, although the comparison between children born into low-status families and reared in either low- or high-status adoptive families was significant (t [18] = 1.773, $p < .05$, one-tailed test; from Capron & Duyme, Table 2), it accounted for only 9 percent of the variance in IQ scores.

31. This estimate is lower still than recent and more moderate estimates of 20 to 25 points. See, for example, Zigler, E., & Seitz, V. (1982). Social policy and intelligence. In R. J. Sternberg (Ed.), *Handbook of human intelligence* (pp. 586–641). New York: Cambridge University Press.

6

Social Class and IQ

Henry Higgins' mother confronts the Professor and his friend Colonel Pickering about their experiment with young Eliza.

Mrs. Higgins. You certainly are a pretty pair of babies, playing with your live doll.

Higgins. Playing! The hardest job I ever tackled: make no mistake about that, mother. But you have no idea how frightfully interesting it is to take a human being and change her into a quite different human being by creating a new speech for her. It's filling up the deepest gulf that separates class from class and soul from soul.

—G. B. Shaw, 1916

THE IMPORTANCE OF SOCIAL CLASS

No factor has attracted more attention from social scientists than has social class. It is used variously and often indiscriminately to describe and explain differences between individuals ranging from intelligence to child-rearing practices to the susceptibility to mental and physical illness. With respect to IQ, there is, on the face of it, good reason to be so respectful of social class differences, for it is one of social science's most reliable findings that differences in social class are associated with differences in IQ.

The data summarized in the left-hand panel of Figure 6 for fathers (shaded bars) and their sons (open bars) are typical of the results reported in many studies over the past sixty years.[1] Considering the data for the fathers first, it is clear that their IQs, sorted according to social class, span a rather large range. The fathers in the highest represented social class averaged 114; those in the lowest represented class averaged 81.[2] The vertical lines within each bar, representing one standard deviation, indicate that there also is considerable overlap in the distributions for each class. The standard deviations in each class averaged about 12 to 13 points, meaning that there is considerable variability within each social class, and as a consequence, relatively high and low IQs can be found within

Figure 6
Social Class and IQ for Fathers and Their Sons

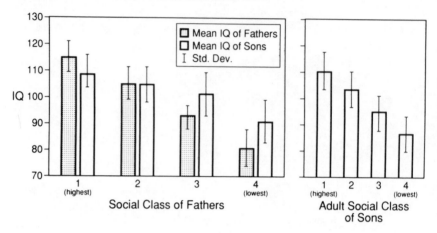

each class. As a case in point, for this sample about 11 percent of the children in the lowest social class (average IQ = 91) exceed the average IQ (110) of the children in the highest social class. This fact alone implies that the relation between IQ and social class is far from perfect, a point we will have good reason to reconsider.

The pattern of the sons' IQs in the left-hand panel generally follows that of their fathers, with one significant exception: In each class the average IQs of the sons deviates from their fathers' average. Sons in the higher social classes tend to average somewhat lower IQs than their fathers. The reverse is true in the lower social classes, where sons tend to average higher IQs than their fathers. The result is that the differences between the sons in different social classes are about one-half as large as the differences observed in their fathers' IQs. The explanation of this pattern is nothing more than the phenomenon of regression toward the mean. As noted earlier, all scores that are imperfectly correlated, as are the IQs of fathers and sons (the average r is about .35 to .45), will show some regression owing to factors affecting one set of scores and not the other. Scores at the extremes will show somewhat greater regression than those near the mean, a pattern evident in Figure 6.

From the facts of regression alone we might be led to wonder whether social class differences in IQ are shrinking over the course of generations, but that is not the case, at least for this sample. In the right-hand panel of Figure 6 the IQs of the sons are plotted as a function of their own adult social class, not the class of their fathers. It is remarkably clear that the sons have, as it were, recreated the social class–IQ pattern of their fathers.

The discrepancy between the distribution of the sons' IQs in the left- and right-hand panels is the result of social mobility. In each generation some of the sons in each social class have moved up or down into new social classes. Social mobility implies that the social class of the parents may only be a moderate predictor of the child's eventual social class, and this is true. Not surprisingly, the child's own IQ seems to be, by and large, an equally good predictor. There is evidence in fact that an individual's social mobility is predictable, to some extent, from his or her IQ.

For the data in Figure 6, for example, IQ differences between fathers and sons seemed to be related to the social mobility of the son. There was a correlation of .37 between the father-son difference in IQ and the corresponding father-son difference in social class. The direction of the difference in IQ also seemed to predict whether the son rose or fell in social class relative to his father. In the middle classes sons with higher IQs than their fathers tended to move upward, whereas sons with lower IQs tended to move downward. In the extreme classes matters are a bit different. In the highest class children either stay in the same class or move down; in the lowest class children either remain in that class or move up. The general point, however, is the same for the extreme classes as for those in the middle: Social mobility seems predictable, to some extent, from the child's own IQ—even if that IQ is measured as early as age six or seven.[3]

To the extent that social mobility depends on IQ, it also depends on there being sufficient variability in IQ within each social class. As noted earlier, the children in each social class, as do their fathers, span a rather wide range of IQs. There is, it would seem, much room for social mobility within each generation. It has been estimated in fact that as many as one-fourth to one-half of the children born into each class will eventually wind up in a social class different from that of their parents.[4] So, for example, the sons in the highest social class in the right-hand panel probably come originally from all four social classes. Many, to be sure, are the sons of fathers in the highest class, but others are not. And it is this social mobility that retains the social class–IQ pattern over succeeding generations.

Interpretative Complications

This point may seem to bring us a step closer to evaluating the contention made in the French adoption studies that social class differences produce IQ differences. Nothing we have examined thus far, however, supports or refutes that contention. We have seen that social class and IQ correlate, but we don't know *why* they correlate. Simply given that correlation, we might argue the reverse, that IQ differences themselves produce adult social class differences. But the data we've seen thus far don't support that contention either. The reason lies in the nature of correlational data. It is a simple fact of correlations that they do not themselves indicate causation. If two factors correlate, the first may cause the second (social class differences may cause IQ differences), the second may cause the first (differences in IQ may lead to differences in social class), or the correlation may be the result of a common third factor, a possibility to be discussed soon. These three outcomes are equally possible irrespective of the magnitude of the correlation. In the extreme case, were the correlation between social class and IQ perfect, we would still have no sufficient basis for inferring causation.

To further explore the relation between IQ and social class, the first step is to complicate matters by introducing a third factor that might influence the relation between them: education. The argument might be made that IQ and social class of origin are important principally in affording different levels of educational opportunities. Education in turn is the gateway to success in most societies.

In the case of IQ there is good reason in fact to believe that education might be the route through which IQ exerts its effects on eventual social standing.[5] IQ tests historically were intended to predict educational success, and it should come as no surprise that they do so rather well, particularly in elementary school, where the correlation between IQ and educational achievement is .40 to .60 or better. That correlation is lower at higher educational levels, partly as a result of the fact that individuals with lower IQs are eliminated from the student population. The result is that the remaining students have a smaller range in IQs, and it is more difficult to show a significant correlation between two variables if one is greatly restricted in range. As a hypothetical example of this difficulty, consider correlating the height of all men with their ability to play basketball. In general, there would probably be a moderate positive correlation because basketball success depends in part on height, and those who are taller are more likely to have played the game. But consider correlating basketball ability and height only for men who are between six feet and six feet two inches tall. If it could be measured, the correlation would be nearly zero because such a small range in height probably does not confer much advantage.

This caveat aside, it is generally true that individuals with higher IQs do better in school. The correlation between social class and IQ in adults, then, may be due to IQ's effects on educational success. This argument sounds intuitively reasonable, and there is evidence that IQs do in fact exert their influence in this manner.[6] But there also is clear evidence that an individual's social class of origin affects educational attainment. The data in one often-cited study demonstrated that point for a group of male high school seniors in Wisconsin in the late 1950s. These students were tracked during their subsequent careers in higher education, and the likelihood of their college graduation was studied as a function both of their own IQ and of the social class of their parents (see Appendix 8).[7]

Both factors clearly affected the percentage of students who were successful in college. As social class increased, so did the likelihood of graduation—from 7 percent for students in low-status families to 42 percent for students in high-status families. As IQ increased, a similar trend was evident: from 3 percent for students with low IQs to 47 percent for students with high IQs. Examining the effects of one factor while holding the other constant still revealed a discernible effect for each factor. For example, if social class were held constant by, say, examining only the lower class, IQ still had strong effects: The percentage of students graduating college with low IQs was only 0.3 percent, whereas students with high IQs had a 20 percent graduation rate. Similarly, if only students with high IQs were considered, the effects of social class were still apparent. Students from the highest class had better than a threefold chance (64 percent vs. 20 percent) of graduating, even given equivalent IQs.[8]

In interpreting these data it is vital to keep in mind that these students had already completed high school. In effect, they had been equated in terms of some prior educational achievement and were then studied to discover the effects of IQ and social class on further educational achievement. Reasonably, both factors might contribute to differential success before high school graduation. Students with higher IQs or those coming from higher social classes might receive better grades and be encouraged to take a more college-oriented curriculum. The authors of this study in fact noted that for male students, social class seemed to affect the likelihood of initiating plans to attend college, whereas in college, IQ seemed to predict success better than social class. For females the same general trends were noted, although social class seemed to exert more influence during college than did IQ.

Teasing apart the separate effects of IQ, social class of origin, and education on eventual success seems rather impossible from these data as well as from other attempts to do so. Generally, it has been found that much of the influence of IQ on adult status seems tied to educational success. Even when factors like grades and social class of origin are controlled, however, IQ can be shown to have identifiable effects on eventual success.[9] There are regularities in the average IQ level associated with different social classes, but IQ seems to be more than merely the by-product of differences in social class of origin. The body of evidence, although complex and open to various interpretations, suggests that, to some degree, *a child's IQ in itself is a predictor of eventual success, quite apart from that child's social class of origin or the impact of IQ on educational attainment.*[10]

THE ENVIRONMENTAL INFLUENCES OF SOCIAL CLASS

This argument has been derived from children and parents who share both common environments and a common heredity. The argument by environmentalists centers on the dominance of shared environment and on the supposed irrelevance of shared genes. Although it is standard practice in social science to explain differences between families in different social classes as environmental in origin, that assumption requires empirical justification. The children in intact families may come to have IQs similar to those of their parents for genetic or environmental reasons. Indeed, the different environments created by families in different social classes may themselves owe their origins, at least in part, to genetic differences between families. Nothing thus far discussed reveals that point, but it is certain that genetic and environmental effects cannot be disentangled from the types of evidence thus far presented. A start at an acceptable analysis can be made by looking again at adopted children.

Table 2
IQs and Environmental Status Scores in Leahy's (1935) Adoption Study

Fathers' Occupation	Adoptive Families		Control Families	
	Adopted Children's IQ	Environmental Status	Control Children's IQ	Environmental Status
Professional	113 (12)	195 (27)	119 (13)	180 (29)
Business Manager	112 (11)	171 (40)	118 (16)	161 (31)
Skilled Trades	111 (14)	133 (35)	107 (14)	106 (43)
Farmers	------	------	------	------
Semi-Skilled	109 (12)	94 (30)	101 (12)	78 (37)
Slightly Skilled/ Day Laborers	108 (14)	75 (29)	102 (11)	40 (27)

Source: *Genetic Psychology Monographs*, 17, p. 285, 1935. Reprinted with permission of the Helen Dwight Reid Educational Foundation. Published by Heldref Publications, 4000 Albemarle St., N.W., Washington, D.C. 20016. Copyright circa 1930.

As noted earlier, adoptive families in most studies span a range of social classes that runs roughly from working class to highly advantaged. If the environment is predominant in producing the pattern of IQ differences across social classes, we might expect adopted children to exhibit the same range as that found for the children in intact families. Information on this point was provided by two of the major adoption studies, those of Alice Leahy and Barbara Burks. Both studies included adoptive families and intact families that were matched to the adoptive families on educational and occupational levels and, in the Leahy study, parental IQ. Complete matching was not possible on every factor, and as we will see, imperfect matching between adoptive families and their controls makes interpretation problematic.[11]

Both studies reported similar data with respect to the social class patterning of IQs for adoptive and control children. The data for Leahy's study are presented in Table 2. In this study the adopted children were separated from their biological parents at birth and placed before the age of six months. All children were tested at about ten years of age. Leahy used adoptive fathers' occupational level as her measure of social class. For each level, running from slightly skilled/day laborers to professionals, the average IQ of the adopted children is given along with an environmental status score, a composite measure that included occupation, education, economic status, child educational facilities, and various aspects of the cultural status of the families.

For the children in control group families the range in IQs across father's occupations (102 to 119) was similar to that found in other studies of social class, with the exception that the lowest represented occupational levels are average in IQ, not below average. This relatively high base reflects the afore-mentioned fact that adoptive families often do not span the entire range of social classes, but exclude those below average. Families matched to them might similarly be expected to be average, but not below average.

The pattern of IQs across occupational levels for adopted children was quite different. The range was comparatively narrow (108 to 113), 5 points compared with 17 points in control group families. This difference in range is accentuated by comparing only those families rated the very highest and lowest in environmental status within the adoptive and control groups. Leahy arbitrarily defined these families as those that were, respectively, one standard deviation above and below their group averages in environmental status. For adoptive families the IQs of the children in the most advantaged environments averaged 113, only 3 points above the overall group average. Children in the least advantaged environments averaged 106, only 4 points below the group average. For control families children in the most advantaged environments averaged 127, 18 points above their group mean. Children in the least advantaged environments averaged 99, 11 points below the overall group average.

Simply stated, there was a far greater range in children's IQs evident in the control group families than in the adoptive families (28 points vs. 7 points). Before we delve further into the intricacies of Leahy's data we might pause a moment and ponder this singular fact, for one implication of it is indeed startling: *Adoptive children tested at above average IQs almost irrespective of the occupational levels of the families into which they had been placed.* Differences in social class, here indexed by occupational level, are the cornerstone to the interpretation of IQ differences offered by environmentalists. If social class differences are the major determinant of IQ differences, and if the effects of social class are principally environmental, then the range in adopted children's IQs might be expected to be equivalent to that of control children.

This argument requires that the two groups are equivalent environmentally. They are with respect to measures of occupation, education, and parental IQ, but not with respect to environmental status. On this measure the adoptive families were higher than control group families at each occupational level. This difference between adoptive and control group families illustrates the special nature of adoptive families, and the difficulty of matching control group families to them on every possible variable. The question is whether this difference between adoptive and control group families accounts for the restricted range in IQs across occupational levels of the adopted children as compared with control group children.

The answer, I believe, is no. The range in environmental status scores in adoptive families does in fact span nearly four standard deviations from the lowest to the highest occupations. A similar range is evident in control group families. It appears, then, that although differences in environmental status between families occupying different occupational levels were quite appreciable in both groups, these differences simply did not result in much variation in the adopted children's IQs.

Still, there is a 5-point difference across occupational levels in adoptive families. We might, however, question whether the 5-point difference between the children of day laborers and professionals was in any part due to the influence of the adoptive families. Recall that adoption agencies practice selective placement. In Leahy's study there is evidence of selective placement, and we might guess that the small range in IQs across occupational levels is due at least in part to it. It might be tempting, therefore, to argue simply that, at least as evidenced by these data, IQs are not at all malleable. Perhaps adopted children are already above average when they are adopted, and it is these above average IQs that we see years later when the children are tested. The small range in average IQs across different social classes is due to selective placement. Apart from that, social classes—and the environmental factors of education, occupation, and cultural status that covary with them—do not affect the adopted children's IQ.

AN INTERPRETIVE PUZZLE

This interpretation has the advantage of simplicity, but it is unquestionably incorrect as a generalization. It does, however, illustrate the existence of a puzzle, this one composed of two seemingly incompatible facts. The first fact is that in most adoption studies that have examined a range of social classes, there is indeed a weak relation between the adoptive family's social standing and the IQs of their adopted children. The second fact, however, is that the two French adoption studies, particularly the cross-fostering study, revealed significant changes in IQ that appear to be a direct function of social class. Judging from the French studies alone it would be entirely reasonable to conclude that the environmental effects of social class directly produce differences in IQ between social classes.

The Adoption Constancy Effect

The first fact to be examined, the weak correlation in most studies between measures of social standing and the adopted child's IQ, is nothing more than the unanswered question remaining from Skodak and Skeels. From that study the curious fact emerged that the average IQs of the adopted children seemed elevated, although they did not correlate with the educational levels of the adoptive parents. Those correlations were .04 and .06 for adoptive mothers and fathers, respectively. Stated another way, Skodak and Skeels found no differences in IQ between children reared in families representing the highest and lowest educational levels in their study (less than ten years vs. seventeen to twenty years of education). In fact, in both extreme types of families the adopted children's IQs averaged 109.[12]

An explanation of that curiosity can now be suggested. Correlation states the degree of relation, the rank-ordering between two sets of numbers. It is a statistical property of correlations that adding a constant to one set of numbers (or performing any other manipulation that does not alter the rank-ordering of the pairs of numbers) does nothing to alter the correlation. In other words, if each child gained about the same IQ advantage from his or her adoptive family, that constant added to their IQs would not necessarily show up in any correlation. This statistical truism we might call the "adoption constancy effect." It does not demonstrate that a constant *was* added to each child's IQ; it merely makes that effect possible. It suggests that the adoptive families in Skodak and Skeels, for example, irrespective of their particular social class, each had about the same enhancing effect on their adopted children's IQs.

That is, clearly, a rather striking idea, and before it is accepted we might wonder whether the correlations found in Skodak and Skeels are representative of adoption studies in general. Perhaps for one reason or another they are uncharacteristically low, and other adoption studies have shown more powerful effects of at least some aspects of the environment on adopted children's IQ scores. The Skodak and Skeels correlations, however, although lower than average, are not unusual (see Appendix 9).[13] Simply stated, a variety of evidence points to the fact that the social status of adoptive parents, as rated by their educational level, occupation, or income, seems to correlate rather modestly with their adopted children's IQs.

It would seem, then, that in many adoption studies much of the variation in adopted children's IQs is unaccounted for by these environmental measures. Many hereditarians use these low correlations to suggest that individual differences in IQ are largely determined by genes. Environmentalists have been quick to suggest that these correlations are artificially low owing to the restricted range in IQs found in adoptive families. There is in fact evidence of restricted range in most adoption studies as judged by the standard deviations of parental and children's IQs. But restricted range is not true in each study. Moreover, these correlations might be expected to be artificially inflated by selective placement, also a factor present in most adoption studies.

We also might consider the possibility that something has been missed. It has been argued, rather reasonably, that measures like education and occupation are rather blunt indices of the intellectual levels found within adoptive families. Perhaps, then, there are powerful undiscovered environmental factors that do strongly influence individual differences in adopted children's IQs. If there are such global factors, however, they are indeed odd, for consider their properties: They must significantly influence individual differences in adopted children's IQs but at the same time not be captured by, that is, bear no appreciable correlation with, parental IQ, educational level, income, or occupational level. After more than a half-century of adoption work it would indeed be rather extraordinary if factors of this nature remain undiscovered.

If we discount the possibility of having overlooked some singular yet heretofore untapped global factor that really does distinguish one family from another, and dismiss the possibility that these correlations are largely artifactual, we are left with the two points that spawned the adoption constancy idea: In at least some studies adopted children's IQs seem elevated; these IQs, however, do not substantially correlate with any obvious aspects of the adoptive family environment. The adoption constancy effect in turn suggested an intuitively implausible conclusion: *Families widely divergent in social class may nonetheless provide equally advantaged environments for the development of their children's IQs.*

This idea does not imply that working-class and professional-class families are in fact equivalent in every respect. They are probably different in all the obvious ways that these families are typically distinguished from one another, meaning that different social classes do afford children different *kinds* of opportunities. Yet whatever the effective environments are with respect to raising the IQs of children, over a broad spectrum of social classes all families may be equally capable of providing them. In other words, *the range of opportunites within most social classes may be sufficient to allow for the enhancement of IQ. "Good families," whatever their nature, at least with respect to the enhancement of IQ, may be found in a wide range of social classes.*

One way to think about this implausibility is to assume that there are a number of factors in any environment that may act in concert to enhance a child's IQ. No one of them alone accounts for a significant proportion of the individual differences in IQ, but together they combine to constitute a sort of threshold.[14] Above it, all environments are *potentially* equal, at least across a broad range, in producing the same increment in children's IQs. Below it we might find environments that are ineffective in this respect, or perhaps worse environments within which we see deficits over time. Unfortunately we do not know what factors compose this threshold. At the least we can say that over a broad range of social classes, they are not, by and large, the global factors that we usually rely on to distinguish one family from another.

The Remaining Puzzle Posed by the French Adoption Studies

All well and good for many of the classic adoption studies, but the French Cross-Fostering Study and perhaps as well the French Adoption Study certainly do not seem to fit this mold. Although they did not systematically examine a wide range of social classes, the 12-point difference that they reported between children reared in high and low social classes is appreciably greater than that reported by other studies.

The explanation of the differences between the French studies and others likely rests in part on the fact that the French studies examined more extremely separated groups along the social class continuum as compared with other studies. In point of fact, the French studies were expressly designed to examine the extremes in social class. That difference in itself, that is, without an additional assumption, does not, however, entirely explain the differences between the French studies and others. The reason it does not is that the French studies revealed rather larger changes in IQ as a function of social class compared with other studies, given what appears to be relatively small differences in the "extremeness" of their groups as compared with the most widely separated social classes in other studies, including those of Leahy and Skodak and Skeels.

There are, naturally, differences owing to culture as well as to generations between the French studies and these other studies, rendering exact comparisons impossible. These caveats aside, however, the resolution of the apparent differences between the French studies and others also invites a rethinking of the general relation between the environmental influences of different social classes and changes in IQ. The usual assumption about such relations is that they are *linear*, meaning that environmental differences between social classes produce a constant change in IQ anywhere along the social class continuum. If so, it is difficult to understand why most adoption studies reveal virtually no effects of differences in social class across a rather wide range of classes, whereas the French studies show large effects when examining the extremes.

An alternative relation between changes in IQ and environmental differences between social class, one that offers an explanation of this apparent puzzle, is shown in Figure 7. In this relation there are relatively small environmental effects on IQ, given changes in social class, across a broad range of classes, roughly from working class to upper middle class. At the extremes matters are quite different: Highly disadvantaged as well as highly advantaged environments have comparatively strong effects on IQ's malleability.

That is to say, *differences in social class at the ends of the continuum matter far more than those same differences in the middle of the continuum*. It is this sort of idea that may best express the relation between the environmental effects of social class and changes in IQ. The midrange of the continuum represents the relation found in most adoption studies and is the area within which the adoption constancy effect is visible. Within this range a "typical" adopted child may gain about an equal intellectual enhancement from his or her adoptive family almost irrespective of the particular status of that family. The extremes of the continuum are indicative of the comparison examined in the French adoption studies. At these extremes environmental differences between social classes do indeed have comparatively strong effects on children's IQs.

As by now may have become apparent, the solution to one puzzle in matters related to IQ often conjures up another. In this instance the idea revealed in Figure 7, although suggesting a resolution to the problem posed by the French studies, does nothing to suggest *why* many adoptive families are in fact effective

Figure 7
Theoretical Relation between the Environmental Influences of Social Class and IQ

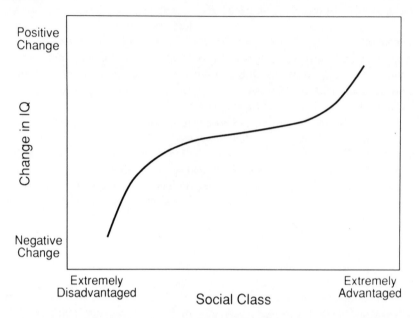

in enhancing their adopted children's IQs. If, over a broad range, the typically measured differences between families are not influential, then what *is* effective? In other words, what is the source of the adoption constancy effect?

The answer to that puzzle, a tentative answer to be sure, awaits some additional thinking and admittedly more than a bit of speculation—some having to do, oddly, with genetics. For the moment, though, it might be added that the theoretical relation shown in Figure 7 need not be confined to the environmental effects of social class. In place of social class substitute the number of books in the home, parental attention, nutrition, or any other environmental factor. The theoretical relation depicted in Figure 7 may also represent the influence of these factors on IQ, a possibility that would make the idea presented in the figure a general statement of environmental influence. That possibility is examined again in the final chapter.[15]

THE SPECTER OF GENETICS

These ideas are perhaps sufficiently unexpected in their own right, but the data upon which they rest pose additional interpretative problems that return us to Leahy's study. As noted earlier, in that study there was a greater range in the IQs of children in control group families across social classes as compared with adoptive families. This greater range, and the rather orderly changes in average

IQ across occupations of different status that are evident in control group families, is certainly not explained by the adoption constancy effect, or by the hypothesized nonlinear relation between the environmental effects of social class and IQ shown in Figure 7. There were other clear differences in Leahy's study between adoptive and control group families as well. Environmental status correlated much higher with children's IQs in control families ($r = .53$) than in adoptive families ($r = .19$). In addition, parent-child correlations that averaged about .15 to .20 in adoptive families were in the neighborhood of .50 for control group families. This latter correlation is within the range of average correlations typically found for parents and children in intact families.[16]

Were there unmeasured environmental differences between control group families that spread out the IQs of their children and produced the more substantial correlations with measures of family environment? Or was there something else, something that we've been gingerly sidestepping our way around? Intact families share genes as well as environments.

The possibility that these distinguishing characteristics of intact families as compared with adoptive families may have a genetic basis, at least in part, has long been studied and, as expected, has brought with it the usual rhetorical storms. With respect to social class differences in IQ perhaps the most controversial statement of genetic influences came in 1971 when Richard Herrnstein offered the following syllogism to summarize the evidence on this issue:

1. If differences in mental abilities (as measured by IQ) are inherited, and,

2. If success requires those abilities, and

3. If earnings and prestige depend on success,

4. Then social standing (which reflects earnings and prestige) will be based to some extent on inherited differences among people.[17]

We have yet to investigate the first premise, but we have explored the second and third. Together, they summarize the relation between IQ as a measure of mental ability and social standing as expressed through occupational status and income. If the first premise is accepted, the conclusion follows unsurprisingly: Social standing, as the result of the combined influences of IQ and other factors, will, to some extent, reflect inherited differences between individuals.

To say that the conclusion follows from the premises is simply a statement of logical necessity, not a comment on the social significance of the syllogism. Even if the first premise is indeed accepted, it might well be argued that the resulting influence of heredity on social standing is indirect and modest. Indirect because, as noted earlier, IQ has its influence on eventual social standing principally through education. Given the less than perfect correlation between educational attainment and IQ, it is clear that many factors in addition to IQ influence educational success. For example, a classic analysis by O. D. Duncan indicated that although IQ had the single largest influence on educational success, alone it accounted for only about 16 percent of the individual differences in educational attainment.[18] Three other measures of family background and social standing combined with IQ accounted for only 42 percent of the variation in educational success. That leaves important influences to other factors, and we might guess what they are. An individual's motivation, study habits, social skills, and overall maturity and self-discipline each plays a role in determining educational success, and none seems captured in large measure by IQ.

Similarly, Duncan found that educational attainment correlated only moderately with occupational level, indicating that factors other than one's education are influential in occupational success. Even combined with IQ and the three measures of family social standing, the resultant four factors barely accounted for half of the variation in occupational level. And to complete the picture, IQ, education, and the family factors together accounted for less than 20 percent of income differences.

Simply stated, by the time the *diminishing influence* of IQ is traced through education, occupation, and income, and the nonintellectual components of eventual success are factored in, there is a rather tangled web of interconnected influences that leads somehow to social standing. To say, then, that because individual differences in IQ have a genetic component, resultant social standing somehow reflects inherited differences, is to state a rather modest conclusion. It does little, if anything, to demonstrate genetically determined success.

Although Herrnstein emphasized the role played by IQ in each stage of the process leading to social standing, he also noted these caveats. Nonetheless, when published, Herrnstein's syllogism caused a volatile reaction, so much so that he was forced to cancel invited lectures at several universities and was the focus of student unrest at Harvard University, where he is a faculty member. In subsequent years he reportedly found it difficult to receive a hearing for his ideas.[19]

Why? For one thing Herrnstein assumed a rather generous inherited component to IQ. Given the prevailing spirit of environmentalism, it is little wonder that his argument met with something less than enthusiasm in some quarters. Then, too, in light of the historical arguments of hereditarians, even the hint of genetic influence was interpreted to mean that IQ is immutable. As we will see, assuming some genetic influence need not imply immutability. Yet, as it stood, that argument alone would probably not have resulted in so much controversy, for other psychologists had at that time concluded something similar to Herrnstein about genetic influences on IQ.

It was Herrnstein's emphasis on the link between social standing and heredity that caused the uproar—that and a corollary that Herrnstein offered concerning the future influence of heredity on social standing. He pointed out that if by some stroke of realized dreaming the environment for all were somehow made highly advantaged, then genetic differences between individuals would play an even greater role in determining individual differences in IQ and, therefore, social standing. This uncomfortable fact follows from the assumption that if there are two influences on IQ, heredity and environment, making one of them a constant (e.g., a highly advantaged environment for all) leaves the other as the only factor left to produce individual differences.

The implication of this corollary aroused the fear that the very realization of the American dream of a favorable environment for all would have the by-product of increasing the genetic influences on success. That fear was unwarranted on several grounds, not the least of which is the aforementioned modest link between IQ and eventual social standing. Then, too, we might reasonably suppose that an ''advantaged environment'' need not imply the *same* environment for all individuals, but divergent paths leading to equal opportunity.

These ideas, though interesting in their own right, are far removed from the basic contention regarding the heritability of IQ that underlies Herrnstein's syllogism. It may seem to be the highest form of irony yet encountered, but evaluating the influence of presumably the most powerful of environmental factors, social class, has most clearly necessitated a consideration of genetics. But so be it. It is time to confront that contention directly.

NOTES

1. From Waller, J. H. (1971). Achievement and social mobility: Relationships among IQ score, education, and occupation in two generations. *Social Biology, 18*, 252–259.

2. The term ''represented'' social class is used because this sample does not span all possible social classes. The data were gathered from white males in Minnesota as the result of a mailed questionnaire. Social class was determined from a combined educational and occupational index. There was in fact one higher social class reported in Waller's study than is shown in Figure 6. The sample size ($n = 1$) was too small for inclusion, but the data for this class were consonant with the other results: The IQ for the father was 140; his son's IQ was 127.

3. Jensen, A. R. (1981). *Straight talk about mental tests.* New York: The Free Press; McCall, R. B. (1977). Childhood IQ's as predictors of adult educational and occupational status. *Science, 197*, 482–483.

4. Jensen; Herrnstein, R. J. (1973). *I.Q. in the meritocracy.* Boston: Atlantic Monthly Press.

5. Sewell, W. H., & Shah, V. P. (1967). Socioeconomic status, intelligence, and the attainment of higher education. *Sociology of Education, 40*, 1–23.

6. Any attempt to sort out the interrelated effects of IQ, education, and social class is admittedly open to alternate interpretation. Compare, for example, Herrnstein with Bowles, S., & Gintis, H. (1973). I.Q. in the U.S. class structure. *Social Policy, 3*, 65–96.

7. Sewell & Shah.

8. There are several ways in which the data in Appendix 8 can be viewed. Undoubtedly they might be used to support an extreme position regarding the importance of either social class or intelligence as measured by IQ. One way to test the comparative importance of these two factors might be to look at extreme combinations of them. For example, we might ask whether it would be better to be of high intelligence and low social class or the reverse, low intelligence and high social class. That comparison points to a nearly

2:1 advantage for high intelligence (20 percent vs. 10.5 percent), at least with respect to completing college.

9. Again, this conclusion is much challenged by those who view IQ as epiphenomenal and social class as fundamental. Compare, for example, Jensen, pp. 194–196, with Lewontin, R. C., Rose, S., & Kamin, L. J. (1984). *Not in our genes*. New York: Pantheon Books.

10. There is surely no single line of evidence or reasoning that in itself demonstrates this conclusion. There are, however, two sorts of findings that support at least a weak form of it. The first is that for adopted children, adult social class is not well predicted by the social class of their adoptive family, or for that matter by the social class of their biological parents (e.g., Teasdale, T. W., & Owen, D. R. [1984]. Social class and mobility in male adoptees and non-adoptees. *Journal of Biosocial Science, 16*, 521–530; Teasdale, T. W., Sorensen, T.I.A., & Owen, D. R. [1984]. Social class in adopted and nonadopted siblings. *Behavior Genetics, 14*, 587–593; Teasdale, T. W., & Owen, D. R. [1986]. The influence of paternal social class on intelligence and educational level in male adoptees and nonadoptees. *British Journal of Educational Psychology, 56*, 3–12). The simplest conclusion is that something in addition to received social class—from either the biological or the adoptive parents—affects adult success. Reasonably, one of those factors might be intelligence as measured by IQ. There also is evidence that parental social class has only modest effects on a child's academic achievement in intact families. See Longstreth, L. E., Davis, B., Carter, L., Flint, D., Owen, J., Rickert, M., & Taylor, E. (1981). Separation of home intellectual environment and maternal IQ as determinants of child IQ. *Developmental Psychology, 17*, 532–541; White, K. R. (1982). The relation between socioeconomic status and academic achievement. *Psychological Bulletin, 91*, 461–481.

11. See Kamin, L. J. (1974). *The Science and Politics of IQ*. Potomac, MD: Lawrence Erlbaum Associates.

12. See Locurto, C. (1988). On the malleability of IQ. *The Psychologist, 11*, 431–435, especially Table 1.

13. These correlations are the averages taken from the adoption studies listed in Appendix 4 with the addition of Skodak and Skeels. See also Bouchard, T. J., Jr., & Segal, N. L. (1985). Environment and IQ. In B. B. Wolman (Ed.), *Handbook of intelligence: Theories, measurements, and applications* (pp. 391–463). New York: John Wiley & Sons.

14. The idea that there is a sort of environmental threshold composed of many distinct influences was elaborated—perhaps surprisingly—by Jensen, A. R. (1969). How much can we boost IQ and scholastic achievement? *Harvard Educational Review, 39*, 59ff.

15. See also Scarr, S., & Arnett, J. (1987). Malleability: Lessons from intervention and family studies. In J. J. Gallagher & C. T. Ramey (Eds.), *The malleability of children* (pp. 71–84). Baltimore: Paul H. Brooks, especially Figure 3, in which a similar function expresses the relation between "genetic potential" and IQ. Figure 7 is idealized in that it represents the changes in IQ that might be expected for a "typical" adopted child. Presumably, children with different genotypes for IQ might be represented by different functions, that is, different "reaction norms," to borrow a term familiar in behavior genetics research.

16. There is good evidence that there was restricted range within the adoptive families. In turn this restriction may have lowered the correlation between adoptive parents and their own children. See Kamin, Table 9, p. 124.

17. Herrnstein, R. J. (1971, September). IQ. *Atlantic Monthly*, pp. 43–64.

18. Duncan, O. D. (1968). Ability and achievement. *Social Biology, 15*, 1–11.

19. Herrnstein, R. J. (1982, August). IQ testing and the media. *Atlantic Monthly*, pp. 68–74.

7
Genetics and the Malleability of IQ

To the real work of man for man—the increase of achievement through improvement of the environment—the influence of heredity offers no barrier.
—E. L. Thorndike, 1914

In the actual race of life, which is not to get ahead, but to get ahead of somebody, the chief determining factor is heredity.
—E. L. Thorndike, 1916[1]

THE CASE OF KAJ AND ROBERT

There are few more provocative illustrations of the promise of adoption research in understanding the roots of individual differences in intelligence than the cases of two Danish adoptees, Kaj and Robert. Kaj was adopted soon after birth by distant acquaintances of his father and was raised as an only child in what were described as humble circumstances in a rural village in Denmark, where he received a minimum education. He was by nature temperamental and restless, a loner who never settled into a steady occupation, a "womanizer" who had been married three times and had fathered three children. At age nineteen he was convicted of grand larceny. At age thirty-eight he was charged with larceny and embezzlement by an employer who later dropped the charges. In one psychiatric diagnosis he was described as a vacillating psychopath.

Robert, too, had been adopted soon after birth, by a family that had been recruited through a newspaper advertisement. He was reared in advantaged circumstances in the home of a naval officer in Copenhagen. He grew up with adopted brothers and sisters, received an above average education, and completed an advanced training program as a draftsman. Robert described himself as constrained and shy in the presence of women.

Despite these apparent differences, Kaj and Robert were, in some ways, remarkably similar. Robert, despite the seeming stability in his professional life, also was restless, changing jobs frequently, although always within the same profession. He confessed to being indifferent to work and admitted to having a difficult time getting along with colleagues. Despite his shyness around women he had, like Kaj, been married three times, and had fathered five children. And, like Kaj, he had received psychiatric treatment; his illness was described as anxiety neurosis. He had as well been prosecuted, once for assault and battery and on another occasion for the theft of money from work. A case report on Robert described him as extremely sensitive, overly conscientous, emotionally isolated, and lacking adaptability.

Kaj and Robert shared more than their status as adopted children, far more in fact than their inability to develop settled lives. As may have been guessed by now they shared identical genes as well.[2] Although each brother knew for many years that he was an identical twin and had been adopted, they were not reunited until the age of forty, when Robert sought out Kaj. It might be thought that a reunion of long-separated identical twins would initiate the development of close contact between them or at the least evoke intense curiosity on the part of each twin. That was not the case, however, for Kaj and Robert. Their reunion was much of a disaster. Both soon admitted to feeling happier when apart. After each meeting with Kaj, Robert would repeat to himself, "Am I really like that?"[3] He "regretted ever having looked Kaj up," and described Kaj's unstable character as repellent. Kaj, for his part, described his identical twin as "the most unpleasant person I have ever met."[4]

Soon after their reunion they terminated their relationship. Five years later the Danish psychiatrist Juel-Nielsen asked Kaj and Robert to take part in a study of identical twins reared apart. The twins agreed, but only on condition that they did not have to meet. In a twenty-five-year follow-up study Juel-Nielsen reported that during one interview, Kaj casually mentioned, without visible emotion, that Robert had died. Upon subsequent investigation Juel-Nielsen found that Robert had died of angina pectoris and during the last years of his life had complained of lumbar pains, two conditions that Kaj suffered from as well.

Irrespective of their aversion to each other the twins could not help but admit to some uncanny resemblances. Robert observed that they both lacked "a practical fitness for life," and predicted at the time of their testing by Juel-Nielsen that although they both wanted to be independent, their restlessness and failure to commit—even to independence—made this goal all but impossible. "I believe," Robert observed, "that we will continue to vacillate all our lives, changing jobs, and, perhaps, wives too. It is symptomatic of us that we always leave a door ajar."[5]

Despite these similarities, Juel-Nielsen noted that Kaj appeared more extroverted and self-assertive than Robert, "psychopathic," whereas Robert was "neurotic." Their differences extended as well to their performance on psychological tests. Juel-Nielsen noted that the twins seemed to differ noticeably in unstructured situations such as those present on a well-known projective test, the Rorschach. These differences Juel-Nielsen termed "superficial." Beyond them the twins were, he concluded, fundamentally similar, a fact he illustrated by diagnosing both twins as "characterologically deviant personalities."

Their similarities extended as well to their IQs. Kaj's IQ was 111; Robert's was 117 on a first testing and 115 on a second testing. The difference of only

4 or 6 points in their test scores is both instructive and dramatic. For any test there is an error in measurement that refers to the expected differences in two scores obtained from the same individual. For most IQ tests that error is about 5 or 6 points. Kaj and Robert, then, raised in seemingly divergent social classes, never having met until the age of forty, and repelled by each other, differed about as much in IQ as would two scores obtained from the same individual taking the same intelligence test twice.

THE HERITABILITY OF IQ AS JUDGED FROM IDENTICAL TWINS REARED APART

The similarity between Kaj and Robert in IQ was not unusual in Juel-Nielsen's study. For the twelve pairs of separated twins studied, their correlation in IQ was .62.[6] Nor is the Juel-Nielsen result itself unusual. It is in fact the lowest correlation reported for the four major studies of identical twins reared apart. Those correlations range from .62 to .77, with a weighted average of .71 for a total of ninety-seven pairs of twins (see Appendix 10).[7] The overall agreement in these four studies is, on the surface, quite remarkable, particularly when we consider the interpretation of this correlation. Given that the twin pairs were reared in separated environments, the correlation in their IQs has been argued to be a direct estimate of genetic influence on individual differences in IQ. Stated another way, the correlation between identical twins reared apart estimates the *heritability* of IQ, a quantitative description of genetic influence on individual differences that ranges from 0.0 to 1.0, with higher numbers indicating greater genetic influence.

Heritability is perhaps most easily seen in the correlation of identical twins reared apart, but it also can be calculated from other kinship relationships and from adoption studies other than those that involve identical twins.[8] The simplest interpretation of the heritability estimates taken from the studies of identical twins reared apart suggests that somewhere between 62 and 77 percent of the individual differences in IQ are due to genetic differences between individuals, that is, to differences in genotype, the genetic constitution of an individual. *Note that this interpretation is confined to describing differences between individuals as measured within a particular population at a specified point in time. As such, changes in that population may well alter estimates of heritability. Defined in this way heritability is not a constant, nor is it immutable. It also does not reveal anything about the origin of differences between groups, say, the origin of race or social class differences within that population. Nor does it tell us to what extent a single individual's intelligence may be genetically influenced.*

As a further restriction, this interpretation depends importantly on the assumption that the separated twins have truly been separated, that is, raised in environments that are not similar (that is, uncorrelated in a statistical sense). Although the requirement seems to have been met by Kaj and Robert, given the selective placement practices of adoption agencies, it seems reasonable to suppose that identical twins are often placed in similar environments. Even when the adoption is done more informally, by families themselves, for example, we might expect the twins to be placed selectively, perhaps even within branches of the same family.

This possibility does not seem to be the case for Kaj and Robert, but critics of these data have pointed to environmental similarity as the "fatal flaw" and the "overwhelming flaw" in studies of identical twins reared apart.[9] The description might be overly dramatic to make a point, but there is no doubt that the problem is an important one, for the presence of selective placement might mean that the correlation between the twins is not due solely to their genetic identity, but to environmental similarity as well. The result might be to invalidate or at least question the use of the correlation between identical twins reared apart to estimate heritability.

There is in fact one study of identical twins reared apart that might seem to have settled the importance of the fatal flaw of correlated environments. The noted British psychologist Cyril Burt, a follower and acquaintance of Francis Galton, collected data on fifty-three pairs of identical twins reared apart and reported that although the correlation in their IQs was .771, there was virtually no correlation in their environments of rearing. Burt's data have not been included in the studies of reared-apart identical twins cited here, and it would naturally seem to be a rather curious omission. Even aside from the evidence of rather complete environmental separation in his sample, Burt's correlation is quite like those reported in other studies, and his sample size of fifty-three twin pairs was the largest single data set ever reported.

Unfortunately, Burt's data were a bit too clear, as a chronological examination of his work revealed. In 1943 Burt first published data on identical twins reared apart, and for fifteen pairs reported a correlation of .77. In 1955 he reported that the sample size had now grown to twenty-one pairs, yet the correlation remained at .771. In 1958, with data on more than thirty pairs, the correlation was again reported to be .771. In 1966, as though the point needed further demonstration, for the final sample of fifty-three pairs the correlation remained at that unalterable value.

What may be most remarkable about these data is not their impossible consistency, but that this uniformity went unnoticed until after Burt's death in 1971. It was a most tragic oversight, not simply because of the distortion that Burt's data represented in the scientific literature, but more important because of the impact that Burt's work had, at least indirectly, on public policy in Great Britain. For many years British schoolchildren were given a standard placement test called the "11 +" to denote the average age at which the examination was administered. To some extent, the examination determined children's subsequent educational paths—whether they would be allowed to pursue a college preparatory curriculum or would be assigned to trade schools. The usefulness of the test for this purpose rested to some admittedly limited degree on the acknowledged strong genetic influence on individual differences in intelligence, as was so cleanly demonstrated by Burt's work. It was not until 1965 that a Labour government refused to continue the examination, but by then it is not mere hyperbole to suggest that considerable damage may have been done to generations of British children who had been tracked, and perhaps many probably denied advanced educational opportunity at least in part because of the 11 + examination.

Soon after Burt's death Leon Kamin did notice the all-too-clear nature of Burt's work. Based on a meticulous analysis of the many flaws and impossibilities in Burt's results, Kamin wrote in 1974: "The conclusion cannot be avoided: The numbers left behind by Professor Burt are simply not worthy of our current scientific attention."[10] It took but a short time thereafter for the Burt story to unravel. In 1976 Olliver Gillie, the medical correspondent for the *Sunday Times* of London, charged not only that Burt had fabricated much of his data, but also that he had invented two collaborators, Margaret Howard and J. Conway, whose names appeared many times on articles written by Burt.

If there were any remaining doubts about the fraudulent character of Burt's work, they were dispelled in 1979 when Burt's biographer, Leslie Hearnshaw, published the definitive accounting of Burt's career.[11] It is virtually certain now that, at the least, Burt collected no data between 1955 and 1966 when the sample sizes in his reports grew by 60 percent. Hearnshaw, moreover, was unable to locate the elusive collaborators, Howard and Conway, or for that matter to find evidence of their existence. Perhaps most damaging, Burt's diaries, to which Hearnshaw had access, reveal one instance in which Burt described himself as "calculating data" over the course of a ten-day period to meet the request of a fellow scientist for the IQ scores and social class ratings of Burt's final sample of twins. As Hearnshaw notes, it was a request that could have been fulfilled in less than an hour had the data been available. Then, too, there is Hearnshaw's observation that Burt seldom, if ever, answered requests for information, a pattern that should by now sound familiar.

THE REANALYSES OF HERITABILITY ESTIMATES

The aftermath of the Burt scandal was predictable. Hereditarians continued to cite the remaining identical twin studies as evidence that removal of Burt's data did little to change the overall picture regarding the heritability of IQ. They argued as well that regardless of Burt's data, another English study of identical twins reared apart by Julian Shields (summarized in Appendix 10) had probably included many of the same twin pairs that Burt might have tested. There also were those who continued to cite other aspects of Burt's work, some of it on other kinship relationships, all of it nicely pointing to the high heritability of IQ. This latter reaction seems unfortunate and, at the least, improper. The same pattern of irregularities and all-too-clear data is evident in some of Burt's other work. Simply stated, whether or not hereditarians are correct in assuming that individual differences in IQ are largely determined by genetic differences, their case cannot be made on the basis of any data collected by Burt.

For environmentalists the Burt scandal did nothing less than spawn a cottage industry in the re-evaluation of the existing data on identical twins reared apart. Not surprisingly, the heritability of IQ seemed to fall lower with each succeeding publication. The whole of them pointed in a predictable direction as the following quotes, chronologically arranged, attest:

"There exists no data which should lead a prudent man to accept the hypothesis that I.Q. scores are in any degree heritable" Kamin (1974).

"There is no hard and convincing evidence that the heritability of IQ is anywhere near substantial" Taylor (1980).

"The hypothesis that IQ is determined primarily by heredity appears untenable" Farber (1981).

"It seems clear that the study of separated identical twins has failed to demonstrate a heritable basis for IQ test scores" Lewontin, Rose, & Kamin (1984).[12]

These quotes reveal the same sort of strident tone that has become familiar in the history of IQ. There are, to be sure, many tangential issues associated with this controversy, some political and explosive, but the single substantive question to be considered is direct, if not simple: To what extent do the re-evaluations of the identical twin data damage the hereditarian case?

The re-evaluations began with Kamin's observation that in the study by Shields, of a total of forty pairs tested, twenty-seven of them were raised in related branches of the biological parents' families. For those twenty-seven pairs the correlation in IQ was .83. For the remaining thirteen pairs raised in unrelated families the correlation was .51. In only ten of Shields' forty cases had a twin pair never attended the same school or been reared by related families. For those ten pairs the correlation was .47.[13]

Kamin's observations were suggestive, though incomplete. Among the more systematic and often-cited re-evaluations were those of Howard Taylor and Susan Farber. Taylor sorted the twin pairs according to four criteria, each bearing in some way on possible similarities in the twins' circumstances of rearing.[14] Two of the criteria, age of separation and the relatedness of adoptive families, proved nonsignificant. Two others, however, reunion in childhood and similarity in social environment, did result in lower heritability estimates. The correlation for twins reunited in childhood was .85; for children not reunited in childhood the correlation was .57. For twins reared in a similar social environment the correlation in IQ was .86; for twins reared in dissimilar environments the correlation was .52.[15]

We might note that neither of these lower correlations, nor Kamin's observations for that matter, in themselves suggest that the heritability of IQ is trivial, as the above-quoted statements might lead one to believe. Even the lowest correlations still attribute about one-half of the variability in IQ to genetic differences. The implication, however, is that if these sorts of reclassifications lower heritability estimates, a more complete reanalysis—one that removed all sources of environmental influence—might lower heritability to near-zero. Taylor in fact reported that there were eleven twin pairs for whom a more complete reanalysis might be possible. For these eleven pairs there were no reunions in childhood, they were reared in unrelated families, and they lived in minimally similar social environments.[16] Curiously, Taylor did not report the correlation for these eleven pristine pairs of separated twins. That correlation is .66.

Equally curious, among these eleven twin pairs one would not find Kaj and Robert, although there seems no obvious reason, based on Taylor's criteria, to have excluded them. They were not reunited until the age of forty, they were not raised in related branches of the same family, and they were reared in what would seem to be dissimilar social environments. Taylor, however, chose to classify them as having "possible similarity in social environment." Taylor's choice of classification is not perhaps unjustified, but it does illustrate the point that the reanalyses—as well as the initial testings of the twins—were not done blindly and one's preconceptions may well influence the outcome.

A similar reanalysis and outcome was reported by Susan Farber.[17] Farber constructed two global categories that she termed Separation I and II. Each category may be seen as a way of judging the similarity in rearing and degree of contact that twins experienced before testing. The heritability estimates resulting from her analysis indicated that for all twin pairs combined, the heritabilities averaged about .78 whether or not either type of separation was taken into account. Heritability estimates were significantly lower when males and females were separately considered, dropping to about .50.

In another analysis Farber included only what was termed a "pure sample," thirty-four pairs, all of whom were separated early, none of whom evidenced any illness or language difficulties that might compromise the reliability of testing. Results for this subsample provided yet more modest heritability estimates, averaging below .50, with one, for twelve pairs of males under Separation II, falling to .14.

Farber's reanalysis points, as did Taylor's, to the possibility that similarity in rearing and degree of contact between identical twins reared apart accounts for at least some of the impressive correlation in their IQs. Unfortunately the precise interpretation of these data depends, to a large extent, on one's preferred orientation, and hence on which set of numbers to focus upon. As an example, for Farber's combined sample the heritability estimates are still rather impressive. It is only when smaller subsamples are constructed—males under Separation type II, for example—that much lower heritability estimates are found. If one chooses to focus on those subsamples, one might conclude, as did Farber, that upward of 25 percent of the correlation between reared-apart identical twins is due to some manner of contact between them before testing.

There are two sorts of peculiarities in Farber's analysis that might give one pause before accepting that conclusion. One concerns the results of personality assessments made on many of the twins. As part of this assessment Farber reclassified all the twin pairs into one of three degrees of separation: highly separated, mixed separation, or little separated. Oddly, when the twin pairs were then rated in terms of similarity in global personality within each of these categories (on a 3-point scale with "1" meaning "most similar," the rating given to Kaj and Robert), there was a slight tendency for greater separation to be associated with greater similarity in personality.[18] Twins who had been highly separated before testing were rated as most similar. In fact, within the category of "highly separated" a subgroup of the most highly separated pairs (n = 9) received an average rating of 1.55, the highest similarity rating of any subgroup reported by Farber (see Appendix 11).

Paradoxically, in fact, as Farber noted, "as a group the more time monozygotic twins spent with no contact with each other, the more similar they seem to become [in personality]."[19] Several additional observations supported that idea. Among the most similar pairs fully one-third had no contact before testing. The comparable figure for the least similar pairs was 13 percent. Moreover, no twin pair rated as most dissimilar (a rating of "3") spent their childhoods apart. Indeed, *lack of contact specifically during the preschool years distinguished the most similar twins.*

Much of this argument must surely sound paradoxical. If similarity in environment and contact among twins produces similarity in IQ, as some of the reanalyses of the twin data suggest, why should personality seem to be unaffected, or affected somewhat differently? Shouldn't contact in childhood, being reared in similar families, produce similarity in personality, as it seems to in IQ?

An argument could be made that treats personality as fundamentally different from IQ. Perhaps contact between twins usually has the effect that it did on Kaj and Robert, repelling them, or for younger twins, causing them to develop their individuality and seek to be treated differently. We have, then, to suppose that this striving toward individuality, while producing differences in personality, leaves IQ unaffected. Indeed, we have to suppose that IQ is affected quite differently by the same environmental processes that produce individuality in personality.

There is no evidence available to indicate that this paradoxical pattern should be so. In fact, some of Farber's data point in the opposite direction. Grouping the twin pairs according to their personality ratings reveals that the more similar the twins were in personality, the higher were their correlations in IQ and the smaller were their average differences in IQ (see Appendix 12). In fact, the correlation between average difference in IQ and similarity in personality was .38, meaning that generally the more similar twins were in personality, the more similar they were in IQ.

With this pattern in mind it might be worthwhile to have a second look at Farber's IQ analyses with respect to the effects of separation. This second look brings us to the second curiosity about these data. As noted earlier, as one portion of her analysis Farber categorized all twin pairs into one of three types of separation. It might be noted in passing that Kaj and Robert were placed in the category of "mixed separation," defined as "no knowledge of twinship; much contact after reunion in adulthood." Regardless of the correctness of that classification, the simplest analysis of the effects of separation on heritability would be to present the correlations for each category of separation.

Those correlations indicated that degree of separation had no effect on heritability (see Appendix 13). If anything, there was a slight tendency for the more highly separated twins to be more similar in IQ, a pattern in line with the ratings of similarity in personality. An additional observation supports that possibility. Among the twin pairs classified as "little separated" there were five pairs who had not been separated until after four years of age. Their data were omitted in each of the calculations here discussed, but had they been included the correlation for "little separated" twins would have remained the same.

It also might be noted that the average pair-difference in IQ for the different categories of separation suggests that separation had little effect. The average difference between the "highly separated" and "little separated" categories was only 1 point. Considering only Farber's pure sample of thirty-four twin pairs, a strikingly paradoxical pattern emerged: The average pair-difference in IQ for "highly separated" twins was 7 points (n = 24); for "least separated" twins the difference, based, however, on only three pairs, was 14 points.

BEYOND IDENTICAL TWINS

There are now three conflicting analyses of the literature on identical twins reared apart. The original studies, if taken at face value, seem fully compatible with an appreciable estimate of heritability. The reanalyses by Kamin, Taylor, and Farber, among many others, suggested that environmental factors may have produced a portion of the similarity in IQ evident in the twin correlations. Finally, there is what we might call a "second look" at the reanalyses. Using the critics' own classification schemes for sorting the separated twins it is possible to demonstrate that substantial heritability estimates do not depend, to any large extent, on degree of contact among twins, their degree of overall separation, or the similarity in their environments of rearing. In fact, combining Farber's data on similarity in personality with the correlations in IQ for different categories of separation might lead to the rather extraordinary conclusion that more highly separated twins are slightly more similar in both IQ and personality.

And so, whom to believe? What would seem to be called for would be a study that is neither tainted by fraud nor susceptible to endless reinterpretation. Nothing of the sort exists, and it is certain that attempts to add to the literature on reared-apart identical twins will be met by the strongest possible criticisms. That very scenario is in fact now occurring. At the time of this writing the largest-scale study of identical twins reared apart is in progress. Conducted by Thomas Bouchard and colleagues at the University of Minnesota, it has as its goal the collection of data from one hundred pairs of identical twins reared apart. The IQ results this far reported (summarized in Appendix 10) indicate that the overall finding for the first twenty-nine twin pairs is fully consistent with previous work.

And like previous work, the Minnesota study is already receiving severe criticism. Michel Schiff, author of the French Adoption Study, suggested that the public attention already accorded the Minnesota study conforms to a type of "sensational journalism," given that one early report of the study appeared in the same issue of a widely read science magazine with an article on sperm banks.[20] The intent of this sort of criticism seems all too clear when it appears, as did Schiff's, beneath the title "Identical Twins Strike Out Again."

There seems, in short, no simple answer to the question of whom to believe. When given conflicting interpretations of the same data one approach might be to average all the data together to arrive at a sort of Solomon-like conclusion. In the current case that might mean averaging the upper heritability estimates of .70 to .78 or so with the lower estimates of .14 to .50 provided by the reanalyses. We might then say that the heritability of IQ, as judged from identical twins reared apart, seems to be roughly about .40 to .60 or so.

We might do something else as well. We might look for other sources on which to base estimates of heritability. The analysis of other kinship relationships might suffice, but true to our reliance on studies of adoptions we might look at adoptions other than those that involve identical twins. It is a far more extensive data base to be sure, and for that reason alone it might be a more useful place to look. Then, too, considering more standard adoptions allows us to return once again, however briefly, to Skodak and Skeels.

In adoption studies heritability estimates can be determined by comparing the correlation between biological parents and their adopted-away children with the correlation between adoptive parents and those same adopted children. In Skodak and Skeels, for example, the correlation between biological mothers' educational levels and their adopted-away children's IQs was .31 on the fourth and final testing of the adopted children. The comparable statistic for adoptive mothers and adopted children was .04. A caution is in order in interpreting these statistics because selective placement may inflate each of them.[21] If we assume selective placement to be equally influential in both correlations, the resulting heritability estimate derived from comparing them is .54.

Adoptions, in addition, provide sources of evidence of genetic influence that go beyond heritability estimates. As an example, based on the IQ data available for some of the biological mothers, Skodak and Skeels composed two groups of adopted children. Group "a" consisted of children whose biological mothers were judged to be "mentally defective," and whose IQs and educational levels were below average for the entire sample of biological mothers. The children in group "b" had mothers who were above average in IQ and education for the sample. Although the two groups of adopted children differed with respect to their biological mothers' IQs and educational levels, they seem to have been placed into adoptive families that differed little with respect to the adoptive parents' educational levels or the occupational ratings for the adoptive fathers. The IQs of the children in group "b" were substantially higher than those of the children in group "a" at each testing (see Appendix 14).

Although the comparison of these subgroups does not yield an estimate of heritability, it has been said of it that "although the samples are small, the data are compelling" for indicating a strong genetic influence on IQ.[22] That conclusion becomes perhaps less compelling if we consider some additional observations made of these two groups by Skodak and Skeels. The observations are themselves provocative and deserve to be presented in Skodak and Skeels' words:

If reliance were to be placed on these data alone, the inference would be fairly clear. However, comparison of the actual situation in the [adoptive] homes leads to a different conclusion. As a group the homes of Group (b) are superior to the homes of Group (a) on every count on which homes can be evaluated. . . . In the number of books, the extent of participation in church, civic, social, recreational, and cultural organizations, participation in Child Study and PTA groups, familiarity with and application of approved child rearing practices and attitudes, the number of toys, school equipment, typewriters, personal radios, the degree of freedom in spending allowances, deciding recreation, hours to be kept and other factors now believed to be essential for optimum social and emotional adjustment, the homes in Group (b) were definitely superior to the homes in Group (a).[23]

Skodak and Skeels are here illustrating a point that we will have good reason to reconsider soon. Based on obvious environmental indices like occupation and education, the circumstances of rearing for the two groups of children seem virtually identical. Yet the *effective environments* of these adoptive families may have differed appreciably, and these differences may have influenced the observed differences in the adopted children's IQs in the two groups. These descriptions do not themselves demonstrate that these hidden environmental differences were in fact influential in this manner, but they, at the least, reinforce the point that the standard ways of measuring environmental influence—that is, various indices of social standing—may indeed miss important facets of the family environment.

They also reaffirm the idea that taken as a whole, Skodak and Skeels leaves the relative influence of genetics and environment on individual differences in IQ open to question. As is invariably the case, we need a study whose results are less susceptible to alternative interpretations. Precisely that sort of study was apparently provided in 1975 by Harry Munsinger, who reported on the resemblance of white and Mexican-American adopted children to their biological and adoptive parents.[24] The results for both subgroups were virtually identical: The adopted children's IQs bore a near-zero correlation with the social standing of their adoptive parents, but correlated .70 with the social standing of their biological parents. Moreover, Munsinger reported that there had been no selective placement for these samples, thereby making the interpretation of these correlations uncommonly straightforward. They seemed, perhaps more than any previous study, to suggest that the heritability of IQ was dramatically high.

Not surprisingly, Munsinger's study was soon cited by hereditarians as perhaps the clearest evidence yet produced of gentic influence on IQ. Not surprisingly either, there soon developed an alternative interpretation of Munsinger's results. There are, in fact, several peculiarities in the data. For example, the correlation between social status and IQ even within the same individuals is on the order of only .40 to .60. That Munsinger would obtain a correlation of .70 across generations for children and the parents who did not raise them is truly remarkable. There are as well peculiarities in the social standing rankings of adoptive and biological parents. Those rankings for the eighty-two sets of parents in the study were done on a scale of 1 to 6. For forty-eight couples the ratings for mother and father were the same. In itself that uniformity is not unusual, given the natural tendency toward assortive mating among parents that often produces a correlation in IQ among parents that approaches .25. For the remaining thirty-four sets of parents in which the ratings for mother and father differed, the difference was always two ranks, never more, never less. To paraphrase Leon Kamin, who first noticed this unlikely consistency, parents in Munsinger's study seemed to have a marked disaffinity for mating with members of adjacent social classes.[25]

Munsinger had published the entire set of raw data in the original report of his study and undertook a reanalysis based on Kamin's criticisms that at least in part supported his original conclusions. The damage to the study's credibility was, however, already accomplished by the time of his reanalysis. Munsinger's study was openly compared with Burt's twin studies, with the obvious implication that Munsinger's work meet the same discredited fate.

Irrespective of the proper disposition of Munsinger's study, we need not hint at any impropriety to conclude that data so extreme and apparently so clear cannot be relied on in determining the heritability of IQ. Any single study, and therefore any single estimate of genetic influence on individual differences in IQ, might be regarded much like a single score in a distribution of scores: Although most scores fall near the middle of a distribution, some are indeed extreme. It is in the nature of distributions and perhaps the messy nature of the real world that this should be so. For the purpose of determining heritability, a single study might be thought of as an attempt to estimate heritability in the entire population by examining a quite small and often select sample. That sample—or for that matter any sample—may produce an extreme result. To obtain a fair estimate of heritability, then, the average taken from a range of heritability estimates is needed; any single, extreme outcome should evoke due caution.

In this context we might regard Munsinger's result, apart from its peculiarities, as setting an (admittedly artificial) upper limit on estimates of heritability. If so, we might ask whether there exist results that indicate a lower limit to heritability. As it happens, there are data that nicely provide just that sort of boundary. They do not, however, come from any of the reanalyses of reared-apart identical twins. In point of fact, they come from a most unlikely source.

THE PARADOX OF ADOPTED SIBLINGS

That source is two adoption studies we have considered previously: the Texas and the Transracial adoption studies.[26] In those two studies the correlations among biological siblings (the biological children of adoptive parents) were .35 and .37, respectively. For adopted siblings living in these same families, that is, families with two (or more) adopted children, the respective correlations were .26 and .49. The remarkable fact about the correlations for biological and adopted sibs in each study is that they did not much differ. More to our purpose, when compared *they yield heritability estimates of near-zero.*[27]

To be sure, there are complications attendant to using these sibling comparisons. Correlations of adoptive siblings may, as has been noted previously, be inflated by selective placement. Moreover, if we focus on the parent-child correlations in these same studies, the resulting heritability estimates average about .50. The difference between the near-zero estimates derived from the sibling comparisons and the higher estimates taken from the parent-child correlations underscores the point that heritability estimates derived from different sources may not agree. The near-zero estimate derived from the sibling comparisons, however, seems buttressed by several sorts of other findings regarding young children, and seems to raise a quite unanticipated point: *Genetic differences appear to have little effect on individual differences in IQ early in life.*

It is possible that comparisons among adopted siblings are themselves special and might invariably yield uncommonly low heritability estimates. To evaluate that possibility we would like to see correlations among adopted siblings at several different ages. Unfortunately most adoption studies, like the Texas and the Transracial studies, have included only young siblings. Skodak and Skeels did follow their sample of adopted children into adolescence but did not report comparisons among adopted adolescents within the same family.

There is, however, a study that did so: the Minnesota-Adolescent Adoption Study. The adopted children in that study ranged from sixteen to twenty-two years of age. At the time of testing they had lived with their adoptive families for an average of eighteen years. The correlation among biological siblings in the adopted families was .35, not much different from that seen in other adoption studies. And heritability estimates derived from parent-child comparisons averaged about .50, again fully consonant with previous studies. There was, however, one startling, distinguishing feature of this study, and it came from the correlation among adopted siblings living in the same families. That correlation, surprisingly, was − .03. *After eighteen years of living together adopted siblings were as similar in IQ as two unrelated individuals who have never met.* When that correlation is compared with the correlation for biological siblings, the resulting heritability estimate is nearly .70.[28]

It has been argued that there is precious little corroboration for this finding, as though it stands as an outlier data point that should be regarded with healthy skepticism. Undoubtedly it is a troublesome finding, particularly for environmentalists, who would naturally expect that adopted children living together should, because of their common family environment, show an appreciable correlation in IQ in adolescence. Troublesome or not, there are in fact now three other studies that have reported the same finding. One study of adopted adolescents aged thirteen revealed a correlation in IQ of − .16, whereas the comparable correlation for biological siblings was .38. A large-scale study of Danish adults (aged eighteen to twenty-six) who had been adopted together by, on average, the age of six months revealed a correlation of .02. A recent ten-year follow-up of the Texas adoption project also has reported a zero correlation between adopted sibs in adolescence.[29]

THE TWO SURPRISES OF NATURE AND NURTURE

If we combine the pattern of findings for adopted adolescents with that for young adopted siblings, it yields two unexpected ideas. The first idea, already discussed, is that we might assume that the influence of genetic differences on individual differences in IQ would be most visible early in life, before the cumulative effects of the environment begin to exert their influence. Yet just the opposite seems to be true: *Genetic influences on IQ are more apparent in adolescence than early in childhood.*[30]

As a second surprise, we might reasonably think that the effects of common environment, that is, living in the same family, might become more visible over time, affecting adolescents more than young children. Again, precisely the opposite seems to be true, at least as judged by the data for adopted siblings. Based on this pattern alone, we might suggest a rather odd idea: *the longer unrelated individuals live together, the more dissimilar they become.*[31]

Among all the unexpected findings we have come across in the journey from preschool programs through adoptions and identical twins, these last two ideas are perhaps the most unexpected of all. It seems that genes do not act in a manner we might have expected, and neither does the environment. It is not, to be sure, the first time the environment has behaved unexpectedly. It was suggested earlier, when discussing the small differences among adopted children placed into families of different social standing, that across a broad range, the environment as typically conceived—in the form of differences *between* families of different social standing—did not have the influence one might expect in terms of producing differences between individuals living in different families. The data for adopted adolescents expresses that idea in another way: Living within the same family does not produce the similarity among family members that we might expect.

These speculations about the role of the environment might seem unimportant, given that the majority of the data here surveyed point directly to a rather visible role for genetics in determining individual differences in IQ. Even with generous acknowledgments to the interpretative problems posed by the identical twin data and to those results that suggest low or near-zero heritability estimates, there is little doubt that an averaging of all the data leaves 40 to 50 percent of the individual differences in IQ as owing to genetic differences. One might go somewhat higher or lower, depending on which aspects of the data are emphasized, but to suggest that the heritability of IQ is much below .40 is to dismiss or to selectively evaluate much of the data.

Given that the idea of heritability seems to connote something fixed and unalterable, there might seem relatively little influence left for the environment. In point of fact, nothing could be further from the truth. One way to understand what particular heritability estimates mean with respect to the malleability of IQ would be to think of what is left over. In the case of a heritability estimate of .50, one-half of the individual differences in IQ are due to influences that are presumably not directly genetic, leaving, it would seem, a rather substantial role for the environment.

We might add to this the clear indication from the adoption literature that there is *at least* moderate malleability to IQ. From the four adoption studies of contrasted environments it seems evident that children's IQs may change by as much as 10 to 12 points. Aside from the French Cross-Fostering Study, that sort of malleability often is not evident without appreciable interpretative caveats. It does, however, happen to be the IQ difference reported by the Milwaukee project It also is close to the difference between Taylor's eleven pairs of most highly separated twins. Although their correlation in IQ was .66, their average difference in IQ—a piece of information not previously mentioned—was 13 points. That pattern demonstrates once again the independence of correlation from the magnitude of scores. It demonstrates as well the conceptual independence of the heritability of IQ from the malleability of IQ.[32]

The point might be made in another way by looking at what particular heritability estimates predict about malleability if it is assumed that the remaining influences are entirely environmental. Total variation in IQ is given by a statistic known as the variance, the square of the standard deviation. In the case of IQ, the variance is $(15)^2 = 225$. Assume that one-half of that variance, 112.5, is genetic in origin, that is, reflects a heritability of .50. If the remaining variation is composed entirely of environmental influences, the environment might be thought of as a variable influencing IQ that has a variance of 112.5 and a standard deviation equal to the square root of 112.5, or about 10. So, if heritability were .50 an improvement in the environment of one standard deviation would be needed to produce an IQ gain of 10 points. If heritability were higher, it would simply mean that a more extreme environmental change would be needed to produce a 10-point change. *The more fundamental point is that any heritability estimate can be rephrased in terms of the environmental change needed to produce a given change in IQ.*

Phrased in that manner it does not seem, on the face of it, impossible to produce an improvement in IQ almost irrespective of any heritability estimate. Our problem is that we have no understanding of how to change the environment effectively, much less how to measure it in units precise enough to reveal what constitutes a standard deviation. More important, looking directly for environmental factors that might produce changes of that magnitude have not suggested any factor or set of factors inside or outside the family that seem impressively influential. Apart from the extreme results of the Milwaukee project, the results of preschool programs do not suggest that educational interventions are effective. From the adoption literature it appears that within a broad range of social classes, adopted children's IQs are not markedly influenced by typically measured indices that distinguish one family from another. In fact, based on that literature, one might conclude that across a broad range of social classes, the direct effects of the environment (as judged by the correlation of adopted children's IQs with various indices of their adoptive environments) account for no more than about 10 percent of the individual differences in IQ in adulthood.

It may seem counterintuitive, but it is nonetheless true that *our best estimate of the influence of the environment on individual differences in IQ comes not from any direct attempt to measure environmental influence, but indirectly, from estimating the effects of genetic influence and then considering what must be left over.* It may seem far more counterintuitive to suppose that if, on average, direct genetic influences account for only about 40 to 50 percent of the individual differences in IQ, and typically measured environmental influences account for only about 10 percent of those differences, something quite important is still left over. That "something" seems not to be simply genetic or environmental, at least in the manner in which we typically conceive of the environment.

So, we need to ask, What is left? The question might seem like an open invitation to conjure up unusual sources of influence, the magical explanatory power of free will, or perhaps even the satisfying vagaries of mysticism. For better or worse, nothing of the sort is in the offing. What is to be considered, however, may prove to be just as powerful and satisfying, if not as mystical, and will return us to the environment but in a quite unexpected way. We will see it only by entering uncharted territory: the nature and nurture of uniqueness.

NOTES

1. Thorndike, E. L. (1914). *Educational psychology, Vol. 3.* New York: Teachers College; Thorndike, E. L. (1916). *Educational psychology: Briefer course.* New York: Teachers College.

2. This case history was taken from Juel-Nielsen, N. (1965). Individual and environment: A psychiatric-psychological investigation of monozygotic twins reared apart. *Acta Psychiatrica et Neurologica Scandinavica Monograph, 183* (supplement). Reprinted in 1980 with a twenty-five-year follow-up by International Universities Press, New York.

3. Ibid., (1965), p. 136.

4. Ibid., p. 132.

5. Ibid., p. 134.

6. Juel-Nielsen reported two correlations: .62 for a first testing; .68 for a combined first and second testing. Correlations between identical twins are not computed as a standard Pearson product-moment correlation because there is no rule for sorting members

of each pair into x and y columns. Instead, twin correlations are reported here and elsewhere in this work as intraclass correlations, computed as a one-factor analysis of variance (with each twin pair constituting a level) and takes the form:

$$\frac{\text{MS between } - \text{ MS within}}{\text{MS between } + \text{ MS within}}$$

7. Sources for Appendix 10 are Bouchard, T. (1984). Twins reared together and apart: What they tell us about human diversity. In S. W. Fox (Ed.), *Individuality and determinism: Chemical and biological bases* (pp. 147–184). New York: Plenum; Farber, S. L. (1981). *Identical twins reared apart: A reanalysis*. New York: Basic Books; Newman, H. H., Freeman, F. N., & Holzinger, K. J. (1937). *Twins: A study of heredity and environment*. Chicago: University of Chicago Press; Shields, J. (1962). *Monozygotic twins: Brought up apart and brought up together*. London: Oxford University Press. See also Bouchard, T. J., Lykken, D. T., McGue, M., Segal, N. L., & Tellegen, A. (1990). Sources of human psychological differences: The Minnesota study of twins reared apart. *Science, 250*, 223–228 for confirmation of the basic findings discussed here regarding identical twins reared apart.

8. The correlation between identical twins, not its square, directly estimates heritability because the intent is to determine shared variance between twins, not "variance accounted for." Heritability determined in this manner is much like the determination of the reliability of a test. There is a general heritability formula that takes the form

$$\frac{r_{ab} - r_{cd}}{G_{ab} - G_{cd}}$$

where r_{ab} is the correlation obtained from any biological reared-together relatives, r_{cd} is any reared-together relatives with less biological relatedness than r_{ab}, and G_{ab}, and G_{cd} are the theoretical genetic correlations expected in a population for those relationships. For example, if for identical twins reared together $r = .85$ and for fraternal twins reared together $r = .60$, the resulting heritability estimate is .85, $- .60/1.00 - .50$. Heritability in this case would equal .50. This is equivalent to $2(r_{id.} - r_{frat.})$, a familiar formula for computing heritability from twin data.

9. Lewontin, R. C., Rose, S., & Kamin, L. J. (1984). *Not in our genes* (pp. 108–109). New York: Pantheon Press. These authors emphasize that heritability estimates are not immutable within a given population but may change given changed environmental circumstances within that population.

10. Kamin, L. J. (1974). *The science and politics of IQ* (p. 47). Potomac, MD: Lawrence Erlbaum Associates. Much of the description of Burt's work comes from Kamin. For an equally condemning view see Gould, S. J. (1981). *The mismeasure of man*. New York: W. W. Norton. For a more sympathetic appraisal see Hearnshaw, L. (1979). *Cyril Burt: Psychologist*. Ithaca, NY: Cornell University Press.

11. Hearnshaw. See also Joynson, R. (1989). *The Burt affair*. New York: Routlege, for a strenuous attempt to defend Burt.

12. Kamin, p. 1; Taylor, H. F. (1980). *The IQ game* (p. 206). New Brunswick, NJ: Rutgers University Press; Farber, p. 208; Lewontin et al., pp. 109–110.

13. In Appendix 10, Shield's study is listed as containing thirty-seven, not forty, pairs. The discrepancy derives from three pairs eliminated by Shields because he judged their test scores to be unreliable.

14. Taylor.

15. These correlations were recomputed from Taylor's data as intraclass correlations

by Bouchard, T. (1983). Do environmental similarities explain the similarity in intelligence of identical twins reared apart? *Intelligence, 7*, 175–184. Taylor's computations were double-entry correlations in which each twin pair was listed twice.

16. Three pairs came from Newman et al., five from Shields, and three from Juel-Nielsen.

17. Farber.

18. Personality ratings are taken from ibid., Table 9.1, p. 248.

19. Ibid., p. 249.

20. Schiff, M., & Lewontin, R. (1986). *Education and class: The irrelevance of IQ genetic studies* (pp. 219–220). Oxford, England: Clarendon Press.

21. It was previously noted that selective placement may inflate adopted children–adoptive parent correlations. It may do the same to correlations between biological parents and their adopted-away children, if we assume that selective placement results in adopted children being reared in families that are similar to the children's biological families.

22. Scarr, S., & Carter-Saltzman, L. (1982). Genetics and intelligence. In R. J. Sternberg (Ed.), *Handbook of human intelligence* (p. 842). New York: Cambridge University Press.

23. Skodak, M., & Skeels, H. (1949). A final follow-up study of children in adoptive homes. *Journal of Genetic Psychology, 75*, 112.

24. Munsinger, H. (1975). Children's resemblance to their biological and adopting parents in two ethnic groups. *Behavior Genetics, 5*, 239–254.

25. Kamin, L. J. (1977). Comment on Munsinger's adoption study. *Behavior Genetics, 7*, 403–406; Munsinger, H. (1977). Reply to Kamin. *Behavior Genetics, 7*, 407–409.

26. Data are taken from Horn, J. M., Loehlin, J. C., & Willerman, L. (1979). Intellectual resemblance among adoptive and biological relatives: The Texas Adoption Project. *Behavior Genetics, 9*, 193, Table 10, and Scarr, S., & Weinberg, R. A. (1977). Intellectual similarities within families of both adopted and biological children. *Intelligence, 1*, 187, Table 6.

27. It should be noted as well that these adopted sib correlations are another way to estimate the effects of differences between families. Other correlational data—the relation between adoptive children's IQs and various aspects of their adoptive environments—suggest a far different picture. The discrepancy suggests that some ways of measuring common family influence may be more potent than others.

28. Scarr, S., & Weinberg, R. A. (1978). The influence of "family background" on intellectual attainment. *American Sociological Review, 43*, 685, Table 6.

29. Kent, cited in Plomin, R. (1986). *Development, genetics, and psychology*. Hillsdale, NJ: Lawrence Erlbaum Associates; Teasdale, T. W., & Owen, D. R. (1984). Heredity and familial environment in intelligence and educational level—a sibling study. *Nature, 309*, 620–622; Loehlin, J. C., Willerman, L., & Horn, J. M. (1988). Human behavior genetics. In M. R. Rosensweig & L. W. Porter (Eds.), *Annual reviews of psychology* (pp. 101–133). Palo Alto, CA: Annual Reviews.

30. See also Honzik, M. (1957). Developmental studies of parent-child resemblance in intelligence. *Child Development, 28*, 215–228, for corroborating evidence about trends in parent-child correlations that comes from a familiar source. Honzik published a comparison between the correlations of biological parents and their adopted-away children reported by Skodak and Skeels, and the parent-child correlations in intact families that she had obtained from her own California Guidance Study. Generally, similarity between

parents and their biological children grew with age, even for biological parents separated from their children. On the other hand, the correlations between adoptive parents and their adopted children declined with age. A similar decline in the correlations between adoptive parents and their children has been reported in the ten-year follow-up of the Texas Adoption Project: Loehlin, J. L. (1987). Twin studies, environment differences, age changes. *Behavioral and Brain Sciences, 10,* 30–31. See also Wilson, R. S. (1983). The Louisville Twin Study: Developmental synchronies in behavior. *Child Development, 54,* 298–316, for similar data taken from twins.

31. To complete the paradoxical nexus, this striking fact should be considered in conjunction with the equally odd idea discussed earlier concerning identical twins reared apart, where it was noted that, at least with respect to personality, less contact seemed to lead to greater similarity.

32. The 13-point difference also illustrates the fact that some methods of classifying or measuring twins can indeed yield evidence for the effects of separation.

Part III

Uniqueness and the Status of IQ

8

The Nature and Nurture of Uniqueness

Everyone's an environmentalist until the birth of their second child.
—Anonymous in origin; acknowledged by countless parents

Most environmentalists . . . have felt obliged to argue that genes do not affect IQ scores—or at least not much. It does not seem to have occurred to them to concede that genes might be important and then to argue that genes could exert their influence primarily by determining a child's environment. Given the environmentalists' extraordinary ingenuity in explaining away evidence that genes are important in the first place, their failure to argue that genes may exert their impact largely through the environment is puzzling.
—Christopher Jencks[1]

THE FAILURES OF RECEIVED WISDOM

Some ideas force themselves on us with all the drama and power of an erupting volcano. So it is with the idea of genetic influences on individual differences in IQ. From Galton through Goddard, to Jensen and Herrnstein, whenever that idea has surfaced the political and scientific repercussions have been immediate. From the evidence surveyed in the previous chapter it would seem that we are perhaps cautiously approaching a time when the idea that there is genetic influence on individual differences in IQ is more acceptable and less explosive than in the past. More acceptable because the weight of current evidence appears in its favor, particularly so since the meticulous criticisms by environmentalists have forced hereditarians to sharpen their arguments and the strategies used to gather relevant data. Less explosive because, as we have seen, heritability estimates themselves tell us little about the malleability of IQ and leave a large proportion of the individual differences in IQ unexplained. *Paradoxically, heritability estimates are our best evidence that there is much left to be understood that is not directly genetic.*

Other ideas slip up on us catlike and unexpected. So it is with what is left to be understood about individual differences in IQ. It is an idea that has been growing ever more visible in the journey from preschool programs to adoptions, and finally through the heart of our discussion of heritability estimates. Its power and influence should not be judged by the time it has taken to germinate, but following its slow development may make its final impact all the more lasting.

It began with the ineffectiveness of preschool programs to produce long-term changes in IQ or school achievement. That outcome was characterized as an attempt to take something obvious and distinctive about advantaged families— their emphasis on education, for lack of a more precise specification—and bring it to disadvantaged children. The ineffectiveness of preschool programs does not of course mean that education is unrelated to realizing a child's potential, but in other respects it should make us wonder. Perhaps we have not extracted the critical environmental feature or features of advantaged families as compared with disadvantaged families. More to our point, we now have good reason to question whether there are any singular and critical features to be extracted from advantaged families that will produce the common result of raising IQ or school achievement in all children.

That idea was suggested forcefully by the adoption literature. Children placed into families of varying social standing ranging roughly from working class to upper class showed, on average, few differential effects of their environments of rearing. The usual environmental factors that seem to distinguish one family from another—social class and its indices of education, occupation, and income—seemed, over a broad range, to be relatively unimportant in producing differences in IQ between adopted children raised in different families.

That same idea, albeit in different form, can be found in the "second look" at the reanalyses of the data for identical twins reared apart. It was suggested that living in the same neighborhood, even in related branches of the same family, that is, experiencing a similar environment, did not appreciably affect the similarity of separated identical twins with respect to IQ or personality. There was in fact some evidence, though incomplete and at best suggestive, that precisely the opposite might be true.

In an equally provocative but indirect way the idea we are pursuing was also evident in the correlations for adopted siblings reared together. Interpretative problems aside, that correlation provides the complement to the correlation of identical twins reared apart: The latter estimates heritability; the former provides an estimate of the effects of common environment. That correlation approaches zero as adopted siblings reach adolescence.

These different bits of information coalesce to suggest something rather extraordinary. Common environment refers to factors that members of the same family *share*. It includes all the various aspects of family life that traditionally have been thought to be important in producing individual differences in IQ: not only traditional social class indices, but also common child-rearing practices, the opportunities afforded siblings, the common influence of neighborhoods and schools. In short, these factors that now seem comparatively weak in their effects on IQ constitute nothing less than the shared culture of a family. Given traditional

Table 3
Correlations and Average Expected Differences in IQ for Various Family
Relationships

Relation	r	Difference in IQ
Identical Twins Together	.85	6
Identical Twins Apart	.76	8
Fraternal Twins	.50-.62	10-12
Biological Siblings	.34-.50	12-14
Parents - Children	.35-.45	12-14
Adopted Siblings (Young)	.25-.50	12-14
Adopted Siblings (Adolescents)	.00	17

social science approaches to the study of intelligence, it seems heretical to suggest precisely what these results reveal: *Exposure to a common environment does not in itself ensure commonality in IQ.*

By "commonality in IQ" we mean in turn two sorts of evidence: the correlation between individuals sharing the same environment and the average IQ difference between those individuals. We know from other evidence that these two ways of measuring commonality do not necessarily yield the same conclusion. That point is underscored by the data presented in Table 3, which shows the correlations and average expected IQ differences for various family relationships.[2] The most curious feature of these data concerns the average IQ difference between fraternal twins and between biological siblings reared together. Although the correlations for both relationships are, on average, significantly above the correlation for young adopted siblings, the average difference in IQ for fraternal twins and sibs is rather large, as is in fact the average expected IQ difference between parents and their children. Fraternal twins differ by, on average, 10 to 12 points; biological siblings by 12 to 14 points, not far different from the average difference between young adopted siblings.

These observations strongly suggest something hinted at by other data: The *most powerful influences producing individual differences in IQ lay within families.* It cannot escape attention that a pair of fraternal twins, born at the same time, sharing, on average, half their genes, and raised in a common environment, may differ in IQ about as much as a pair of reared-apart half-siblings in the French Adoption Study. A pair of biological siblings, born at different times but equally similar genetically to fraternal twins, may differ in IQ more than the half-sibs in that adoption study.

Figure 8
Influences on Individual Differences in IQ as a Function of Age

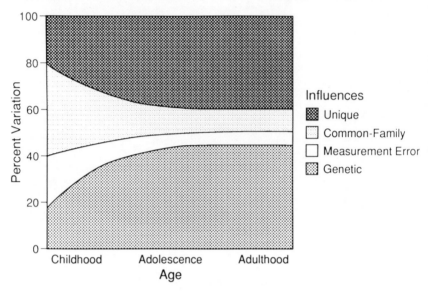

Environmentalists have made much of the malleability in IQ as judged from the data in the French Adoption Study. But the differences between biological siblings should alert us to the misleading label of ''genetic identity'' given to the half-sibs in that study. A pair of half-sibs would be expected to differ, on average, by about 15 points. If in the French study the fitter of each pair of half-sibs had been adopted, we might expect an average 15-point difference between adopted and nonadopted children irrespective of any influence of their adoptive environments. That fact alone demonstrates the lack of certainty that surrounds any estimate of malleability taken from that or any other adoption study. More to our point, in light of the interpretative problems of that and other adoption studies, the environmental influences associated with different social classes of rearing appear to be, on average, less influential than whatever forces are operative *within* families that spread the IQs of fraternal twins and biological siblings apart, or for that matter produce equally large differences between parents and their children.

SPECULATIONS ABOUT THE ORIGINS OF INDIVIDUAL DIFFERENCES IN IQ

To capture this idea as well as some of the others that have been coursing through the last few chapters, we might conceive of the various influences on individual differences in IQ in the form shown in Figure 8. The figure is not so much a summary of known facts as it is a way of representing possibilities. It does, however, provide a starting point for a highly speculative discussion of the origins of what I will call *uniqueness*. The figure reflects the idea that genetic influences appear to grow in importance from infancy through adulthood until they account for, conservatively, about 40 percent of the individual differences in IQ. Conversely, the environmental factors that distinguish one family from another, shared or common-family influences, appear to diminish in importance, accounting for perhaps 30 to 40 percent of the individual differences in IQ in childhood (as judged by the correlation of young adopted siblings) and falling to about 10 percent by adolescence.

Based only on the data from adopted sibs, we might have reduced the influence of shared environment to zero by adolescence. But recalling the quote by Skodak and Skeels in the previous chapter, there are undoubtedly shared influences that go undetected by our usual ways of measuring differences between families according to indices of social status. Then, too, most adoption studies sample a restricted range of families. There would undoubtedly be larger between-family differences if less selected families and truly disadvantaged families were included in our estimates. The effects of measurement error have also been included; these are largest in infancy and early childhood and fall to about 5 to 10 percent of the total variation in IQ by late childhood.

Lastly, there is a broad and as yet ill-defined category of factors that in one way or another produce what we might call unique influences on IQ, that is, influences not shared by different individuals living within the same family. Figure 8 reflects the idea that these influences grow in importance from early childhood through adulthood, eventually constituting at least as important an influence on individual differences in IQ as do direct genetic influences.

Before exploring the nature of these unique influences an admission of sorts is offered. It is, unfortunately, true that social science at times may seem to consist of the tortured restatement of the obvious. Before slipping into precisely that trap it should be made clear that all of this examination of correlations and average differences in IQ and the drawing of abstract figures is a complicated way of attempting to understand something that is rather straightforward and obvious: We are, all of us, unique. And so the fundamental question, if not its answer, should be equally straightforward: From where does our uniqueness arise?

As a corollary to that admission we might reasonably wonder whether the ideas expressed in Figure 8 are themselves unique to IQ. Perhaps the sorts of differences evident between family members in IQ are not indicative of their similarities in other respects—in personality, for example. After all, aren't family members really quite a bit alike? Isn't it in the nature of families to ensure just that? Like father like son, and so forth . . .

Perhaps not. Consider this quote taken from an article that summarized much of the recent evidence regarding similarity in personality among siblings: ''Upper middle class brothers who attend the same school and whose parents take them to the same plays, sporting events, music lessons, and therapists, and use similar child rearing practices on them are little more similar in personality measures than they are to working class or farm boys, whose lives are totally different."[3]

The quote has an air of unreality about it. Surely it can't be precisely true. Can growing up in the same family have as little effect on similarity in personality as it seems to on IQ?

An example may bring these unrealities to life. The example comes from the family of Jessica Mitford, an Englishwoman who, along with her five sisters and a brother, experienced just the sort of childhood that might be expected to produce considerable similarity among siblings.[4] The example, of necessity, focuses on personality and character differences among the Mitford family members, yet we might speculate that the factors producing those sorts of differences may also be influential in producing differences in IQ.[5]

The Mitford family lived for most of each year during the 1920s and 1930s in the Cotswolds, an isolated part of the English countryside, "old and quaint, ridden with ghosts and legends." The family home, Swinbrook House, resembled a medieval fortress, set apart from the town and sufficiently self-contained to include a schoolroom for the Mitford children and bedrooms that converted to hospital rooms as needed to avoid the necessity of family members leaving Swinbrook House. Outsiders, defined as Huns, Frogs, Americans, other people's children, and for that matter "most other inhabitants of the planet," were decidedly unwelcome.

Until the age of eight or nine Jessica and her five sisters were educated solely by their mother in the family drawing room (her brother, Tom, escaped by being sent to boarding school). At that age the sisters were turned over to a governess, who conducted classes in the Swinbrook House schoolroom. Aside from classes, life for Jessica and her sisters revolved around the church, the Conservative party, and the House of Lords, of which their father was a member. It was a life so predictable and dull, a solid "unchanging monotony," that Jessica envied Oliver Twist, "so lucky to live in a fascinating orphanage."

If nothing else, the Mitford sisters are a reminder that even uniform boredom has its surprises. Despite their common, cloistered lives, Jessica and her sisters evolved their individuality as much as, if not more than, other siblings. Although other children their age might have been occupied with dolls, group sports, and piano lessons, the Mitford sisters, particularly the three youngest, who were educated together—Debo, Jessica, and Unity—found other things to occupy themselves. Youngest sister Debo spent silent hours alone in the Swinbrook House chicken coop learning to imitate a hen's precise expressions when laying eggs. To fill in the times when the hens were unproductive, Debo kept precise logs of the stillbirths reported in the vital statistics section of the London *Times*. Jessica gave her father hours of "palsy practice," shaking his hand while he drank tea in preparation for his old age, when the shaking would become involuntary. And Jessica and Unity invented their own language with which to translate dirty songs so that they might safely be sung in the presence of their parents.

We might note as well that the presence of a governess did not mean that there was uniformity in the sisters' education. Governesses seemed to come and go with unusual rapidity at Swinbrook House. One, a Miss Whity, left after the sisters discovered that she was afraid of snakes. One morning soon thereafter Debo conveniently wrapped her pet snake, Enid, around the water closet chain. Miss Whity was found unconscious after the door to the water closet had been pried open with a crowbar.

Jessica's individuality as well as that of Unity and Debo was evident at preciously early ages. At age nine Jessica found herself on a rare trip outside Swinbrook House to attend a dance class. The teacher was late, and Jessica felt compelled to lead the other children up on the roof, there to share in intimate detail her newfound information regarding the origin of babies, concluding with the observation that ''and even the King and Queen do it!'' Her participation at dance class soon ended when one of the children broke down and revealed this discovery and its source to her governess. Lest the importance of this incident be minimized in light of modern standards of tolerance, it should be added that Jessica's revelations had a lasting impact on the neighborhood: At age seventeen, when she was a debutante, Jessica found out that two neighborhood boys were still forbidden to associate with her as a result of that rooftop indelicacy.

At age twelve Jessica chanced to read a book about astronomy. In the way that the past can with hindsight seem like a window to the future, that singular event foretells much about her eventual life path. An interest in astronomy was in and of itself uncommon enough for a young girl of Jessica's upbringing. Her decision to become an astronomer after reading it was far more uncommon. As a first step she wanted to attend the nearby grammar (public) school to gain the necessary education in science but was forbidden to by her mother. That book, and her mother's reaction to Jessica's request, set in motion a chain of events that would push her from her family and into the swirl of events that was leading Europe inexorably into World War II.

Determined to escape the suffocating sameness of Swinbrook House, Jessica went promptly to the family bank after her mother's decision and opened a Running Away Account for herself. The use to which this account was to be put occupied much of her thinking during the next few years. She never expressed much interest in the settled-in country life-style of her older sister Pam, but was for a time enamored with the life that older sister Nancy was leading as a flippant and sacrilegious novelist, one of England's ''bright, young people'' of the 1920s. The life-style of another older sister, Diana, who had married wealth, also for a time had its appeal.

Ultimately, however, Jessica turned away rather dramatically from her older sisters' comforting and comfortable ways of life. Like many of her generation, she became first an avid pacifist and then a socialist, a path that had much to do with the direction Unity had taken. Unity Mitford, just as rebellious as Jessica and searching for something to shock her parents, turned in her own unique direction to fascism, embracing the emerging Third Reich in Germany. Unity's interests nicely complemented Jessica's decision to become a communist. In mid–1930s Europe no two ideologies could possibly be further apart, yet Unity and Jessica managed an accommodation at Swinbrook House before Jessica left for Spain, there to involve herself in the Spanish Civil War. The sisters divided an unused sitting room down the middle: a German swastika and photograph of Mussolini on one side; a bust of Lenin and the Hammer and Sickle on the other. And while these ideological wars raged, Debo was said to be dreaming of her fairytale duke who would be coming to take her away.

The younger sisters' eventual life paths could not have been more dissimilar. Unity moved to Germany and for a time became part of Hitler's inner circle. Tragically, after a falling out with Nazism, Unity attempted suicide. She survived, only to live with debilitating injuries until her death years later in England. Jessica immigrated to America and became an active force in the American Communist party. Debo became a duchess.

SIBLING UNIQUENESS

The Mitford sisters are a sort of prototype of sibling uniqueness, one that allows rephrasing of the question regarding the origins of uniqueness: What factors within the Mitford family, despite the cloistered nature of the family environment, produced six sisters among whom were a novelist, three politically unconcerned members of the English gentry, a fascist, and a communist?

We should begin by recognizing that there was probably some influence of the Mitford's common family environment, at least on Jessica's and Unity's general interest in politics. Jessica's father was, after all, a member of the House of Lords and was described by Jessica as "one of nature's fascists." Both parents were apparently sympathetic to fascism, and older sister Diana, referred to above as an apolitical member of the English gentry, did in fact take as her second husband the head of the British Union of Fascists.

Another common influence must have been the dominant social forces of the different eras in which the younger and older sisters were raised. The three older sisters, none of whom evidenced a clear interest in politics, were part of the postwar 1920s with its euphoric disregard for seriousness. The younger sisters grew up in the more somber 1930s, when unavoidable political and ideological currents swept across Europe. That leaves Debo, "unclassifiable" according to Jessica, as the outlier among the younger sisters.

Yet, even granting these common influences, the sisters' differences seem more remarkable than do their similarities. Jessica and Unity might have developed a common interest in politics owing to their family environment and the charged political climate of the thirties, but their incompatible commitments to communism and fascism are not easily explained by common influences. It was perhaps their differing *reactions* to the common influences at Swinbrook House and the *Zeitgeist* of the 1930s that require explanation. *If so, to understand the origins of uniqueness we need to identify factors that foster differences, not similarities, among individuals living in an apparently similar environment.*

One need not to be a social scientist—it may indeed be an advantage not to be one—to guess at some of these factors. As a start there is the obvious idea that the differences between Jessica and Unity seem to fit the stereotype of sibling rivalry. We might speculate that in the average family, the presence of other siblings has the common effect of forcing each sib to seek his or her individuality. Perhaps so, but in itself sibling rivalry, despite its ubiquity in psychological explanations of sibling differences, is uninformative about the direction or nature of most such differences. Which particular rivalries might, for example, be predicted to blossom among six sisters? And how might those rivalries influence IQ and personality differences between siblings?

There is, however, a related idea that does concern multiple siblings in the same family and returns us more directly to IQ differences among sibs: It is birth order. Most earlier-born sibs evidence higher IQs than later-born sibs, a rank-ordering that has proved reliable enough to spawn a theory to explain it, one known generally as the confluence model.[6] The model assumes that a sibling's intelligence is a function of the average intellectual level of the family. Average intellectual level is defined simply as the sum of the intellectual levels of all family members divided by the number of family members. The model measures intellectual level usually in terms of mental age, with an average adult score of, say, 16 (Terman's original mental age for the average adult) and a newborn's score of 0.

To see how the model works, we might calculate the expected intellectual levels for two sibs. The firstborn sib comes into a family whose average intellectual level is $16 + 16 + 0/3 = 10.67$. If the second sib is born when the mental age of the firstborn sib is, say, 4, the average intellectual level for the second sib would be lower, $16 + 16 + 4 + 0/4 = 9.0$.

Note that the second sib's intelligence need not necessarily fall below that of the firstborn sib. What matters in the model is the spacing between siblings, not birth order per se. If the secondborn sib is born when the older sib's mental age is sixteen, then the secondborn might be expected to evidence higher intelligence, since the average intellectual level of the family would then be $16 + 16 + 16 + 0/4$, or 12.0. There is a caveat to this prediction because the model also assumes that older sibs benefit from the opportunity to teach younger sibs, a benefit denied only to the youngest sib. Despite that caveat, the general predictions of the confluence model are easy to follow. Later-born sibs usually would be predicted to have lower IQs than earlier-borns because each new sib adds a 0 to the numerator and a 1 to the denominator, thereby lowering the overall intellectual level of the family.

For our interest in understanding uniqueness, the confluence model deserves considerable attention, for it attempts to explain the influence of what appears to be a prototypical environmental nonshared factor among siblings—birth order, or more generally sibling spacing. Unfortunately, despite initial enthusiasm for the model, it appears that birth order or sibling spacing does not explain much of the variation in IQ within families, perhaps as little as 2 percent. There is, to be sure, a slight negative relation between IQ and birth order, but the differences between earlier- and later-born sibs are not great, perhaps 1 point or so across successive pairs of sibs. There are as well some specific problems with the model's predictions.[7] Moreover, the model would have no way to explain the average 10- to 12-point difference in IQ between fraternal twins, who, being born at the same time, would be expected to experience equal family intellectual levels. Nor would it provide any information as to why parents differ from their children about as much as do two sibs from each other.

Perhaps the confluence model has simply focused on the wrong nonshared factor within a family. Perhaps the ordinal position of a sib does not so much matter; what may be more influential is that parents, for one reason or another, treat their different children differently. Parenting styles might change over time, parents may have preconceived ideas about treating firtborn and later-born children differently, or parents might treat children differently based on characteristics of the children.[8]

Gender differences would be one obvious case in point for this latter possibility. In the Mitford family Jessica's brother, Tom, the only male among seven sibs, also was the only sibling to be sent away for formal education. Not surprisingly, there is abundant evidence that parents are likely to treat males and females differently. The impact of this differential treatment on IQ is probably quite small. It may be influential in producing differences in specific abilities—the advantage that females exhibit in some aspects of verbal ability; the advantage for males in some cases in mathematical reasoning. But many of the major intelligence tests are designed intentionally so as to eliminate, or at the least minimize, gender differences in IQ, meaning that test items that distinguish the sexes are eliminated during the process of standardizing the test. The result is that gender differences, much like birth order differences, account for, at best, a small percentage of the individual differences in IQ.[9]

There are any number of other nonshared environmental factors that we might consider, but many of them bring along a rather curious interpretative problem, a contradiction of sorts. Parental treatment, as an example, is undoubtedly a factor that varies between families. As we have seen, across a broad range, the obvious differences between families, including different parenting styles, are comparatively weak and do not contribute much to the variation in IQ between families. If factors of this sort are weak between families, how can they be strong within a family?

It might be so. Within a family a small difference in treatment between two sibs, a slight favoritism, for example, might be perceived by the neglected sib as quite important, whereas the same difference spread across different families might not matter. Simply put, factors that are important within families might be less so between families. The particular dynamics of a family might magnify the impact of factors that are otherwise silent. Unfortunately, this sort of explanation places a healthy burden on the family dynamics that create influential effects out of factors that are otherwise weak. More important, there is precious little evidence that factors such as different parenting styles for different sibs do in fact exist within the family in sufficient magnitude to produce rather dramatic differences in IQ.

The beauty of explanations of this sort is that they are endlessly available. If one factor proves insignificant, there are always many more within easy reach. But that availability is also a danger, possibly obscuring the overall weakness of these influences. It is likely that a number of such nonshared environmental factors do exist within families, and each of them influences IQ to some extent. Birth order contributes something, differential parental treatment something else, and perhaps a whole range of chance factors unique to an individual's experience something more. Taken together, my guess is that they make a modest contribution to the overall variance in IQ.

The failure to as yet identify environmental factors—either between or within families—that are powerful influences on IQ within their normal range of variation must lead in another direction. To be sure, that other direction may well include genetic influences. Fraternal twins and biological siblings share, on average, only half their genes; some of their differences in IQ may be related to genetic differences. It also is possible that genes that are shared may express themselves differently in different individuals, producing what is termed ''nonadditive genetic variance,'' a formal way of saying something curious: *Some individual differences may be genetically based, but they may not run in families.*[10] Much like unique environmental factors, however, there is no evidence that these genetic differences or nonadditive effects between sibs are themselves sufficiently powerful to produce the sorts of differences in IQ between siblings that are evident in Table 3. It seems quite likely, in other words, that uniqueness of the sort evident between siblings or between parents and their children is due in significant degree to sources that are not directly genetic.

This approach to uniqueness means simply that neither genetic nor environmental influences in themselves are sufficient as explanatory mechanisms. An effective analysis of uniqueness, in other words, requires something else: genes and environment acting in concert, producing outcomes not ascribable to either source alone. To be sure, this argument, like much of this chapter, is derivative in nature, and therefore uncomfortable in the way that hunches lack the certainty of direct proof. The very idea of unique influences in IQ exists as a sort of remainder after the direct influences of genes and the environment have been taken into account. Now the idea that uniqueness is explicable only with reference to the mutual influence of genes and environment emerges as what remains after attempting an explanation based solely on the isolated influences of each factor.

INTERACTIONS AND COVARIANCE

Admittedly, the idea of a mutual influence between genes and environment is not new. It is common even among social scientists committed to environmentalism to speak of the fact that genes and the environment *interact*, meaning generally that the outcome of any genotypic differences between individuals depends on how these genotypes react in a given environment. With respect to uniqueness, interaction suggests that particular environments may either accentuate or diminish genetic differences between individuals. If so, then two sibs living in the same environment may react very differently to that environment, thereby producing larger (or smaller) differences between them than would be predicted by their genotypes alone. In other words, interactions might well contribute to some of the variation in IQ within families.

To see a demonstration of interaction, imagine that in an adoption study we classify adopted children into groups of "above average" and "below average" genotypes for IQ on the basis of their biological parents' IQs. (Admittedly, this classification rule is imprecise, and it assumes a certain genetic influence on individual differences in IQ—still a highly contentious issue.) Imagine as well that we expose one-half of each group to an above average environment and the other half of each group to a below average environment. Interaction in its technical sense might mean, as an example, that individuals with below average genotypes would "improve" far more in the above average environment than would individuals with above average genotypes, thereby greatly reducing or even eliminating the differences between these two genotypic groups based solely on the IQs of their biological parents.

The example outlined above is not simply a thought experiment, but in fact represents the design of the French Cross-Fostering Study. If interaction were present in that study, children coming from low-status backgrounds might improve far more than children from high-status backgrounds when both groups were reared in families of high status. That result, however, did not occur: Rearing in a high-status family did not eliminate the differences between these two groups of children. (Conversely, rearing in a low-status environment also did not eliminate these differences.)

We have previously seen a second piece of evidence that also indicates a lack of interaction between genotypes and environment. It came from the examination of the results of Head Start programs. It was noted that Head Start seemed to have the same effect on children's IQs—an initial boost followed by a decline—irrespective of children's initial IQs. That is, children with above and below average initial IQs seemed to benefit equally from Head Start. If there were an interaction, we might expect one group to improve more than the other: Perhaps lower IQ children have more to gain, or perhaps children with initially higher IQs can take better advantage of Head Start. Neither possibility seems to be true.

Given the common use of the term "interaction" by social scientists, it may seem odd that direct evidence for interactions is quite difficult to uncover. My guess is that interactions would be more evident if more fine-grained ways of specifying the environment were developed. Blunt indices like social class, within a broad range, simply do not represent effectively different categories. As a result, graphing different genotypes—themselves certainly not well specified by measures of parental IQ—against different social classes is unlikely to reveal differential effects of the environment.[11]

There is, however, a second and more powerful way in which genotypes and environments may mutually influence each other and contribute to uniqueness. They may, in a sense, "piggy-back," meaning that different genotypes for one reason or another experience particular environments. Consider a sibling who is an active and exploratory baby, easy to care for, self-reliant, if not a bit too independent. Imagine, say, Jessica Mitford. The baby's parents and others in the baby's environment soon began reacting to that baby in a particular manner, providing opportunities for her to explore, leaving her on her own more and more. As she grows older she will on her own seek out opportunities to express her inquisitiveness and independence.

Imagine her sister to be a quite different baby, quiet and moody, more dependent on parental stimulation, slow to react to new situations. As she grows older her parents as well as others in her environment treat her quite differently than her active sister, providing more attention and direction, perhaps exposing her to less challenging learning situations. She herself adds significantly to this treatment by seeking unchallenging environments. In short, each baby's own characteristics—her temperament and other genotypic characteristics related to personality and intelligence—determine, to a large extent, how she will be reacted to and what types of environments she experiences. The end result is that each sibling experiences environments that match their abilities and dispositions. This result means in turn that differences within those effective environments, in parental treatment, for example, may indeed be influential when combined with children's unique genetic dispositions.

TYPES OF COVARIANCE

This sort of piggy-backing is termed gene-environment correlation, or *co-variance*. In the example above of sibling sisters two sorts of covariance are illustrated: *reactive* covariance, in which an individual's genetic characteristics determine how others treat that individual, and *active* covariance, which describes the fact that individuals to some extent, determine their own environments.[12] Focusing on these forms of covariance admittedly leads to a somewhat different and perhaps uncomfortable view of the child and the factors that influence development than is typically conceived. It is a more active and engaging view, one in which a child's genetic predispositions combine with chosen and received environments to produce unanticipated outcomes. As uncomfortable as this view may be, I suspect it is a necessary one. We will not get far in understanding uniqueness by viewing children as passive receptacles of the treatment afforded them by their environments, or for that matter as largely determined simply by their genotypes.

Discomfort may be temporary, but another criticism of this view may be more enduring. Identifying reactive and active covariance as principal sources of unique influences on IQ may appear to be a subtle way of saying that most of the variance in IQ is, in one way or another, genetic in origin. Given the arguments of some staunch hereditarians, that inference is not entirely unfounded, and there are legitimate quantitative issues in deciding how to treat covariance.[13] Not surprisingly, environmentalists counsel us that covariance as well as inter-action may be interpreted to mean that the environment is ultimately predominant in determining the fate of any genotypic differences between individuals. It is but a short step from there to the idea that since genotypic differences and the environment are inexorably linked, their respective influences cannot be separated to provide independent estimates of heritability (see note 14). Hereditarians counter that because genes clearly come first in the order of development, cov-ariance is properly considered a "gene-drive" idea, one that retains the pre-eminence of genotypes in determining IQ.

In practice, reactive and active covariance as they have so far been described may result in an enhancement of differences between individuals based solely on their genotypes and therefore may contribute to the total variance in IQ. The enhancement is not, strictly speaking, due to genes any more than it is due to the environment. It seems, then, most reasonable to treat these forms of cov-ariance as constituting separate sources of influence on IQ. As separate sources of influence their effects should be measurable apart from estimates of heritability or (common-family) environmental influence.

Unfortunately, to obtain direct measures of covariance, far more precise ways of specifying both different genotypes and different environments are needed— the requirement also needed to provide better evidence for interaction.[14] Lacking that evidence we can only speculate as to the importance of these forms of covariance in producing uniqueness. It seems reasonable to suppose that both reactive and active covariance grow in importance during development, partic-ularly active covariance. If so, by adolescence they together may well constitute a most important source of influences on individual differences in IQ.[15]

As was shown in Figure 8, early in development a child's family environment has its maximal effects in producing similarity. The effectiveness of the family environment in this respect is probably aided by a third form of covariance during the early years of development. Children are born into environments provided by their parents. Reasonably, the parents' genetic dispositions may influence the types of environments they provide. The child, then, is born into an environment that is, to some extent, already correlated with his or her genotype.

This type of covariance has been called *passive*, and it may enhance the similarity between genetically related individuals. It also renders interpretation of the influence of family environment rather difficult. Family environment usually is regarded as constituting a purely environmental influence on IQ. In point of fact, that influence may be genetically mediated. As an example, parents with above average genotypes for IQ provide an environment for their children that undoubtedly reflects, to some extent, the parents' own intellectual dispositions—a rich array of reading materials, an emphasis on education, perhaps an interest in the discussion of stimulating issues around the dinner table. Traditional social science interprets the above average IQs of the children in these families as owing to those salient aspects of the family environment. Yet the children's genotypes are correlated with those of their parents as well as with those intellectual aspects of the family environment. The parents' genotypes also are correlated with the environments they have provided. The interlocking correlations preclude any straightforward causal interpretation, but it is clearly incorrect to ascribe the children's intellectual status solely to the family environment.

ON THE PROPER EXPLANATION OF UNIQUENESS

We are, let us imagine, painting a picture depicting the sources of uniqueness that conjointly affect a given individual's IQ. It is, of necessity, very much a mosaic, with no single inlaid component dominating the design. There are some purely environmental influences coursing through the design; color them white. There are as well some purely genetic influences; for contrast, color them black. Imagine now a rounded frame with small streams of black flowing through it, smaller rivulets of white running in other directions, together forming the major arteries and veins that give definition to an otherwise inarticulate form.

The streams and rivulets cross and merge over and again throughout the frame; from their joinings burst not predictable grays, but the colors of the rainbow. The colors, the interactions and covariances that form the heart of uniqueness, spread across the frame, forming psychedelic spirals that turn in upon themselves, sunbursts with colored petals shooting from their core. It is, to be sure, an uncommon design.

The most uncommon thing about it is that, like a snowflake, its particulars are themselves unique. There is, of necessity, a differently contoured design for each of us. The differences are, in some cases, difficult to detect; the white and black veins may follow common paths, cross at common locations for twins and siblings. Their intersections may yield common bursts of color, especially in the case of identical twins. But if we could line up a number of designs, each from a member of the same family—perhaps the Mitford family—we would come away impressed with their differences rather than with their similarities.

Those differences, and particularly their growth in late childhood and adolescence, are a difficult matter to resolve for any theoretical position. Hereditarians, relying, of necessity, on predictions based on genetic similarity, cannot easily explain the rather impressive differences between biological siblings, or why there are changes in the similarity between adopted siblings over time.

Environmentalists are less hampered, in that a variety of explanations are available to them. They might conjure up the "deidentification" between siblings in
adolescence or describe with unblinking eloquence the subtle parental treatment
differences within a family that somehow produce effects larger than those owing
to differences in social class. The ready availability of these explanations should
itself make us cautious. Their inability to explain anything other than a small
part of the puzzles posed by uniqueness should leave us downright cynical.

The problem is not only to explain differences between siblings, biological
or adopted. It is to explain as well the differences between fraternal twins, and
between parents and children, including parents and single children. Birth order
contributes a small bit to some parts of that problem, parental treatment differences another, sibling deidentification another. We might add in yet other environmental factors, perhaps even the unpredictable chance happenings that
appear at times to be so much a part of our individual destiny. Chance undoubtedly plays its role, but I suspect that its importance often is overstated. It may
have been chance that Jessica Mitford picked up a book on astronomy, although
even that choice seems to tell us much about her. The problem is that chance
connotes randomness, and Jessica's eventual life path was anything but random.
As a poker-playing friend once remarked after a particularly bad run of cards,
random events cluster. And so it is with life experiences.

In short, the choice of an astronomy book, like other aspects of Jessica's life
path, requires a more deterministic treatment than that offered by chance alone.
The same book read by a different twelve-year-old would probably have had a
much different effect, or none at all. Then, too, if it were not that chance event,
I suspect that it would have been another that eventually led her from Swinbrook
House. As was first articulated by Pasteur, chance favors the prepared mind. Or
as we might rephrase it, *chance favors the predisposed mind*.

It is one thing to ruminate academically—the word is used with all its ivory
tower connotations in place—about the wonder and pitfalls of uniqueness. It is
quite another to take those ruminations and use them to say something about
our original concern, the malleability of IQ. Yet we began with that issue, with
the Pygmalion myth nurtured to life in the Depression era Chicago slums by
Bernardine Schmidt. We followed it through preschool programs, then through
adoptive families, to disadvantaged and privileged social classes. The myth in
all its full-bodied splendor did not long survive that journey, but the malleability
of IQ in more modest form certainly has.

Can we alter the potential of children? A final answer to that question remains,
still hovering in our midst, demanding an answer. It is only proper to end by
saying something more about it, and about the related question of what IQ means,
and, finally, something about the scientists who provide the answers.

NOTES

1. Jencks, C. (1980). Heredity, environment, and public policy reconsidered. *American Sociological Review, 45*, 730.

2. Data are averaged from Plomin, R., & DeFries, J. C. (1980). Genetics and intelligence: Recent data. *Intelligence, 4*, 15–24; Loehlin, J. C., Willerman, L., & Horn, J. M. (1988). Human behavior genetics. In M. R. Rosensweig & L. W. Porter (Eds.), *Annual reviews of psychology* (pp. 101–133). Palo Alto, CA: Annual Reviews.

3. Scarr, S., & Grajek, S. (1982). Similarities and differences among siblings. In M. E. Lamb & B. Sutton-Smith (Eds.), *Sibling relationships: Their nature and significance across the lifespan* (p. 36). Hillsdale, NJ: Lawrence Erlbaum Associates.

4. The portrait of the Mitford family and associated quotes comes from two sources: Mitford, J. (1977). *A fine old conflict*. London: Michael Joseph; and Mitford, J. (1960). *Daughters and rebels: The autobiography of Jessica Mitford*. Boston: Houghton-Mifflin.

5. The similarity between IQ and personality in this way cannot be demonstrated. Considering them to be affected similarly by the same influences is derived from the argument made in Chapter 7 concerning the covariation of IQ and personality in the case of identical twins reared apart. At the least there is little evidence to indicate that IQ and personality require wholly independent treatment.

6. Zajonc, R. B. (1976). Family configuration and intelligence. *Science, 192*, 227–236.

7. See, for example, Galbraith, R. C. (1982). Sibling spacing and intellectual development: A closer look at the confluence model. *Psychological Bulletin, 18*, 151–173; also, Plomin, R. (1986). *Development, genetics and psychology* (pp. 78–79). Hillsdale, NJ: Lawrence Erlbaum Associates.

8. There is evidence of considerable stability in parenting across siblings. See, for example, Ward, M. J., Vaughn, B. E., & Robb, M. D. (1988). Social-emotional adaptation and infant-mother attachment in siblings: Role of the mother in cross-sibling consistency. *Child Development, 59*, 643–651.

9. See Jensen, A. R. (1980). Bias in Mental Testing. New York: The Free Press.

10. Lykken, D. T. (1982). Research with twins: The concept of emergenesis. *Psychophysiology, 19*, 361–373.

11. There is better evidence of interaction in animal research. A study by Cooper, R. M., & Zubek, J. P. (1959). Effects of enriched and restricted early environment on the learning ability of bright and dull rats. *Canadian Journal of Psychology, 12*, 159–164, is one such example.

12. See Plomin, R., Defries, J. C., & Loehlin, J. C. (1977). Genotype-environment interaction and correlation in the analysis of human behavior. *Psychological Bulletin, 84*, 309–322.

13. Compare, for example, Farber, S. L. (1981). *Identical twins reared apart: A reanalysis*. New York: Basic Books, and Lewontin, R. C., Rose, S., & Kamin, L. J. (1984). *Not in our genes*. New York: Pantheon Books, with Scarr, S., & McCartney, K. (1983). How people make their own environments: A theory of genotype → environment effects. *Child Development, 54*, 424–435.

14. There is evidence, indirect at best, of the potential influence of covariance from the data on identical twins reared apart. Heritability estimates from this source usually are .20 or more above other estimates (about .70 to .75 vs. about .40 to .50). The inflation may be due to an unusual effect of reactive and active covariance in this case. Given the twins' genetic identity, reactive and active covariance would tend to enhance the similarity between the twins, and hence enhance heritability estimates. For example, given their identical genetic dispositions, the twins would be likely to seek out similar environmental niches and to be treated similarly. The result would be to increase the correlation in their

IQs. This argument may sound like a complicated way of simply saying that identical twins reared apart are similar because of their genetic identity, but in this instance their similarity is enhanced over what would be true simply on a genetic basis because of the covariation of the twins' genetic similarity and environmental treatment. This contention has been taken further, to argue that heritability estimates themselves are artifactually inflated by the presence of covariance. If so, the direct effects of genotypic differences per se may be much smaller than they appear in heritability estimates. (See Lazar, D. [1974]. Heritabiilty analyses of IQ scores: Science or numerology? *Science, 183,* 1259–1265.)

15. This analysis owes much to Scarr & McCartney and Scarr, S. (1987). How genotypes and environments combine: Development and individual differences. In Bolger, N., Caspi, A., Downey, G., & Moorehouse, M. (Eds.), *Persons in contexts: Developmental processes* (pp. 217–244). New York: Cambridge University Press. See also Plomin, R., & Daniels, D. (1987). Why are children in the same family so different from each other? *Behavioral and Brain Sciences 10,* 1–60.

9

IQ in Perspective

If you want to try and understand something, try to change it.
—Countless behaviorists, modeling themselves after B. F. Skinner

THE MALLEABILITY OF IQ

Opinions are all too easy to come by in the study of IQ. They are there for the asking, often carrying with them the sureness of science, perhaps even the hint of moral imperative. Worse, they come from every possible direction. In the past decade or so alone scholars from philosophy to physics, paleontology to political science have contributed their putatively seminal thoughts on the matter of IQ. What the study of IQ needs least, it would seem, is one more attempt to tell us how useless IQ is, or how central it is—one of psychology's most profound discoveries, some would say. How IQ is entirely environmentally determined; how it is undoubtedly a highly heritable trait. How it is studied only by racists or angels; why it should not be studied at all.

A good case indeed can be made not only for lowering the volume, but also for lessening the pages printed. The ratio of cant to data, as Sandra Scarr has rightfully pointed out, is entirely too high. In the hope that this work avoids inflating that ratio further, I end with four conclusions and some thoughts derived from them. One or two of the conclusions are themselves unique, or at least cannot be entirely anticipated from what has come before. Others, however, can be found elsewhere. It is their sum that is different.

1. Direct attempts to raise IQ through preschool programs have not as yet worked. Moreover, they have produced few, if any, "beyond-IQ" effects on school achievement or other aspects of intellectual development.

2. Adoptions do provide evidence that IQ is malleable. That malleability is, however, more modest than previously thought and, over a broad range, is not largely a function of typically considered environmental factors associated with social class.

3. The heritability of IQ is at least moderate. This is a relative, not an absolute, statement. Compared with any combination of currently identified environmental factors, heredity seems influential, but . . .

4. A large proportion of the individual differences in IQ is not accounted for by the direct effects of heredity or environment. Unique influences, mostly in the form of covariances, play a significant, perhaps decisive role in producing individual differences in IQ.

A first thought about these conclusions is whether some of them are linked. A common linkage—among laypeople as well as some social scientists—is between the first and third conclusions. If IQ is highly heritable, does this not imply that preschool efforts are wasted? The answer is simple and straightforward: No. Even if the heritability of IQ is .40 to .50 or so, that fact alone tells us no more than did Bloom's idea of half-life. It says only that about half of the individual differences in IQ are due to differences in genotypes. It tells us nothing about the malleability of IQ. In fact, as noted earlier, any heritability estimate can be translated into the environmental changes necessary to evoke a given average change in IQ.

Theoretically, the lower the heritability estimate, the less radical need be the environmental change to produce a given change in IQ. But it also is true that even highly heritable traits can show striking malleability. A good example— and one that is entirely consonant with the ruminations of both Francis Galton and Benjamin Bloom—is height, which has a heritability of about .90. Despite that degree of heritability, some populations, notably the Japanese, have shown a remarkable increase in average height during this century. The basis for this increase probably includes improvements in nutrition and health care in Japan as that country evolved from a closed, almost postfeudal society in the early part of the twentieth century to a major industrial power in the 1980s. Even countries that cannot lay claim to such massive socioeconomic changes, however, show equally impressive increases in height. In England, for example, the average height of males increased from 5 feet 7.5 inches in 1910 to 5 feet 10 inches in 1982, a gain of about one full standard deviation.[1]

The point illustrated by these secular changes in height is crucial for understanding the value and the limits of heritability estimates. Heritability itself provides no prediction about the potential impact of changes in the environment. With respect to IQ we can say only that *current* environmental interventions in the form of preschools are, on average, ineffective. But the failure of preschools to change IQ has nothing directly to do with the heritability of IQ. Indeed, the heritability estimates for IQ indicate that some environmental manipulations must have appreciable influence.

Preschools, Adoptions, and Secular Gains in IQ

And some do, as adoptions demonstrate. Adoptions, moreover, are not the sole source of evidence concerning the malleability of IQ. Surprisingly perhaps, there appear to have been secular changes in IQ that very much parallel secular changes in height. The evidence derives from the observation made repeatedly over the past several decades that if individuals are given the current form of an IQ test and an earlier standardized form of the same test, they tend to score higher on the earlier form. Recall that IQ represents only performance relative to the reference group on which a particular test has been standardized. If individuals score higher on the earlier test, it means that they stand relatively higher in the earlier reference group as compared with that later reference group. In other words, *performance on IQ tests seems to have been improving over time*.

Before accepting that conclusion, a caution is in order: Evidence of this sort may be confounded by differences in the practices used to standardize the different versions of the test. The reference groups may, for example, not be equally representative of their respective populations. If so, no comparisons are possible between scores derived from the two tests. Fortunately secular improvements in IQ have proved to be quite general across different tests and in different countries, thereby increasing the chances that the apparent gains are something more than artifactual. We also should note that although the extent of this improvement varies with the test used and the country studied, on average, the gains are rather robust. In the United States the increase seems to have been somewhere between 5 and 15 points between 1932 and 1978.[2]

If these gains are real, that is, if they are not due to standardization differences or to some as yet undiscovered artifacts, they are indeed most provocative. The gains would undoubtedly be due to environmental factors and would seem to offer the promise that general improvements in the environment may, over the course of many years, result in significant changes in IQ. Interestingly, these gains have been apparently uniform over all segments of the population. They have not, for example, reduced differences between races or social classes over time. It is as if a constant has been added quite regularly to everyone's IQ over the course of the past fifty years. As perhaps no other data, secular gains in IQ exemplify the adage that "a rising tide lifts all boats."

In one sense this finding creates a paradox. Direct attempts to improve IQ in the form of preschool interventions do not work, and yet nonspecific environmental improvements acting over the course of many decades appear to have had a quite positive effect on IQ. The ineffectiveness of preschools in this context may appear all the more puzzling. IQ is clearly malleable, and environmental intervention during the heralded critical period would appear to be precisely what is needed. So, why aren't preschools more effective in those respects? And, as a corollary, to return to a residual puzzle, why are adoptions effective?

These questions undoubtedly have the aura of comparing apples and oranges. Preschools differ from adoptions in any number of ways. Adoptions are assessed after a longer time period. They inevitably immerse the child in a full-scale change of environment compared with the relatively limited changes represented by preschools. Some social scientists have even argued that adoptions result in enhanced IQ precisely because they, in a sense, mimic preschools. Adoptive parents, it is argued, are more likely to engage in intellectually related activities, perhaps even tutor their children, especially their adopted children, who might be judged to need an extra academic boost of sorts. If these arguments are true, they answer our earlier question concerning why adoptions are effective by characterizing them as more and better implementations of the intent of preschools, that is, to provide a pervasive intellectually stimulating environment for the child.

Adoptive families obviously do enjoy the advantages of greater intensity and duration as compared with preschools. In this sense, adoptive families come closer to approximating the conditions that have probably spawned secular improvements in IQ. Adoptions in fact undoubtedly constitute a far more intensive environmental influence than do whatever conditions have acted slowly but surely over many decades to produce secular changes. But even given ample acknowledgment to these aspects of the adoptive family, to these "common-family" influences as they were referred to previously (Chapter 8, Figure 8), there is something left over, something not adequately captured by time and intensity alone. Nor is the "goodness" of adoptive families largely captured by characterizing them as model classrooms, the preschool successfully transplanted right within the family.

Simply stated, the effectiveness of adoptive families, the source of the adoption constancy effect, has as much to do with allowing for the expression of these children's uniqueness as it has to do with any specific sort of "exceptional" environment defined in any conventional sense. Perhaps adoptive parents are, for example, particularly receptive to discovering the nature of their adopted children's predispositions. Adoptive parents may, therefore, be especially good at tailoring their parenting to meet the individual needs of their adopted children, including the use of tutoring in situations where it is judged to be useful and excluding direct tutoring when it is judged unproductive.

To place this admittedly speculative argument in a different context, it might be characterized as linking the second and fourth conclusions. Many adoptive families are successful in raising their adopted children's IQs. They do so, at least in part, by taking into account their children's particular dispositions, by maximizing, that is, active and reactive covariance. This argument does not rule out the advantages of time and intensity, or other obviously advantageous aspects of the adoptive family: the fact that the parents are committed to their children; that many are experienced parents, having raised children of their own before adoption; that the family itself often enjoys advantaged circumstances, traditionally conceived, compared with the adopted child's biological family. But there undeniably is something special about adoptive families, and that "specialness" does not often seem captured in full measure by any of the obvious indices of standard of living or shared family culture that distinguish different families.

To the extent that this idea also is true for intact families, it may well leave us uneasy. For if uniqueness is as important as it has here been suggested, then nothing precise suggests itself about how to maximize a child's intellectual potential. *If the goal is to improve IQ, there is probably no one type of educational program that will work for all children. Nor will any one type of parenting. There is no singular environmental factor that will predictably be associated with improvements in IQ.*

If we follow this idea to its end point, uneasiness may seem to give way to despair, for one implication is that, at least for children within a broad range of social classes, special training will be of no benefit over and above what might be gained within the family environment. Indeed, if taking advantage of co-variance is related to maximizing a child's intellectual development, the best environment in which that might happen is probably not a preschool, but the "normal" environment provided by the biological family in which the child's genetic dispositions are matched, to some extent, with those of the parents and to the environment they have provided.

Similar conclusions do not hold, however, for children whose families are severely disadvantaged. For these children our first reaction is undoubtedly to think that an intensive educational program outside the home is precisely what is needed. Yet, in view of the results of preschool efforts, it is not unreasonable to wonder whether the special attention these children so vitally require would perhaps not be better met in ways other than a preschool, perhaps by focusing on programs that are home-centered.[3]

Effective Preschools? Irrespective of the validity of these ideas, the possibility of developing programs that by-pass the idea of a preschool will not easily meet with approval. Preschools, for many understandable reasons, have become the cornerstone of government-sponsored attempts to aid disadvantaged children. They, as much if not more than any other facet of social assistance programs, seem destined to be kept in place in one form or another for the foreseeable future. Granting that reality, the question is whether they can be altered so as to be more effective.

Given what little we know precisely about the conditions that alter IQ, the answer is not at all clear. One suggestion, however, might come from rethinking the characterization of adoptive families as successful implementations of pre-schools. We might, rather, envision a successful preschool intervention as something like an adoption. To maximize the chances of any such intervention succeeding, it would certainly have to be far more comprehensive than is now the case, far more so than even the Milwaukee project.

By comprehensive, I mean two sorts of things. First, in terms of intensity and duration, it is clear that one or two or even five years of intervention, no matter how well structured or planned or intended, may not work. To the extent that intensity and duration matter, an effective intervention would have to be designed in ways that make it truly a form of co-parenting. It would have to begin with parent training before a child's birth, entail not only a few hours a day of classroom work but virtual full-time intervention that focuses not only on the child but, perhaps more important, on the entire family environment as well. It would have to continue past the beginning of the school years, particularly through late childhood and early adolescence as intelligence becomes adultlike in character.

To put it somewhat differently, *we can expect no appreciable and stable change in IQ without appreciable and stable support.* And yet, even if that much were agreed to, it would not be sufficient. The reason has again to do with the importance of unique influences on IQ. I suspect that if there is a successful preschool intervention, it would not be one that simply compounds time and intensity into a form of co-parenting, but one that also incorporates the idea of *tailored parenting* into its programs. That is to say, any successful intervention will have in its own way to recognize the importance of uniqueness, and design opportunities for individualized learning that maximize the chances that a child's particular abilities and dispositions will be realized.

This description of an intervention that might—I stress *might*—be effective raises two reasonable questions. The first is whether, even if this sort of intervention might work, we should initiate it. An intervention of this magnitude would certainly radically alter the fabric of life for these children and their families. It is, at the least, a presumptive and intrusive idea. Whether it should be tried at all is a matter of values, perhaps of politics, but is surely not principally a matter of science.

Should IQ Be Raised?

The second concern is whether IQ gains of the sort possible under this most invasive intervention—10 to 12 points as a guess—would indeed be worth the effort. That answer depends critically on one's view of the value of IQ. Assuming for the moment that IQ is indeed valuable, the answer is clear: yes. Imagine, for example, a group of children whose IQs average 85. Assume that IQs falling below 80 are predictive of special education placement, remedial classes, high failure rates, and the like. For that group of children about 37 percent will experience these severe school problems. If we could manage to raise those children's IQs to an average of close to 100, and if, unlike the Milwaukee Project, the usual school correlates of IQ improve as well, the comparable percentage of children experiencing severe school problems could drop to about 10 percent.

It perhaps did not escape attention that the averages used in the example above roughly correspond to the averages for blacks and whites in the U.S. population. That group difference has been the subject of considerable controversy, beginning well before Jensen's speculations about racial differences and heritability. As has been pointed out, heritability estimates pertain only to *individual differences within a population*; they tell us nothing about the source or sources of differences between groups within that population, or certainly the proportion of genetic influence in a given individual's IQ. The heritability of a trait within a population may be high, and yet differences between groups within that population may be entirely environmental in origin. Heritability estimates simply do not resolve that sort of issue. It also is true that given the current state of our knowledge, and the disinclination of many social scientists to study these matters, we will probably know little more than that about the origins of black and white differences in IQ.

That sort of uncertainty arises because the IQ debate has focused almost exclusively on heritability. If we attend to what I consider to be a more important topic, malleability, a far more certain conclusion is possible. Simply put, *there can be little doubt that the malleability of IQ for blacks and whites is equal.* Indeed, some of the most substantial evidence for the malleability of IQ comes from the black and interracial children in the Transracial Adoption Study. Similarity in malleability does not mean that any group differences are entirely environmental in origin. If we combine the malleability estimates presented here, however, with the average difference in IQ between blacks and whites, it is clear that whatever the reasons for the difference, the malleability of IQ is sufficient to eliminate most, if not all of it. Some might still maintain that a portion of that original difference was genetic in origin, but that point is neither verifiable nor important. It is the malleability of IQ that in fact *is* critical in the debate about racial or other group differences in IQ.

As a related concern we might wonder why, if an intervention of the magnitude described may be effective but is judged too disruptive, a scaled-down version of it—current preschool efforts—do not also work, albeit with more modest results. In other words, if a pervasive intervention might produce a quite positive effect, why wouldn't a more limited intervention produce a smaller, but still positive effect, and so on?

That preschools seem not to work in this manner indicates something important and general about the way the environment effects IQ. The idea was originally presented in the discussion of social class differences (see Chapter 6, Figure 7). It was suggested that the environmental effects of social class were negligible across a broad range of classes and were only appreciable at the extremes. Substitute preschool programs for social classes and the same thought emerges. At one extreme I imagine that poorly designed programs may even have a negative impact on IQ. At the high end of effectiveness our hypothetical form of co-parenting and tailored parenting may produce a positive effect. But within a broad range—the range within which current interventions fall—there is virtually no effect.

Given this idea, one might be led to the conclusion that preschools, in their current form of a one- or two-year intervention, simply represent a well-intentioned idea whose time has now passed. As with any issue related to IQ, this one has more than one viewpoint. From one perspective, it may well be argued that the rationale for current preschools, at least for disadvantaged children, should be based on wider grounds than simply the enhancement of IQ, even setting aside the many interpretative problems associated with measures of social competence. Head Start, as an example, might amply be justified, in that it effectively disseminates a variety of services to children and their families that go well beyond formal educational practices.[4] One-third of Head Start families, for example, report that Head Start was extremely helpful with respect to family and personal problems. Ninety-six percent of the families in need of some form of social services received them through Head Start or through referral by Head Start to the appropriate agency. As well, Head Start often is the first place that these families come in contact with community health services. Virtually all Head Start families report some assistance of this kind.[5] Head Start, as well as other preschool programs, undoubtedly also serve as publicly assisted forms of day care, not a minor contribution when a large proportion of all mothers with children eligible for Head Start have entered the work force.

These considerations aside, there is another, quite different perspective on the value of current preschools. It centers on the question of whether Head Start and other preschool programs are the most appropriate vehicle through which to disseminate the above-described services, since none of those services seems to necessitate a one- or two-year preschool program. If not, we might well wonder whether educational programs that have no identifiable educational impact are best left in place on the basis of their nonacademic merits. At the least, it should not, after more than two decades of these efforts, be forbidden to rethink how best to impact disadvantaged children. *If the appropriateness of preschools is never questioned, it is certain that more innovative forms of assistance—and perhaps more successful forms—will not evolve.*

THE VALUE AND MEANING OF IQ

Everything in the world can be explained by factors about which we know nothing.
—Peter Urbach[6]

Speculations about improving IQ or about eliminating group differences in IQ are naturally predicated on the assumption that differences in IQ are important enough to warrant such serious attention. Little has been said directly about the value of IQ other than to note that it has historically been the most often used outcome measure in intervention and adoption studies. Its popularity has not, however, insulated it from severe criticisms. The rule seems to be that if IQ behaves the way it is expected to—as it does by and large in adoption studies— then use it. If it proves to be a disappointment—as it is in preschool interventions—then find something else to measure and, in the process, characterize IQ as too narrow, biased, or even irrelevant for tapping the subtleties that are to be found.

That characterization is as accurate as it is cynical. But cynical or not, accurate or not, the fact remains that IQ has received sufficient criticisms over the years to warrant serious re-evaluation. That re-evaluation centers on a seemingly answerable question: How do we know that IQ is indeed a measure of intelligence?

The Challenge Posed by Secular Gains

There have been any number of challenges to the importance of IQ. Oddly, perhaps the most provocative challenge comes from the presence of secular gains. To see the challenge posed by this finding, assume for the moment that secular gains in IQ are real and that IQ does indeed measure intelligence. If so, should not such profound changes be readily apparent? After all, an increase of the better part of a full standard deviation would mean that an individual of average IQ today would have the IQ of about the average college graduate of fifty years ago. Should there not be many more geniuses in the population today as compared with fifty years ago? Far fewer individuals in need of special education or remedial instruction? As one critic put it, "Clearly, massive IQ gains should bring a cultural renaissance too obvious to be overlooked."[7] Or, stated somewhat differently, are we really standing on an elevated intellectual platform looking down, benignly perhaps, upon our ancestors?

The last question is facetious, but there is a serious point behind it. Add in another piece of information and the point becomes impossible to ignore. During the period 1963 to 1980 scores on the Scholastic Aptitude Test (SAT), the college entrance test, declined by between one-fourth to greater than one-half of a standard deviation. The decline was evident in both the verbal and the quantitative (mathematical) portions of the test.[8] During that same period IQ gains in the U.S. population were on the order of 2 to 5 points. The SAT and standard IQ tests correlate rather highly; one estimate in fact put the correlation between the verbal portion of the SAT and IQ at .80.[9] How can two tests that correlate so highly show opposing trends?

The SAT decline itself has been the subject of much discussion and theorizing. At last count in fact seventy-nine hypotheses had been put forth to explain it.[10] One of the most plausible explanations is that the SAT decline was produced not by a decrease in scholastic achievement per se, but by a widening of the candidate pool taking the test. As college opportunity expanded, so did the range of students taking the examination. One result of that expansion might have been a lowered SAT average. If true, the gains in IQ and declines in SAT pose no contradiction. Unfortunately changes in the candidate pool seem to be, at best, only part of the answer, since the candidate pool did not expand appreciably after 1972, and the SAT decline is still quite evident from 1972 to 1980. That decline also was evident when quality of education and indices like social class were held constant. That is, the decline was evident even if high-achieving students graduating in different years from similar high schools were compared.[11] In short, the losses in SAT performance seem as valid as the gains in IQ. Indeed, these losses seem entirely consonant with current concerns about the quality of education in the United States, of eroding standards and declining student achievement.

As might be expected, the resolution of the inconsistency between trends in IQ and SAT sorts principally along ideological lines. For some of the critics of IQ, among them a generous sampling of environmentalists, the data on secular changes in IQ and SAT declines confirm what they have all along suspected: Not only is IQ highly malleable, but, happily, it is virtually worthless. If there are no obvious signs of sprouting genius, if one would be hard-pressed to identify evidence of increased national intelligence that is as apparent as it should be if IQ measures intelligence, if indeed there seems to be evidence to the contrary as judged by the SAT erosion, then IQ cannot measure what we have thought it does. Instead of measuring intelligence, it measures something else, something that might improve over time while not revealing itself in any obvious, real-world way. As one critic put it, IQ tests do not measure intelligence, but rather measure "a correlate with a weak causal link to intelligence."[12]

A correlate with a weak causal link to intelligence? Is this possible? Have those who have extolled the virtues of IQ—among whom are principally found, not surprisingly, hereditarians—been fooling themselves for the better part of a century?

The defense of IQ begins by pointing to the fact that the meaning of any test is revealed, to a large extent, by the correlations between scores on that test and other indices. In the case of IQ those correlations provide a defensible picture. As has been noted, IQ does correlate well with a variety of measures of academic achievement, so much so that some psychometricians refer to IQ as a test of "academic intelligence."[13] Beyond that, IQ correlates more highly with the entire nexus of measures of occupational or social success than does any other currently available psychological measurement. If, for example, we ask individuals to rank occupations in terms of their prestige, that ranking reveals an orderly ranking in IQ as well. If we were limited to making one measurement of a seven-year-old child to predict that child's eventual life success, however assessed, arguably the one best measure would be that child's IQ. Without further belaboring the point, IQ seems to behave just the way we might expect a genuine measure of intelligence to behave. If it is merely a mysterious weak sister of intelligence, it is a most fortuitous one, mimicking the real thing rather nicely at times.

Given the array of evidence indicating the validity of IQ, the advocates of IQ have at times argued that the apparent secular gains must be the result of some as yet not understood artifacts—increasing test sophistication across generations, inequalities in the standardization samples used in different tests, and so forth. This argument is possible, but it does place the advocates of IQ, particularly hereditarians, in a rather peculiar position. The reliance on undiscovered factors to explain something about IQ is precisely the criticism hereditarians have long leveled at environmentalists. Hereditarians are now edging themselves into a similar position in alluding to unspecified artifacts that render secular gains unimportant.

It is an untenable position. Secular trends in IQ are simply too pervasive to be dismissed as artifactual to any large degree. There may be some partial explanations that involve artifacts, and these ultimately may lead to a lowered estimate of the real gains in IQ over time. Beyond those caveats there undoubtedly has been true enhancement in IQ test performance.

And so, what to make of that enhancement? Unlike some critics, I do not think that secular changes necessitate the characterization of IQ as a weak sister of intelligence. Ironically, that position comes from an overevaluation of the supposed predictive power of IQ. That overevaluation in turn becomes part of a syllogism that is used to dismiss the value of IQ. The syllogism, which begins with the assumption that there have been substantial secular increases in IQ over time, goes something like this:

1. If IQ measures intelligence, there should be clear signs of increased national intelligence;

2. there are no such clear signs, ergo:

3. IQ must measure something other than general intelligence.

Although assumption of substantial secular gains is true, the first proposition in the syllogism is, at best, only partially correct, thereby rendering the remainder of the syllogism suspect. The first proposition assumes that there is a direct path from intelligence to real-world achievement. That is simply not true, a point that was made previously in the discussion of IQ and social class (Chapter 6). Assuming that IQ measures intelligence, the manner by which IQ has its "real-world" effects on occupational status or social class as examples, is, at best, circuitous. As earlier noted, IQ enters into a pattern of diminishing influence as its path is traced through education to income and eventual occupational success. To summarize this point in another way, factors other than intelligence importantly determine success. If those other factors do not change, or may themselves be on the decline, they may well obscure any improvements that might be predicted based on IQ alone.

Secular Gains and Erosions in Educational Success. All well and good perhaps with regard to occupation and income and perhaps other sorts of real-world indices of achievement, but what about educational success? IQ correlates rather impressively with scholastic achievement, and there seems to be little, if any, evidence of academic enhancement over time. Indeed, as judged by the SAT decline and other indices of educational achievement, there seems to be evidence to the contrary. And so, the question remains: Can this discrepancy be resolved?

The answer is yes, although the apparent divergence between secular gains in IQ and educational erosions is surely a most telling problem for conventional wisdom. But again, the apparent discrepancy depends, to some extent, on an overevaluation of the predictive power of IQ even with respect to education. As noted previously, the correlation between IQ and educational success is anywhere from about .40 to .60 or so on average, depending on the measure of educational success used and the subjects tested; correlations are higher for elementary school children than for more advanced students. The correlations usually are substan-

Figure 9
The "Twisted Pear": A Theoretical Positive Correlation between School
Grades and IQ

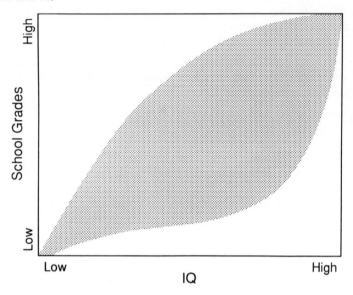

tial, but they also may obscure some interesting divergences. This possibility is shown in Figure 9, which expresses a hypothetical relation between IQ and school success, measured by school grades in this instance, in the form of a type of positive correlation that sometimes is called a "twisted pear."

Overall, Figure 9 demonstrates a positive correlation between IQ and school grades of about .50 or so, but that correlation is more evident at the extremes. At the low extreme IQ is highly predictive of poor school grades. That is to say, there is relatively little variability in school grades among low-IQ individuals. A somewhat comparable, though less precise relation is evident for high-IQ individuals, meaning simply that high IQ seems pretty much to predict significant school success. Most individuals do not fall at the extremes, but in the middle, and in that large middle ground there is considerable variability. If we were in fact to cut off the extremes from Figure 9 and focus only on the middle, the correlation between IQ and school grades would be far less than .50. Simply stated, especially within the average range of intelligence, IQ is only moderately predictive *in itself* of educational success. Other factors—motivation, maturity, goal orientation, and the like—play an important role.

The implication of this idea is that *secular changes in IQ are not themselves sufficient to have produced overall enhancement in educational success.* That there may have been erosions in educational success is not explained by this idea, nor does it necessarily transfer from school grades to other, putatively more objective measures of school success like the SAT. But it does suggest that changes in IQ cannot be used in any simple manner to predict wholesale changes in at least some measures of educational success.

One might still argue that if Figure 9 is indeed accurate, secular changes in IQ should have left us with fewer individuals performing poorly in school over the years and certainly more high-achieving individuals. After all, if the twisted pear is accurate, it means that IQ *is* predictive of school success at the extremes. If so, can we not extrapolate that idea to the real world? In other words, even if things are a bit muddled in the middle, shouldn't secular gains in IQ have left us with, for example, more high-achieving geniuses?

Terman's Termites and a Thought Experiment. The answer is, as we will see, "not necessarily." It is true, however, that supporters of IQ often point to the extremes of IQ to demonstrate their point about IQ's value. They are especially likely to cite a longitudinal study of high-IQ individuals to buttress their case. That study was begun by Lewis Terman in the 1920s when he identified 1,528 California schoolchildren whose IQs averaged 150, within the top 1 percent of all children tested. These children, who became known as "Terman's Termites," were carefully monitored over the next fifty years in what is undoubtedly the single most extensive study of intellectual giftedness.[14]

The results of the study seem, at first blush, to document amply the value of having a high IQ. In childhood Terman's subjects were typically accelerated in grade placement by about two to three grades. Contrary to stereotype, they were above average not only in school achievement, but also in terms of physical health, their proficiency at sports, their emotional maturity, and in ratings of character. They were, in sum, entirely well rounded, giving no support to the idea that giftedness in one respect must be inevitably compensated for by deficiencies in other respects.

Their superior achievements were maintained into their adult years. By midlife 70 percent of them had finished college as compared with only 8 percent of their generation. There were five times as many Ph.D.s among them as among average college graduates. Everything about them, their incomes, occupational levels, overall satisfaction with their lives, was well above average. Even their death rate was one-third less than the population average.

These results are not surprising if one believes that high IQ confers the sorts of advantages that should be the result of genuinely superior intelligence. But these results also are quite predictable on the basis of these individuals' social classes of origin and, as a result, their educational advantages. Nearly one-third of the children came from professional families, only 7 percent from semiskilled or unskilled workers. In other words, on average, these children were advantaged in a number of ways. How do we know that it was their IQs that set them apart?

The answer typically given is to cite other information about the success of these high-IQ individuals that seems not due merely to their backgrounds or educational histories. For example, those high-IQ individuals who earned only a high school degree as adults earned about as much as college graduates in the general population. Also, as adults, members of the sample outperformed colleagues in the same occupation with respect to income. That superiority was even evident in semiskilled and unskilled occupations, where high-IQ individuals outearned their counterparts by about 25 percent. The pattern of these findings often is used to argue that amount of education did not invariably lead to greater income for this sample, and that high IQ itself seemed to predict socioeconomic success.[15]

None of these outcomes means, however, that the same trends would be evident within the average range of IQ. Nor does it indicate that high IQ alone determines success. For women in the sample the relation of high IQ to real-world success was in fact far more difficult to divine. Forty percent of the high-IQ women who had completed advanced degrees were listed as housewives ("not employed" in the vernacular of the times) or employed only part-time by midlife. Nearly 70 percent of the high-IQ women with college degrees were similarly categorized. Interestingly, many of these women found nontraditional channels through which to realize their ability. A number, for example, were described as poets, novelists, playwrights, painters, and sculptors; one was listed as a missionary.

These data amply attest to the lack of opportunities during the earlier part of this century even for women with extremely high IQs. But the fact that high IQ produced a wide variety of life successes was true for males as well. That fact is clear from a study conducted as part of a longitudinal follow-up.[16] For that study, two groups of one hundred males each, labeled groups A and C, were formed from the original high-IQ sample. Although both groups had IQs as children that had fallen within the 99th percentile, there were marked differences between the two groups as adults. The members of group A were far more successful in virtually every respect. Fifty-nine of them had entered professional-level occupations as compared with only five of the group C members. Only one group A member had an occupation in the clerical or skilled trades as compared with seventy of the group C members. Group A members outearned their counterparts $23,900 to $7,178 in 1959, the year in which the study was conducted. Ninety-two of the group A members had earned a college degree or better. Only forty of the group C members had graduated from college.

In attempting to understand the differences between the two groups, the scientists conducting the study spoke of the greater drive to succeed and overall social adjustment of the group A members. They also were judged to be physically healthier than group C members, to exhibit greater perseverance and self-confidence. Group A members also were judged to have come from stable families wherein their parents were more likely to encourage initiative, independence, and school success than was true for members of group C.

To be complete, it should be noted that the group A members also tended to come from families higher in socioeconomic status, and as a group they had higher IQs than did their counterparts in group C (averages of 157 vs. 150). But these differences were slight compared with their life success differences. It seems clear that even for high-IQ individuals, many more factors than sheer intelligence—at least as measured by IQ—entered into success.

And that fact in turn should question the first proposition of the critics' syllogism that so directly links IQ with real-world achievement. To put it somewhat differently, there may well have been some real gains in IQ over the years, but we should not expect to see obvious signs of that change all around us. Not unless the nonintellectual components of success have similarly increased.

We might use Terman's Termites in a sort of thought experiment to question the conclusion of the syllogism on other grounds as well. Imagine for the moment that we transported Terman's Termites into the present and asked them to take a current IQ test. According to the idea of secular changes in IQ, these individuals should score lower, maybe as much as 10 to 15 points lower, rendering them still well above average but perhaps no longer gifted. The question is, Is that really likely? Have they, as it were, lost their giftedness?

The answer is surely no, although if we in fact did transport them to the present and give them an IQ test, they would probably score below their 1930s average. But now alter the situation: What if we transported them, not as adults, but at birth, had them grow up in late twentieth century America, and then gave them a current IQ test? Then they would score just as highly as they did in the 1930s, that is, they would be in the 99th percentile.

What IQ Measures

Sounds perhaps implausible on the face of it, but the apparent implausibility stems from an incorrect view of what IQ measures. If we think of IQ or intelligence in absolute terms, as a sort of *entity* that one possesses in a certain amount, then the secular changes in IQ are indeed puzzling. We now seem to have more of it—whatever *it* is. Earlier generations seem to have had less of *it*.[17] If so, it seems reasonable to ask why there is no greater evidence available about the impact of so many more geniuses in our midst.

But this view of what IQ measures is simply incorrect. IQ must be seen in *contextual terms*, as the ability to master the skills and information necessary to succeed within a given culture, that is, to succeed at a given point in time within a defined context. Terman's Termites would do just as well today in this respect as they did in the 1930s, so long as they had the opportunity to master what it takes to succeed in present-day America. American culture and undoubtedly most, if not all, industrialized cultures have progressed in the manner of demanding more of individuals to succeed. To score 150 today on an IQ test— that is, to score within the top 1 percent—demands more knowledge both in the form of specific information and more general problem-solving skills than was true previously. But Terman's Termites, if raised in today's culture, would have assimilated that increased knowledge and the necessary skills.

We might turn this idea on its head and ask what would happen if we transported an individual who had grown up in modern America and scored 100 on a current IQ test back to the 1930s. We know that our unfortunate transportee (going back to the heart of the Great Depression cannot be seen as a stroke of good fortune) would score well above average if given a test standardized in that era. The argument here is that if that individual had instead grown up in the 1930s, he or she would have been no more than average.

IQ, in other words, tells us something about *potential* to succeed. That potential, like any other human trait, needs a context within which to be realized. The implication of this argument is that individual potential has not necessarily changed, but the conditions under which it is manifested have. The changes in those conditions are what we see as secular changes in IQ. It does not mean that we should expect a greater proportion of geniuses today than yesterday. Nor does it mean that our ancestors need to be protected from their own feeble-mindedness.

It does mean, however, that there are severe limitations in using IQ to compare individuals who have experienced differing intellectual contexts. The easiest way to see this limitation is transgenerationally: IQ simply cannot be used to compare individuals who have grown up in different eras. But that limitations in turn suggests another: If IQ's usefulness is limited to comparing individuals who have experienced the same intellectual context, *perhaps it cannot be used even to compare individuals living within the same generation who may nonetheless have experienced different cultural milieus.*

As an example, even within present-day America it is surely possible that different subgroups—inner-city blacks versus upper middle-class suburban whites, for example—bring appreciably different intellectual contexts to an IQ test. Those differing contexts may result in quite incorrect inferences if IQ is used for purposes of comparison, in the same manner as does the more obvious transgenerational comparison.

Resolution of a Paradox: Secular Gains in IQ and Losses in Educational Achievement. This interpretation of the meaning of IQ, along with a more realistic appraisal of how predictive IQ may be of educational or real-world success, offers a resolution of the apparent paradox between secular changes in IQ and the failure to observe real-world indications of increased intelligence. It does not, however, resolve the discrepancy between secular gains in IQ and apparent decreases in SAT performance, or more generally, declines in educational success. There are some additional considerations that may now make that discrepancy more understandable.

If both the gains and the declines are real, one reason for the discrepancy may be seen by returning to the adoption constancy effect. The failure of adoptions to reveal environmental effects of different social classes over a broad range led to the idea that perhaps a constant had been added to each adoptive child's IQ irrespective of that child's particular social class of rearing. Adding a constant to one factor does nothing to alter the correlations into which that factor enters. So, the adoption constancy effect might mean that there had been average increases in adoptive children's IQs without these increases evidencing themselves in correlations between the adoptive children's IQs and any aspect of their adoptive families.

The same thing would be true if a constant had been subtracted from a factor. And that possibility, that there may have been rather steady declines in some components of academic achievement, is one answer to the IQ-SAT discrepancy. How might that subtraction have come about? The answer requires first an understanding of the differences between an IQ test and a test like the SAT. One way to think about that difference is to consider when an individual has the opportunity to acquire the information demanded by the test.[18] In the case of IQ that opportunity is quite broad-based, extending ideally to every facet of daily living, including, to some extent, information and skills acquired in schools. For the SAT, given that it is intended specifically to predict success in college, that opportunity is far more directly related to information imparted by schools, particularly mathematical skills, the comprehension of written passages taken from literature and science, the rules of grammar, and so forth. The mathematical portion of the SAT, for example, assumes one year of algebra and some geometry. The SAT, in other words, measures what sometimes is called "developed abilities," abilities tied very much to school-related skills. This sort of requirement is less true of IQ tests.

If there was a marked decrease in the effectiveness of schools in the period of 1963 to 1980, perhaps directly related to their success in imparting the specific knowledge demanded by the SAT or tests of scholastic achievement, and perhaps less directly in the form of a lowered emphasis on study skills, motivation, and the like—the non–IQ-related components of educational success—then these tests would be more affected than would IQ tests. Indeed, it might be the case that although general cultural sophistication has increased slightly IQ scores during that period of time, the decline in the effectiveness of schools has entirely negated the impact of those improvements on tests of scholastic success.

This argument admittedly makes a strong assumption about the magnitude of the decline in schools' effectiveness in these respects. The decline must be quite significant, given that the correlation between the two types of tests suggests that improvements in one should show up in the other. The non–IQ-related components of SAT performance must, therefore, have undergone tremendous erosion in the past two decades to produce the IQ-SAT discrepancy. But that erosion is just what has been claimed by critics of modern education in the United States.

Happily, and perhaps surprisingly, there is recent evidence emerging that the erosions in SAT performance may have ended. In fact, slight increases in SAT scores have occurred during the past several years, on the order of one-fourth of a standard deviation in total score between 1980 and 1985. If that trend continues, it would resolve the tortuous discrepancy between secular gains in IQ and declines in SAT performance. It would as well remove one foundation of the critics' case for the irrelevancy of IQ.[19]

The Utility of IQ. Irrespective of the reasons behind the IQ-SAT discrepancy or its recent turnaround, there is another somewhat hidden assumption behind the foregoing argument, and it tells us something about the utility of IQ tests as compared with tests more directly related to school achievement. As we have seen, over a rather large range IQ shows relatively little influence of what we have called common-family environment, factors that distinguish one family from another, including the influence of different schools. Tests of scholastic success, especially achievement tests, however, depending as they do far more on the mastery of specific knowledge, may reasonably be far more influenced by common-family environment, the influence of schools included. In one sense we might say that tests designed to measure scholastic success are more malleable, at least to the extent that we think of malleability as a function of the traditional factors associated with common-family environment.[20]

That sort of malleability in turn creates a paradox of sorts. IQ tests often are derided as being biased against minorities as well as lower and working-class children because the tests differentially tap material more likely to be acquired by middle- and upper middle-class children.[21] This argument is simply another way of referring to the different intellectual contexts that these different subgroups may experience. Whether or not that argument is true, if tests of scholastic success are sensitive to differences between families, that is, if they are affected by typical environmental factors, including differences between schools, they may indeed be *more* biased against minorities and others than are IQ tests.

The implications of this paradox extends to the real-world use of IQ tests. Without taking a survey of any sort, it is apparent that the use of IQ tests is very much on the decline.[22] In some states their use has been abandoned altogether for purposes of assigning children to special education classes, based on the assumption that blacks and others are differentially hindered by the biases of the test. Perhaps so, but some criteria undoubtedly will be used to make these decisions, and one might wonder what measures are to take the place of IQ. If achievement tests or teachers' ratings are used instead, it may be that we have exchanged one biased instrument for even more biased measures. If so, the outcome may not be at all to our liking. In California, for example, where the first court case successfully banned the use of IQ tests for the purpose of assigning students to remedial instruction, there was the same percentage of black children in special education classes two years after the decision as had been enrolled before it.[23]

As a corollary, if IQ tests are less influenced by common-family environment, we might wonder whether something is missed by not using them. The rationale long offered for these tests has rested in part in their ability to identify children who might benefit from special attention but who, for one reason or another, might be passed over in the usual course of schooling. This rational applies as much to children at the higher end of the intellectual scale as to those at the lower end.

It comes as no surprise to know that this rationale is offered more by defenders of the test than by its critics, some of whom would do away with IQ entirely. In trying to decide among these extremes a useful rule of thumb might be that IQ is overrated by its supporters and underrated by its detractors. In the murky middle ground, it might be argued that IQ is probably useful, to some limited extent, in identifying young schoolchildren in the manner just described, so long as it is not the sole instrument used and its predictions are entirely corroborated by other evidence such as teachers' ratings, interviews with parents, etc. Used in that manner the test may fulfill much of Binet's original intent. If, however, the tests also are capable of being misused, then we have a trade-off. If the decision is to avoid them because the misuses outweigh the potential advantages, I, for one, have no quarrel. It is a conservative and conserving decision, but we ought, at the least, to understand what may be lost: an instrument that may be useful in ways that other instruments are not.

That said, there can be no doubt that IQ tests have in fact been misused in the past. The aura of capturing an individual's ability with a single number has proved all too magical and irresistible, and one need not be an extremist to be entirely wary of their use for practical decision making. Yet how one decides on the use of IQ has little to do directly with all the data one might trot out for or against the tests and much to do with one's preferred orientation. As with all other issues related to IQ, ideology is inexorably linked to arguments of substance. And in those arguments it has, unfortunately, been the extremists who have all too often held center stage.

Given their visibility, it would seem impolite to end without taking a final swipe at them.

IDEOLOGY AND IQ

One could not be a successful scientist without realizing that in contrast to the popular conception supported by newspapers and mothers of scientists, a good number of scientists are not only narrow minded and dull, but also just stupid.

—James D. Watson[24]

The Nobel laureate in physics Richard Feynman once characterized much of modern psychology as "cargo cult science." Certain Pacific islanders, he related, wanted the cargo planes to continue landing on their islands after the end of World War II. So they made runways, stationed a man with wooden headphones and bamboo for antennas in position to guide the planes down, lighted some fires, and waited for the planes to land. It was the same, Feynman argued, with cargo cult scientists: "They follow all the apparent precepts and forms of scientific investigation, but they're missing something essential because the planes don't land."[25]

It is difficult to ponder Feynman's characterization without wondering whether there is an airstrip somewhere in the landscape of the endless IQ debate where the planes have safely touched down. Part of the difficulty in locating the planes is, as we have seen, that things are not always as they are presented to be in the science of IQ. Simply put, data can mislead, or perhaps more accurately, the presentation of data can be misleading, if not downright fraudulent. No one camp, environmentalist or hereditarian, has cornered the market on misrepresentation. There are, to be sure, different levels of misrepresentation, and each level is inhabited by members of both extremes. At the level of suspicions of outright fraud there are Bernadine Schmidt and Cyril Burt. At the level of data that look, for whatever reason, simply too good to be trusted without caution, there is Heber's Milwaukee Project and Munsinger's adoption study.

There is yet another level, of data that although reliable and without the taint of suspicion, are presented in so slanted a context that they require reanalysis, if only to strip them of their ideological cover. I'm thinking here principally of the French Adoption Study, although some of the hereditarian presentations of the literature on identical twins reared apart certainly qualify.

Environmentalists may be more prone to fall into this last category, if only because the range of predictions they might make, the number of variables known and unknown they might cite to explain a phenomenon, are nothing less than remarkable. The elusiveness of environmentalists' predictions in this respect is the weakest facet of their argument, and at times threatens to render their position scientifically useless because it leaves environmentalism admitting to no sure and critical test.[26]

There seems, in short, to be nothing that an environmentalist cannot explain. In the mid–1960s, for example, data emerged suggesting that Eskimos living near the Arctic circle evidenced higher IQs than did white Canadians. This finding was indeed puzzling for environmentalists, in that the living conditions of Arctic Eskimos were characterized as extremely poor, with high levels of unemployment and considerable family instability. One environmentalist solved this apparent dilemma by suggesting that "upbringing in an igloo gives just the right degree of cosiness [sic], security and mutual contact to conduce to a good performance in intelligence tests."[27] In fairness, the writer was attempting to illustrate the idea that there often may be unanticipated factors that affect intelligence, and that there can be no substitute for an empirical test of these matters. Surely, that is true. Nonetheless, one has to wonder, given the ease with which environmentalists might be prone to embrace this type of convenient thinking, this "igloo psychology," whether the planes will ever safely land.

Hereditarians, in contrast, seem more locked in to certain specific predictions. If IQ is highly heritable, certain relations must hold: Identical twins even reared apart should correlate highly; there should be an orderly progression in the magnitude of correlations between family members as we ascend the scale of genetic similarity—even if those family members are reared apart. Some of these predictions have been upheld, but not nearly in the neat way predicted by hereditarian thinking. Simply put, there are too many violations of hereditarian predictions for anyone to be comfortable with genetically dominant explanations of IQ. Neither have hereditarians as yet distinguished themselves in their reaction to or explanation of secular changes in IQ. To their credit, in exploring the shortcomings of genetic predictions it was the hereditarians who first noted the relatively weak affects associated with common-family environment, and who first explored the implications of what I have called the nature and nurture of uniqueness. Their work in this respect underscores an irony discussed earlier: Some of our best evidence for the influence of the environment comes not from direct attempts to study environmental influence, but derivatively, from analyzing specific genetic predictions and then observing what is unaccounted for by those predictions. Much is indeed left over, as the strength of unique influences on IQ demonstrates.

Having said that much about the extremists, it is nonetheless oddly comforting to understand that we cannot get along without them. New ways of thinking about IQ are more likely at times to come from the extremes than from the moderate middle. Then, too, each extreme serves to police the worst offenses of the other. We are in this way as much indebted to Leon Kamin for forcing hereditarians to better scrutinize their work as we are to Arthur Jensen for forcing environmentalists to take seriously propositions about human differences that they seem disinclined to explore.

Policing action, unfortunately, exacts its price, molds thought in ways not conducive to respectful dialogue. Correcting excesses becomes unsatisfying: The other side is not simply incorrect, but devious, unworthy of respectful consideration. When a mistake is uncovered it offers the hint of something larger. Such was the case when Leon Kamin noticed a peculiarity in one of the figures published in Arthur Jensen's infamous 1969 paper concerning the failures of compensatory education. The figure in question is reprinted here as Figure 10. Jensen was attempting to demonstrate the fact that there is a relatively modest effect of being raised together or apart on the correlations in IQ between various types of family relations. Identical twins reared together versus reared apart differ a little—but only a little—in their correlations. So, Jensen argued, do fraternal twins (DZ, or dyzygotic twins), siblings, and unrelated individuals. The patterns of the two sets of correlations with their parallel, orderly rise in correlation magnitude as genetic similarity increases, and in the apparent modest influence of separation, are entirely congenial to a strong genetic influence on individual differences in IQ.

There is only one problem with the figure: one of the data points, that for DZ twins reared apart, was fabricated. At the time of Jensen's article no data existed to suggest that DZ twins reared apart would correlate about .45 or so. Indeed, as Kamin pointed out, the only data available at that time came from the study of reared-apart identical twins by Julian Shields, in which four pairs of fraternal twins reared apart also had been located. For those four pairs the correlation was .05. As Kamin described it, "*that* value would wreak havoc with Professor Jensen's figure."[28]

Michel Schiff followed Kamin's lead in reprinting the now notorious figure

Figure 10
Effects of Separation and Degree of Relatedness on Correlations in IQ
Taken from Jensen (1969)

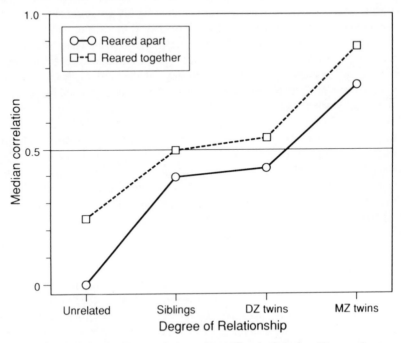

Source: A. R. Jensen (1969). How much can we boost IQ and scholastic achievement? *Harvard Educational Review, 39:1*, pp. 1–123. Copyright circa 1969 by the President and Fellows of Harvard College. All rights reserved. Reprinted by permission of the author, Dr. Arthur R. Jensen, and the President and Fellows of Harvard College.

and taking Jensen to task for the all-too-convenient data point. He also pointed out that another worker congenial to hereditarian thinking, Sandra Scarr, had reproduced Jensen's figure not once, but twice over the ensuing decade. The gravity of this matter is apparently made clear when Schiff informs us: "To place Jensen's 'technical error' in their social [*sic*] perspective, let us note that he was the principal expert consulted by the US Senate, Select Committee on Equal Educational Opportunity (in 1972): his contribution represented half of the approximately 800 pages published by the Committee."[29]

Two observations, each deliciously ironic in its implications: First, although it is true that the data point for fraternal twins reared apart was fabricated, there are now data to indicate that the actual value is about .47. There also are data that place the correlation between half-sibs reared apart at about .22, a value that would fall almost perfectly on the appropriate line.[30] The controversial data point may well have been fabricated, but it also may have been accurate.

Second, and far more interestingly, Jensen was not the person who fabricated the data point. In his 1969 article he noted that the figure was taken "after Erlenmeyer-Kimling & Jarvik, 1963" referring to a summary article on family relations and IQ correlations.[31] In fact, that article did not report data for fraternal twins reared apart. Jensen, however, did not take the figure directly from Erlenmeyer-Kimling and Jarvik. He took the figure, wholly intact, from another article that itself described the figure as "adapted from" Erlenmeyer-Kimling and Jarvik. So, if Jensen or Scarr was guilty of anything, it was in using secondary sources and in relying on the accuracy of another colleague—admittedly deadly sins in the study of IQ.

And the provocative question is, Who originally fabricated the data point? Who provided the missing link for the smooth curves presented in the figure? It is, somehow, a not surprising, but wonderfully revealing touch, the perfect point on which to close, to observe that the original figure, the source of the fabrication, came from an article whose senior author was Richard Heber, the director of the Milwaukee project.[32]

It is undoubtedly a most unlikely case of cross-fertilization. A genetic concept to be sure, but one not realized without the critical involvement of the environment.

A Closing Thought

In Bertolt Brecht's *Life of Galileo* Galileo Galilei is demonstrating his new scientific instrument, the telescope, to a group of onlookers, among whom is a philosopher. The philosopher says:

May I pose the question? Why should we go out of our way to look for things that can only strike a discord in the ineffable harmony? . . . It is a delicate matter . . . but Mr. Galilei was about to demonstrate the impossible. His new stars (the ones visible only with Galileo's telescope) would have broken the outer crystal sphere—which we know of on the authority of Aristotle. I am sorry.

Galileo replies: "Truth is the child of Time, not of Authority. Our ignorance is infinite, let's whittle away just one cubic millimeter. Why should we still want to be so clever when at long last we have a chance of being a little less stupid?"[33]

Just so.

NOTES

1. Lynn, R. (1987). Japan: Land of the rising IQ. A reply to Flynn. *Bulletin of the British Psychological Society, 40*, 464–468.

2. Flynn, J. R. (1984). The mean IQ of Americans: Massive gains from 1932 to 1978. *Psychological Bulletin, 95*, 29–51; and Flynn, J. R. (1987a). Massive IQ gains in 14 nations: What IQ tests really measure. *Psychological Bulletin, 101*, 171–191.

3. At the time of this writing there is in fact a project in progress that seems to have

embodied this home-centered idea. Called the Beethoven Project, it is located in an extremely disadvantaged section on Chicago's South Side and, from initial descriptions, seems to be focusing on parent training and home visits, with a community drop-in center as a component of the project. See *New York Times*, January 13, 1987, p. A26, and July 24, 1988, p. 14.

4. The original goals of Head Start, in the order listed by the program, referred to improvements in cognitive abilities as only the third among seven goals. Those goals were as follows:

1. Improving the child's physical health and physical abilities

2. Helping emotional and social development

3. Improving mental processes and skills

4. Improving self-confidence

5. Improving family interrelationships

6. Encouraging social interest in the problems of the poor

7. Increasing self-worth and dignity

From Zigler, E., & Freedman, J. (1987). Early experience, malleability, and Head Start. In J. J. Gallagher & C. T. Ramey (Eds.), *The malleability of children* (pp. 85–95). Baltimore: Paul H Brooks.

5. Head Start Bureau. (1985). *Final report. The impact of Head Start on children, families, and communities: Head Start Synthesis Project.* DHHS Publication No. (OHDS) 85–31193. Washington, D.C.: U.S. Government Printing Office.

6. Urbach, P. (1974). Progress and degeneration in the "IQ debate" (II). *British Journal of the Philosophy of Science, 25*, 253.

7. Flynn, J. R. (1987b). The ontogeny of intelligence. In J. Forge (Ed.), *Measurement, realism and objectivity: Essays on measurement in the social and physical sciences* (p. 23). Boston: D Reidel.

8. The SAT has an established mean for both verbal and quantitative scales of 500 and a standard deviation of 100. The average score (verbal + quantitative/2) fell from 490 to 445 between 1965 and 1980.

9. Flynn (1984).

10. Zajonc, R. B., & Bargh, J. (1980). Birth order, family size, and decline of SAT scores. *American Psychologist, 35*, 662–668.

11. See Flynn (1984, 1987b).

12. Flynn (1987a), p. 171; (1987b), p. 25.

13. For example, Anastasi A. (1988). *Psychological testing.* 6th ed. New York: Macmillan.

14. There have been many reports of this project. The description here was taken from Terman, L. M., & Oden, M. H. (1959). *The gifted group at mid-life: Thirty-five years' follow-up of the superior child*, Vol. 5. Stanford, CA: Stanford University Press.

15. Herrnstein, J. R. (1973). *IQ in the Meritocracy.* Boston: Atlantic Monthly Press, gives the strongest interpretation of these data along these lines.

16. Oden, M. H. (1968). The fulfillment of promise: 40-year follow-up of the Terman gifted group. *Genetic Psychology Monographs, 77*, 3–93.

17. The hypothetical "it" in this example may be identified with the *g*, or "general factor," that often is hypothesized to underlie performance on IQ tests. See Flynn (1987b) for the implications of assuming that secular gains mean that *g* also has changed.

18. Scarr, S., & Yee, D. (1980). Heritability and educational policy: Genetic and environmental effects on IQ, aptitude and achievement. *Educational Psychologist, 15,* 1–22.

19. See Flynn, J. R. (1988). The decline and rise of Scholastic Aptitude scores. *American Psychologist, 43,* 479–480.

20. See Willerman, L. (1979). Effects of families on intellectual development. *American Psychologist, 34,* 923–929, for a different view.

21. See, however, Jensen, A. R. (1981). *Straight talk about mental tests.* New York: The Free Press.

22. According to one survey, however, "experts" have maintained considerable, though cautious interest in using IQ tests. See Snyderman, M., & Rothman, S. (1987). Survey of expert opinion on intelligence and aptitude testing. *American Psychologist, 42,* 132–144.

23. Scarr, S. (1978). From evolution to Larry P., or what shall we do about IQ tests? *Intelligence, 2,* 325–342. See also Elliott, R. (1987). *Litigating intelligence: IQ tests, special education and social science in the courtroom.* Westport, CT: Auburn House.

24. Watson, J. D. (1968). *The double helix.* New York: New American Library.

25. Feynman, R. P. (1985). *"Surely you're joking, Mr. Feynman": Adventures of a curious character* (p. 340). New York: W. W. Norton.

26. See Platt, J. R. (1964). Strong inference. *Science, 146,* 347–352, for the importance of disproof in science.

27. Medawar, P. B. (1974, Jan. 11). More unequal than others. *New Statesman,* p. 50.

28. Kamin, L. J. (1974). *The science and politics of IQ* (p. 142). Potomac, MD: Lawrence Erlbaum Associates.

29. Schiff, M., & Lewontin, R. (1986). *Education and class: The irrelevance of IQ genetic studies.* Oxford, England: Claredon Press.

30. Teasdale, T. W., & Owen, D. R. (1984). Heredity and familial environment in intelligence and educational level—a sibling study. *Nature, 309,* 620–622.

31. Jensen, A. R. (1969). How much can we boost IQ and scholastic achievement? *Harvard Educational Review, 39,* 50.

32. Heber, R. F., Dever, R., & Conroy, J. (1968). The influence of environmental and genetic variables on intellectual development. In H. J. Prehm, L. A. Hamerlynch, & J. E. Crosson (Eds.), *Behavioral research in mental retardation* (pp. 1–23). Eugene, OR: Rehabilitation Research and Training Center in Mental Retardation.

33. Brecht, B. (1972). Life of Galileo. *Collected poems, Vol. 5* (W. Sauerlander & R. Manheim, Trans.). New York: Pantheon.

Appendices

Appendix 1
Measures of Placement and Retention for the Perry Preschool Project

Outcomes favoring preschool children

1. percent of all years of education in which group

   members were in special education: 16% vs 28% ($p<.05$)

2. classified as mentally retarded: 15% vs 35% ($p<.05$)

Outcomes favoring control-group children or showing no difference

1. preschool children more likely to receive

   remedial education ($p<.05$)

2. number of grades repeated (ns)[a]

3. percent of children classified as handicapped (ns)

4. percent of children ever receiving any kind

   of special services (ns)

5. percent of all years of education in which group

   members received special services (ns)

6. days absent/year (ns)

7. years spent in special education for children

   classified as handicapped (ns)

---

[a] ns = not significant at $p=.05$ here and elsewhere

Note: data are taken from Berrueta-Clement et al. (1984, Table 6).

Appendix 2
Measures of Social Competence for the Perry Preschool Project

Name of Scale (Age)	Number of Items Favoring Preschool Children/Total Items
1. Value placed on school (15)	0/7
2. Aspects of school commitment (15)	3/8
3. Self-report of social responsibility (19)	4/19
4. Self-report of delinquency (15)	2/17
5. Police/court records (19)	3/10
6. Summary of official delinquency records (19)	1/8
7. Attitude towards high school (19)	2/16

Note: Data are taken from Berrueta-Clement et al.(1984, Tables 7, 19, 20, & 22); Schweinhart & Weikart (1980, Tables 7, 8, & 11)

Appendix 3
Other Measures of School Performance Reported by the Perry Preschool Project

Aptitude Measures: Summary

Grade	Binet	Leiter	Peabody	Illinois Psycholin- guistic
1<	<.05	ns	<.05	ns
1	<.05	ns	ns	ns
2	ns	ns	ns	ns
3	ns	<.05	ns	ns

Measures of School Performance in

Addition to Achievement Test Results

Grade	Academic Motivation	Potential	Verbal Skills
1<	ns	ns	ns
1	ns	ns	ns
2	ns	ns	<.01
3	ns	ns	ns

Social-Emotional Maturity

Grade	Classroom Conduct	Socio-Emo- tional Status	Personal Behavior	Teacher Dependence	Social Devel- opment	Emot- ional Adj.
1<	ns	ns	ns	ns	ns	ns
1	ns	ns	<.05	ns	ns	ns
2	ns	<.05	<.05	ns	<.01	ns
3	<.05	ns	ns	ns	ns	ns

Note: Data taken from Schweinhart & Weikart, 1980, Table 7; Weikart, Bond & McNeil, 1978, Tables 15 and 18, and Figures 13 - 18.

Appendix 4
Results from Seven Major Adoption Studies

Study	Adopted Children's IQ	Adoptive Parents' IQ	Adoptive Parents Own Children's IQ	Comparison Group: Children's IQ
Freeman Holzinger, & Mitchell (1928)	95 (16)[a]	---	112 (14)	---
Burks (1928)	107 (15)	---	---	115 (15)
Leahy (1935)	110 (12)	---	---	110 (15)
Scarr & Weinberg (1976)	106 (14)	120 (10)	117 (14)	---
Schiff et al. (1978)	107	---	---	115
Scarr & Weinberg (1978)	106 (9)	115 (11)	---	113 (10)
Horn et al. (1979)	111 (12)	114 (8)	112 (11)	---
unweighted means	106	116	114	113

[a] Numbers in parentheses here and elsewhere are standard deviations.

Source: C. Locurto (1990). The malleability of IQ as judged from adoption studies. *Intelligence, 14*, 275–292. Reprinted with the permission of the Ablex Publishing Corporation.

Appendix 5
Summary Data for Black and Interracial Subsamples in the Transracial Adoption Study

Group	IQs		Educational Levels			
	Adopted Children	Adoptive Parents	Adoptive Parents Mother	Father	Biological Parents Mother	Father
B/B (N=29)	97 (13)	118 (9)	14.9 (2.3)	16.5 (2.7)	10.9 (1.9)	12.1 (1.4)
W/B (N=68)	109 (11)	120 (10)	15.3 (2.0)	17.2 (2.8)	12.4 (1.8)	12.5 (2.2)

Source: C. Locurto (1990). The malleability of IQ as judged from adoption studies. *Intelligence, 14*, 275–292. Reprinted with the permission of the Ablex Publishing Corporation.

Appendix 6
French Adoption Study: Summary of Results for Group Test

Group	Verbal	Performance	Total
Adopted children	104	107	107
Nonadopted half-sibs	91	101	95
Control (class-matched schoolmates of adopted children)	111	115	115
Control (class-matched school-mates of nonadopted half-sibs)	95	103	100

Source: C. Locurto (1990). The malleability of IQ as judged from adoption studies. *Intelligence, 14*, 275–292. Reprinted with the permission of the Ablex Publishing Corporation.

Appendix 7
Parenting of the Twenty Nonadopted Half-Sibs in the French Adoption Study

Subject No.	Parenting	Status
1B2	(2 parents)	R
2B	(nurses) (mother + aunt + uncle)	N
3B	(grandmother) (mother + second husband)	N - L
4B4	(2 parents) (father + uncle + grandmother)	L
5B3	(2 parents) (mother + second husband)	L
6B	("mainly maternal grandparents")	N - L
7B	(nurse paid by mother)	N
8B	"alternately:" mother + stepfather, grandparents	N - L
9B1	(nurse) (mother + stepfather)	N - L
10B1	(grandparents) (mother)	N
11B3	(nurses) (mother) (institutional home)	A
12B	(2 parents) (mother + grandmother) (mother + second husband)	L
13B	(widowed mother) (grandparents) (mother + second husband)	L
14B	(stable nurse)	N
15B2	(2 parents) (father)	L
16B	(widowed mother) (mother + companion)	L
17B2	(2 parents)	L
18B	(2 parents)	L
19B1	(2 parents)	L
20B	(grandparents)	N

Note: Status designations employed by Schiff & Lewontin (1986) are as follows: "R" refers to a child "born before marriage, recognized at the time of marriage; "L" designates a legitimate child born during a marriage; "N" refers to a biological child of a single mother; "A" refers to an "adulterine child."

Source: C. Locurto (1990). The malleability of IQ as judged from adoption studies. *Intelligence, 14*, 275–292. Reprinted with the permission of the Ablex Publishing Corporation.

Appendix 8
College Graduation Rates as a Function of Social Class and IQ

		Level of Intelligence				
		Low	Low Middle	Upper- Middle	High	Weighted Mean
	Low	.3	7.9	10.9	20.1	7.5
	Low Middle	2.3	7.4	16.7	34.4	14.2
Socio- economic level	Upper Middle	4.4	9.8	24.4	46.7	21.7
	High	10.5	23.3	38.5	64.0	42.1
	Weighted Mean	3.2	11.5	23.9	47.2	21.8

Note: From Sewell & Shaw (1967)

Appendix 9
Correlation of Adopted Children's IQ with Aspects of the Adoptive Environment

Dimension	Correlation (Mean)
Adoptive Mother's IQ	.20
Adoptive Father's IQ	.20
Adoptive Mother's educational level	.19
Adoptive Father's educational level	.19
Occupational Status	.15
Income	.10
Environmental Ratings	.26

Note: These averages were taken from the seven adoption studies listed in Appendix 4, with the addition of Skodak and Skeels (1949)

Appendix 10
Summary Correlations in IQ for the Major Studies of Identical Twins Reared Apart

Study	Pairs(n)	r
Newman, Freeman, & Holzinger. (1937)	19	.67
Shields (1962)	37	.77
Juel-Nielsen (1965)	12	.62
Bouchard (1984)	29	.71
Farber (1981)[a]	79	.78

[a] Summary study of first three studies listed and a number of case studies and smaller-n studies.

Appendix 11
Ratings of Similarity in Personality as a Function of Degree of Separation in Farber's (1981) Study

Degree of Separation	n	Similarity in Personality (1 = highly similar)
Highly Separated	20	1.85
Mixed Separation	11	2.00
Little Separated	16	2.06

Appendix 12
Correlations and Average Differences in IQ as a Function of Similarity in Personality in Farber's (1981) Study

Personality Rating of similarity	N	r(IQ)	Average difference in IQ
1 (most similar)	15	.91	4
2	19	.79	6
3 (least similar)	13	.43	9

Appendix 13
Correlations and Average Differences in IQ as a Function of Degree of Separation in Farber's (1981) Study

Degree of Separation	N	r	Average Difference in IQ
Highly Separated	40	.78	8
Mixed Separation	19	.85	7
Little Separated	20	.71	7

Appendix 14
Summary Data for Subgroups "*a*" and "*b*" in Skodak and Skeels (1949)

Group	Biological Mothers' IQ	Biological Mothers' Ed. Level	Adoptive Midparent Ed. Level	Adoptive Father's Occupation (1-4 Scale)	Adopted Children's IQ (4th Test)
a	63	7	12.0	3.2	96
b	111	12	12.5	3.3	118

Selected Bibliography

Begab, M. J., Haywood, C. H., & Garber, H. L. (Eds). (1981). *Psychosocial influences in retarded performance, Vol. 2.* Baltimore: University Park Press.

Berrueta-Clement, J. R., Schweinhart, L. J., Barnett, W. S., Epstein, A. S., & Weikart, D. P. (1984). Changed lives: The effects of the Perry Preschool program on youths through age 19. *Monograph of the High/Scope Educational Research Foundation, No. 8.*

Block, N. J., & Dworkin, G. (Eds). (1976). *The IQ controversy.* New York: Pantheon.

Bloom, B. (1964). *Stability and change in human characteristics.* New York: John Wiley & Sons.

Bouchard. T. (1983). Do environmental similarities explain the similarity in intelligence of identical twins reared apart? *Intelligence, 7,* 175–184.

Bouchard, T. (1984). Twins reared together and part: What they tell us about human diversity. In S. W. Fox (Ed.), *Individuality and determinism: Chemical and biological bases* (pp. 147–183). New York: Plenum.

Bouchard, T. J., Jr., & Segal, N. L. (1985). Environment and IQ. In B. B. Wolman (Ed.), *Handbook of intelligence: Theories, measurements, and applications* (pp. 391–463). New York: John Wiley & Sons.

Brigham, C. C. (1923). *A study of American intelligence.* Princeton, NJ: Princeton University Press.

Burks, B. S. (1928). The relative influence of nature and nurture upon mental development: A comparative study of foster parent–foster child resemblance and true parent–true child resemblance. *Twenty-Seventh Yearbook of the National Society for the Study of Education, 27,* 219–316.

Capron, C., & Duyme, M. (1989). Assessment of effects of socio-economic status on IQ in full cross-fostering study. *Nature, 340,* 552–554.

Chronbach, L. J. (1975). Five decades of controversy over mental testing. *American Psychologist, 30,* 1–13.

Clarke, A. M. (1984). Early experience and cognitive development. In E. W. Gordon (Ed.), *Review of research in education, 11,* 125–157.

Dumaret, A. (1985). IQ, scholastic performance and behavior of sibs raised in contrasting environments. *Journal of Child Psychology and Psychiatry, 26,* 553–580.

Duncan, O. D. (1968). Ability and achievement. *Social Biology, 15,* 1–11.

Elliott, R. (1987). *Litigating intelligence: IQ tests, special education and social science in the courtroom*. Westport, CT: Auburn House.

Eysenck, H. J., & Kamin, L. J. (1981). *The intelligence controversy*. New York: John Wiley & Sons.

Fancher, R. E. (1985). *Makers of the IQ controversy*. New York: W. W. Norton.

Farber, S. L. (1981). *Identical twins reared apart: A reanalysis*. New York: Basic Books.

Flynn, J. R. (1984). The mean IQ of Americans: Massive gains from 1932 to 1978. *Psychological Bulletin, 95*, 29–51.

Flynn, J. R. (1987a). Massive IQ gains in 14 nations: What IQ tests really measure. *Psychological Bulletin, 101*, 171–191.

Flynn, J. R. (1987b). The ontogeny of intelligence. In J. Forge (Ed.), *Measurement, realism and objectivity: Essays on measurement in the social and physical sciences* (pp. 1–40). Boston: D. Reidel.

Freeman, F. N., Holzinger, K. H., & Mitchell, B. C. (1928). The influence of environment on the intelligence, school achievement, and conduct of foster children. *Twenty-Seventh Yearbook of the National Society for the Study of Education, 27*, 103–217.

Gallagher, J. J., & Ramey, C. T. (Eds.). (1987). *The malleability of children*. Baltimore: Paul H Brooks.

Galton, F. (1869). *Hereditary genius: An inquiry into its laws and consequences*. London: Macmillan Co.

Garber, H. L. (1988). *The Milwaukee Project*. Washington, D.C.: American Association on Mental Retardation.

Goddard, H. H. (1912). *The Kallikak family: A study in the heredity of feeble-mindedness*. New York: Macmillan.

Gould, S. J. (1981). *The mismeasure of man*. New York: W. W. Norton.

Head Start Bureau. (1985). *Final report. The impact of Head Start on children, families, and communities: Head Start Synthesis Project*. DHHS Publication No. (OHDS) 85–31193. Washington, D.C.: U.S. Government Printing Office.

Hearnshaw, L. (1979). *Cyril Burt: Psychologist*. Ithaca, NY: Cornell University Press.

Hebb, D. O. (1949). *The organization of behavior*. New York: John Wiley & Sons.

Herrnstein, R. J. (1973). *I.Q. in the meritocracy*. Boston: Atlantic Monthly Press.

Herrnstein, R. J. (1982, August). IQ testing and the media. *Atlantic Monthly*, pp. 68–74.

Horn, J. M., Loehlin, J. C., & Willerman, L. (1979). Intellectual resemblance among adoptive and biological relatives: The Texas Adoption Project. *Behavior Genetics, 9*, 177–207.

Hunt, J. McV. (1961). *Intelligence and experience*. New York: Ronald Press.

Jencks, C. (1980). Heredity, environment, and public policy reconsidered. *American Sociological Review, 45*, 723–736.

Jensen, A. R. (1969). How much can we boost IQ and scholastic achievement? *Harvard Educational Review, 39*, 1–123.

Jensen, A. R. (1974). Cumulative deficit: A testable hypothesis? *Developmental Psychology, 6*, 996–1019.

Jensen, A. R. (1981). Raising the IQ: The Ramey and Haskins study. *Intelligence, 5*, 29–40.

Jensen, A. R. (1981). *Straight talk about mental tests*. New York: The Free Press.

Jensen, A. R. (1989). Raising IQ without increasing g: *A review of The Milwaukee*

Project: Preventing mental retardation in children at risk. Developmental Reviews, 9, 234–258.

Juel-Nielsen, N. (1965). Individual and environment: A psychiatric-psychological investigation of monozygotic twins reared apart. *Acta Psychiatrica et Neurologica Scandinavica Monograph, 183* (supplement). Reprinted in 1980 with a twenty-five-year follow-up by International Universities Press, New York.

Kamin, L. J. (1974). *The science and politics of IQ.* Potomac, MD: Lawrence Erlbaum Associates.

Kelves, D. J. (1985). *In the name of eugenics: Genetics and the uses of human heredity.* New York: Alfred Knopf.

Kirk, S. A. (1948). An evaluation of the study of Bernardine G. Schmidt entitled: Changes in personal, social, and intellectual behavior of children originally classified as feebleminded. *Psychological Bulletin, 45*, 321–333.

Lazar, D. (1974). Heritability analyses of IQ scores: Science or numerology? *Science, 183*, 1259–1265.

Lazar, I., & Darlington, R. (1982). Lasting effects of early education: A report from the Consortium for Longitudinal Studies. *Monographs of the Society for Research in Child Development, 47* (2–3, Serial No. 195).

Leahy, A. M. (1935). Nature-nurture and intelligence. *Genetic Psychology Monographs, 17*, 236–308.

Lewontin, R. C., Rose, S., & Kamin, L. J. (1984). *Not in our genes.* New York: Pantheon Books.

Locurto, C. (1988). On the malleability of IQ. *The Psychologist, 11*, 431–435.

Loehlin, J. C., Willerman, L., & Horn, J. M. (1988). Human behavior genetics. In M. R. Rosensweig & L. W. Porter (Eds.), *Annual reviews of psychology* (pp. 101–133). Palo Alto, CA: Annual Reviews.

Lykken, D. T. (1982). Research with twins: The concept of emergenesis. *Psychophysiology, 19*, 361–373.

Munsinger, H. (1975). The adopted child's IQ: A critical review. *Psychological Bulletin, 82*, 623–659.

Newman, H. H., Freeman, F. N., & Holzinger, K. J. (1937). *Twins: A study of heredity and environment.* Chicago: University of Chicago Press.

Oden, M. H. (1968). The fulfillment of promise: 40-year follow-up of the Terman gifted group. *Genetic Psychology Monographs, 77*, 3–93.

Plomin, R. (1986). *Development, genetics, and psychology.* Hillsdale, NJ: Lawrence Erlbaum Associates.

Plomin, R., & DeFries, J. C. (1980). Genetics and intelligence: Recent data. *Intelligence, 4*, 15–24.

Plomin, R., DeFries, J. C., & Loehlin, J. C. (1977). Genotype-environment interaction and correlation in the analysis of human behavior. *Psychological Bulletin, 84*, 309–322.

Ramey, C. T., & Campbell, F. A. (1984). Preventative education for high-risk children: Cognitive consequences of the Carolina Abecedarian Project. *American Journal of Mental Deficiency, 88*, 515–523.

Ramey, C. T., & Haskins, R. (1981). The modification of intelligence through early experience. *Intelligence, 5*, 5–19.

Ryan, W. (1971). *Blaming the victim.* New York: Pantheon.

Scarr, S. (1978). From evolution to Larry P., or what shall we do about IQ tests? *Intelligence, 2*, 325–342.

Scarr, S. (Ed.). (1984). *Race, social class and individual differences in IQ*. London: Lawrence Erlbaum Associates.

Scarr, S., & Carter-Saltzman, L. (1982). Genetics and intelligence. In R. J. Sternberg (Ed.), *Handbook of human intelligence* (pp. 792–896). Cambridge: Cambridge University Press.

Scarr, S., & Grajek, S. (1982). Similarities and differences among siblings. In M. E. Lamb & B. Sutton-Smith (Eds.), *Sibling relationships: Their nature and significance across the lifespan* (pp. 357–382). Hillsdale, NJ: Lawrence Erlbaum Associates.

Scarr, S., & McCartney, K. (1983). How people make their own environments: A theory of genotype → environment effects. *Child Development, 54*, 424–435.

Scarr, S., & Weinberg, R. A. (1976). IQ test performance of black children adopted by white families. *American Psychologist, 31*, 726–739.

Scarr, S., & Weinberg, R. A. (1977). Intellectual similarities within families of both adopted and biological children. *Intelligence, 1*, 170–191.

Scarr, S., & Weinberg, R. A. (1978). The influence of "family background" on intellectual attainment. *American Sociological Review, 43*, 674–692.

Scarr, S., & Yee, D. (1980). Heritability and educational policy: Genetic and environmental effects on IQ, aptitude and achievement. *Educational Psychologist, 15*, 1–22.

Schiff, M., & Lewontin, R. (1986). *Education and class: The irrelevance of IQ genetic studies*. Oxford, England: Claredon Press.

Schiff, M., Duyme, M., Dumaret, A., & Tomkiewicz, S. (1982). How much could we boost scholastic achievement and IQ scores? A direct answer from a French adoption study. *Cognition, 12*, 165–196.

Schiff, M., Duyme, M., Dumaret, A., Stewart, J., Tomkiewicz, S., & Feingold, J. (1978). Intellectual status of working-class children adopted early in upper-middle class families. *Science, 200*, 1503–1504.

Schmidt, B. G. (1946). Changes in personal, social, and intellectual behavior of children originally classified as feebleminded. *Psychological Monographs, 60* (5, Serial No. 281).

Schweinhart, L. J., & Weikart, D. P. (1980). Young children grow up: The effects of the Perry Preschool Program on youths through age 15. *Monograph of the High/Scope Educational Research Foundation. No. 7.*

Sewell, W. H., & Shah, V. P. (1967). Socioeconomic status, intelligence, and the attainment of higher education. *Sociology of Education, 40*, 1–23.

Shields, J. (1962). *Monozygotic twins: Brought up apart and brought up together*. London: Oxford University Press.

Skeels, H. M. (1966). Adult status of children with contrasting life experiences. *Monographs of the Society for Research on Child Development, 31* (3, Serial No. 105).

Skodak, M., & Skeels, H. (1949). A final follow-up study of children in adoptive homes. *Journal of Genetic Psychology, 75*, 85–125.

Snyderman, M., & Rothman, S. (1987). Survey of expert opinion on intelligence and aptitude testing. *American Psychologist, 42*, 132–144.

Spitz, H. H. *The raising of intelligence: A selected history of attempts to raise retarded intelligence*. Hillsdale, NJ: Lawrence Erlbaum Associates.

Taylor, H. F. (1980). *The IQ game*. New Brunswick, NJ: Rutgers University Press.

Teasdale, T. W., & Owen, D. R. (1984a). Heredity and familial environment in intelligence and educational level—a sibling study. *Nature, 309*, 620–622.

Teasdale, T. W., & Owen, D. R. (1984b). Social class and mobility in male adoptees and non-adoptees. *Journal of Biosocial Science, 16*, 521–530.

Teasdale, T. W., & Owen, D. R. (1986). The influence of paternal social class on intelligence and educational level in male adoptees and non-adoptees. *British Journal of Educational Psychology, 56*, 3–12.

Waller, J. H. (1971). Achievement and social mobility: Relationships among IQ score, education, and occupation in two generations. *Social Biology, 18*, 252–259.

White, K. R. (1982). The relation between socioeconomic status and academic achievement. *Psychological Bulletin, 91*, 461–481.

Willerman, L. (1979). Effects of families on intellectual development. *American Psychologist, 34*, 923–929.

Zigler, E., & Freedman, J. (1987). Early experience, malleability, and Head Start. In J. J. Gallagher & C. T. Ramey (Eds.), *The malleability of children* (pp. 85–95). Baltimore: Paul H. Brooks.

Zigler, E., & J. Valentine (Eds.). (1979). *Project Head Start: A legacy of the war on poverty*. New York: The Free Press.

Index